After his first child became a toddler, Justin Coulson realised he wasn't the dad he wanted to be. To learn more about parenting, he quit a successful radio broadcasting career and started studying, eventually completing a PhD in Positive Psychology and Parenting. Justin is an honorary fellow at the Centre for Positive Psychology at the University of Melbourne.

Justin now lives with his wife and six daughters in Brisbane, Queensland, and travels Australia constantly, giving talks to parents, teachers and professionals. He is the author of *21 Days to a Happier Family*.

Visit www.happyfamilies.com.au

Praise for *9 Ways to a Resilient Child*

'We all want our children to succeed in life but, ultimately, we want them to be happy. And the key to that is teaching them resilience, which is why every parent needs to have this book. Dr Justin Coulson, Australia's number one parenting expert, provides parents with practical advice that is easy to process and implement. As your child grows and learns, you will find yourself referencing this book over and over again!'

Melissa Wilson
Editor of Kidspot.com.au

'Parenting would have to be one of the most rich and rewarding – but also stressful – jobs on the planet. Justin Coulson provides up-to-date research into what helps build emotional resilience and explains clear strategies designed to help parents embody optimism and compassion as they guide their children through the often unpredictable journey of growing up in a very complex world.'

Dr Diana Korevaar
Author of *Mindfulness for Mums and Dads*

'Once again, Justin Coulson has raised critical questions about the way we build relationships with young people. A very useful resource for parents and educators alike, this book unlocks the myths and provides an insight into the way young people think, learn and get on in life.'

Jason Borton
Director of Learning,
Teaching and Early Childhood
ACT Education Directorate

9 WAYS
TO A RESILIENT CHILD

Dr JUSTIN
COULSON, PhD

ABC
Books

Author's note

Several of the stories in this book are on the public record. I hope I have treated them respectfully and accurately. In all other case studies cited in this book, names and other details have been altered to protect the privacy of individuals (except for examples drawn from my own family).

 The ABC 'Wave' device is a trademark of the Australian Broadcasting Corporation and is used under licence by HarperCollins*Publishers* Australia.

First published in Australia in 2017
by HarperCollins*Publishers* Australia Pty Limited
ABN 36 009 913 517
harpercollins.com.au

HarperCollins*Publishers*
Level 13, 201 Elizabeth Street, Sydney, NSW 2000, Australia
Unit D1, 63 Apollo Drive, Rosedale, Auckland 0632, New Zealand
A 53, Sector 57, Noida, UP, India
1 London Bridge Street, London, SE1 9GF, United Kingdom
2 Bloor Street East, 20th floor, Toronto, Ontario M4W 1A8, Canada
195 Broadway, New York, NY 10007

National Library of Australia Cataloguing-in-Publication entry:

Creator: Coulson, Justin, author.
  Title: 9 ways to a resilient child / Dr. Justin Coulson.
  ISBN: 978 0 7333 3482 5 (paperback)
  ISBN: 978 1 4607 0589 6 (ebook : epub)
  Notes: Includes index.
  Subjects: Parenting – Handbooks, manuals, etc.
  Resilience (Personality trait) in children.
  Parent and child.

Cover design by Christa Moffitt, Christabella Designs
Typeset in Sabon LT Std by Kirby Jones
Printed and bound in Australia by McPherson's Printing Group
The papers used by HarperCollins in the manufacture of this book are a natural, recyclable product made from wood grown in sustainable plantation forests. The fibre source and manufacturing processes meet recognised international environmental standards, and carry certification.

For my six precious, precious daughters.
When life puts you in a tight spot, don't ask, 'Why me?'
Instead, stand tall and say, 'Try me!'

We are all inventors, each sailing out on a voyage of discovery, guided each by a private chart, each of which there is no duplicate. The world is all gates, all opportunities.

Ralph Waldo Emerson (1803–1882)

Contents

Introduction

In early 2015 I wrote an article for an online parenting website. As their parenting expert, I am tasked with answering parenting dilemmas and providing inspiring ideas for mums or dads who are struggling. It so happened that this particular article – about resilience – struck a chord. Titled '18 ways to raise a resilient child', it was a hit. When it was shared on social media, its reach was phenomenal. A few weeks after the article was shared, I shared it again. Same result. Then a couple of months later I decided to try it again, and was amazed to see the article going even wider and reaching more people. I've since shared that article several times more, and time and again the response has been enormous.

I'm unconvinced that the article was particularly well written, wise or profound. But it highlighted what resilience is (for now it's enough to say that resilience means that we bounce back from challenges and adversity, and that our developmental progress isn't thwarted by difficult – even traumatic – circumstances), and it tapped into the importance of parents connecting with their children to build up their resilience. There is much more to building resilience than these ideas, but it seems that the idea of resilience resonates with parents who are worried that their children are somehow not coping, or may not be able to cope in the future. Parents and carers want to know how to help their children be more resilient. They ask questions like:

- Why does one child seem capable of thriving in spite of incredible odds while others crumble at the first hint of opposition or adversity?
- How is it that some children relish a challenge and a chance to learn something new – even if that means failure – while others will *not* try anything unless they can be assured of success?
- How can I help my child be resilient when friendships falter?
- How can I help my child stick at something for more than three lessons, or three school terms?
- What can I say to my child when he loses on the sports field or fails an exam? He seems incapable of dealing with failure.

After reading the article, one mother complained to me, 'My daughter Corinne will be 15 years old soon. She's a funny, empowering person – loving, caring, kind and supportive to others. She brings people together. Her coaches, teachers and family see this quality in her as unique and valuable.

'She keeps asking me why she quits everything, why she gives up on everything. She's a swimmer. She's been swimming since Year 2. She got to the top of her game two years ago. In order to be faster she needed to build up her leg strength but she fights it. She wants it but isn't willing to do it.

'In school she starts off really well then gives up and ends up submitting crappy assignments. She won't finish reading a required book or chooses not to read it at all because she doesn't like to read and can't get herself to do it. She'll just refuse to bring herself to study for a test – not all tests, but maybe something she perceives as hard or she is uninterested in. She knows she has to study and tells herself she will but never does it and gets a bad mark. She won't put in the effort in maths. She asks me why she gives up on everything and isn't willing to do what it takes to get what she wants or what she knows is best for her.

'She's stuck! When things get hard, she gives up.'

Perhaps your child gives up too quickly and easily for your liking, moaning, 'I *can't*.' Maybe your child resists going to school because they don't like their teacher, or because the teacher said something that upset them. Your child's resilience may seem low because a friend rejected them, or they failed in a sporting contest or an exam, or missed an opportunity to get a job they desired.

How can we or our children ever do something great, or even mediocre, when the minutiae of family life, school life or work life gives resilience such a hammering? In the following pages we will explore the idea of resilience: what it is and how it works. We'll consider research that shows how well our children are doing – or are not doing – and why. We'll examine the myths that surround resilience, slaying some sacred cows in the parenting-advice world. And we will investigate what researchers have discovered really *does* build resilience – not just in children, but in adults as well.

A resilience problem?

The evidence indicates that we have a resilience problem. Why? One in nine people in Australia experience *high* levels of psychological distress *each year*.[1] To be clear, experiencing depression, anxiety or other forms of psychological distress does not tell us whether someone is resilient. It's how they bounce back and adapt that tells us that. However, this statistic suggests a resilience challenge because in too many instances people are being affected by mental health issues and *not* actually bouncing back. They are not adapting well. Instead, their mental health spiral is negative. They get stuck in rigid stinking thinking, and cannot get out of the rut. Or they find a way to get on with life, simply living with the psychological pain. If an average home and family has approximately five people, based on the numbers mentioned above, one person is experiencing *high* psychological distress in every two households. The numbers are significant. And so is the level of distress.

Let's pick this apart a little more. In 2014–15, 11.7 per cent of people aged 18 years and over experienced *high* or *very high* levels of psychological distress. In a population of just over 23 million people, 3.4 million Australian adults experience depression or anxiety each year. Depression reports are at an all-time high, with 1 in 11 Australian adults reporting having depression or feelings of depression each year. And 1 in 20 Australians reported experiencing *both* an anxiety-related condition and a mood (affective) disorder.[2]

Resilience check-up for our kids

If Australia's adults are struggling rather than flourishing, how are our children doing? Resilient Youth Australia is a not-for-profit group run by highly regarded Australian child and adolescent psychologist Andrew Fuller.[3] The organisation has collected resilience data from over 90,000 Australian children in over 400 communities throughout the country. The data reveals clear and distinct patterns. In Years 3–12, 43 per cent of students (47 per cent of girls and 40 per cent of boys) have good or high levels of resilience. That shows that *just under half* of our children aged 8 through to age 18 are in good shape. Not an ideal picture, but certainly not as bad as it might be.

This is a wide age range, though. We should expect some variability in this age group. Our children experience tremendous developmental changes from ages 8 through to 18. Think of a young Year 3 child and consider the tremendous development that needs to occur for her to become a high school graduate and young adult in a decade's time. So many things will impact on her resilience: physical changes, neurological development, social growth and learning, academic pressures, identity, character and personality development, and more will influence resilience across this age span. So too will the various life experiences that this girl will encounter – in her family, at school, with her friends, and in a range of other settings that can help or hinder her resilience and wellbeing for her entire life.

When we examine the Resilient Youth Australia data by age, we see a distinct pattern emerging. The results show a steady drop from 59 per cent of students reporting good or high levels of resilience in primary school to a lowly 27 per cent by Years 11–12. All of that is concerning – it should be higher throughout these years. Of greatest concern: adolescence seems to be a time where resilience and wellbeing are dropping – significantly.

When our children do not feel hope*ful*, they too often feel hope*less*. Hope*less* children set fewer goals. Their view of the future dims. They perceive pathways as too challenging to traverse, or don't even perceive pathways towards goals at all. Often they doubt themselves and their capacity to accomplish anything of value. In short, that feeling of hope-*lessness* pervades their thinking, their emotions, their actions and their relationships. It affects their approach to school and to life. It reduces their resilience and impacts their wellbeing.

Rather than experiencing adversity and challenge and then finding effective strategies to work through the difficulties, our children are losing the fight against 'stinking thinking', and in too many cases they are losing their lives as well. Suicide is responsible for one-third of all deaths of young people aged 15–24 years. Suicide rates among young people are at the highest they've been for over a decade. And certain parts of our population are at greater risk than others. The rate of suicide among Indigenous young people is significantly higher than among non-Indigenous young people.

These concerning statistics appear consistently in studies of children and young people.[4] It seems to have become 'normal' that our children struggle with adversity, experience low hope and subsequent depression, anxiety and lowered resilience. But simply because it is normal, does not mean it is either appropriate or healthy. And it certainly does not mean we should accept it. The data demonstrates that around a quarter of our children, even during the teen years, maintain high levels of resilience. This small percentage is bucking the trend. How can we make it possible for more of our children to thrive?

We must approach the late primary school years as a golden opportunity to pre-arm our children, to inoculate them against the changes that affect so many so detrimentally. This is a time where we scientists have found a second surge in neuro-development. (The first surge occurs throughout infancy.) As our children enter this early adolescent phase of development (ages 9–13), their brain is beginning to wire itself with changes that will potentially lead to lifelong habits and ways of being. Their identity is still remarkably malleable – and at this stage they are still open to parental influence. We have to capitalise on this critical time in powerful ways to build on the positive foundation of resilience that childhood has provided, and reduce the risks and challenges of adolescence that chip away at resilience.

The good news is that we *know* how to do this. We know what undermines resilience, and we know what builds resilience – in children and in adults. A great deal of it starts well before adolescence – at birth and during infancy. And there is also much that can be done as our children traverse the adolescent years that are so often rocky, challenging and in too many cases tragic.

Because resilience is not just an issue for children but for us as well, some of the stories in this book are not about parenting, but are about adults who have shown extraordinary resilience. They are examples to motivate and inspire us, as adults, towards greater resilience so that we can be better examples of resilience to our children.

The real message of this book is simple: every child has an innate personality and temperament – a disposition – towards resilience that is inbuilt. Some children possess the attributes that promote resilience naturally, and others less so. Every child and every child's circumstances are different. But regardless of that nature-based starting point, the environment in which we raise our children, and the psychological, social and emotional habits that we teach our children can boost their resilience. We have good evidence to show that we can literally make our selves, our children, our families and our communities more resilient. And as we will see throughout this book, there are few legacies we can leave that are greater than the legacy of resilience and wellbeing.

PART ONE

MISUNDERSTANDING RESILIENCE

Some individuals faced with a traumatic
event actually develop new strength.

Nassim Taleb[5]

It's called Post-Traumatic Growth.

In many ways, post-traumatic growth is exactly the opposite of post-traumatic stress. Post-traumatic stress disorder (PTSD) is a serious psychological disorder some people experience after living through significant trauma and hardship. Post-traumatic *growth* is where, instead of experiencing hardship and trauma and turning into a shell of who they once were, people somehow leverage that trauma to their benefit. They live through and experience all of the pain, grief and utter awfulness of their situation. Their pain is as real and profound as it is for those who experience post-traumatic stress. They hurt, shake, and question everything.

Then they rise.

This is the essence of resilience.

Rosie Batty is a person who experienced and demonstrated post-traumatic growth.

Rosie's relationship with Greg Anderson ended two years after it began. It was rekindled several years later and Rosie had a son, Luke. But Greg became unpredictable and violent towards her upon discovering she was pregnant. After multiple assaults on

Rosie over a number of years following Luke's birth, she finally left Greg and obtained an intervention order to keep him away. Greg was only allowed to see their son in public while at sports events.

In February 2014, Greg was watching Luke at cricket practice. As families packed up and left for the evening, Greg isolated Luke in the cricket nets and stabbed him to death. Emergency services were called. Anderson threatened ambulance and police officers, and died that evening in a Melbourne hospital with self-inflicted stab wounds and police gunshot wounds.

The morning following this horrifying attack, as shocked Australians reeled, a grieving Rosie Batty faced the national media and said: 'I want to tell everybody that family violence happens to everybody, no matter how nice your house is, how intelligent you are. It happens to anyone and everyone.'[6]

Rosie spoke clearly. She spoke loudly. She spoke eloquently. She went on to promote change to legal processes related to domestic violence. She pushed for improvements to help victims. Rosie gained national prominence in a remarkably visible and deeply personal effort to stop domestic violence. And in 2015 Rosie Batty was honoured with the mantle of Australian of the Year.

During 2015 I had the opportunity to speak with Rosie a couple of times at various venues as we shared presentations on issues confronting young people. In a break at one of the conferences I asked Rosie if I could share her story as an example of resilience and post-traumatic growth. Rosie responded, 'I've heard of post-traumatic stress disorder. I haven't heard of post-traumatic growth.'

'Well, you're it,' I responded.

Rosie and I spoke briefly about how her trauma, despite being with her every day, had provided a stepping stone to profound purpose, influence, personal growth – and resilience. Rosie wishes, every day, that she had Luke with her, but she explained to me that she feels tremendous gratitude that, because of her pain, she is able to make a difference.

There are so many examples of everyday people overcoming pain, difficult environments, and odds that are stacked against them. They grow through – and in spite of – trauma. They are resilient. Many of them are children. In some cases they endure the worst kinds of adversity and yet they have some capacity to move past their circumstances to create new and better lives.

But would *we* respond like that under similar circumstances? Would *our* children?

We marvel at the resilience shown by those who overcome significant adversity. Could we push through those challenges? What makes those people so remarkable?

One of the most pernicious myths about resilience is that we are either born with it or we are not. Harvard researchers argue that resilience is a combination of qualities we are born with and capacities developed as we live and experience life. Yes, there are some differences in the way people respond to adversity. But to actually develop and strengthen resilience, being born with it is not enough. We need to go through difficult experiences.[7] Carrying a load can, and does, make us stronger. (But not always. More on that in the next chapter.)

A second myth is that resilience cannot be taught. This is an extension of the first myth. But studies have found time and again that resilience can be taught and increased, including in people and populations who are at risk, facing challenges, and have shown limited resilience in the past.[8] Thus, a load is insufficient on its own. We need support and the skills to turn adversity to our gain.

A third myth is that resilience is only necessary in times of significant adversity. While some researchers will argue strongly for this (and Rosie Batty exemplifies this), we actually need resilience every day. Life has a way of demanding lots of us, wearing us down, and asking even more of us tomorrow. When we are resilient we can respond to these demands. We are equipped with capacity and resolve. We develop and enlarge and magnify our ability. In fact, it may be our propensity to do this when times are good (but busy and demanding) that empowers us with the capacity to push through when those significant challenges arise.

So what is resilience?

Most people instantly and unthinkingly define resilience as 'bouncing back' from stress and difficulty. If you're resilient, something bad happens and you 'shake it off'. The resilient person stands tall in the face of adversity, remaining positive and pushing through obstacles. Resilience is like the bungee cord, the rubber band. Challenges stretch us and strain us. But when we are resilient, we move past the challenges and resume our usual shape.

But what *does* it mean to bounce back? If you have a child with anxiety, does resilience mean they just 'get over it'? Or if you suffer depression, does resilience mean somehow just moving past it, and no longer being depressed?

At its simplest, the answer is 'yes'. But as we dive into it, we find that resilience means a little more. Individual resilience[9] is a person's achievement of positive developmental outcomes and avoidance of maladaptive outcomes under adverse conditions.[10] Or to be more precise, it is 'the capacity of a dynamic system to adapt successfully to disturbances that threaten its function, viability or development.'[11]

Bleurgh. That sounds like academic jargon – let's unpack these ideas.

A person is considered resilient if they are doing better than we might expect given the circumstances they are facing, or have faced previously. We see someone born into challenge, and they thrive. The statistics tell us that with the risk factors present in that person's life, they should struggle, fail school, have dysfunctional relationships and never get ahead. But they stand tall, develop well and succeed in school, relationships and life. Thus they are resilient. Something inside them, or something or someone in their environment, or both, helps them find the capacity to 'make it'.

Risk factors

Resilience researchers speak of doing well in spite of the experience of 'adverse' conditions. We typically refer to these adversities as risk factors. Early research into child resilience focused on single risk factors such as foetal alcohol exposure, low birth weight, premature birth, or being born with a genetically transferable illness or disability (such as schizophrenia, dyslexia or depression.) Each of these factors predicts increased risk of undesirable developmental outcomes. In other words, they undermine resilience. For each one of these risk factors a person possesses, their resilience is likely to be lowered, and they are more likely to find it harder and harder to have positive developmental outcomes. And the more researchers investigated these variables and their relationship with child development, the more they realised that these risk factors often co-occur.[12]

Risk factors also occur at the family level. Some are obvious: poverty is regarded as a particularly potent risk factor that undermines resilience.[13] Other family factors related to reduced resilience include living in a home where violence or alcohol and other drug abuse occurs, experiencing parental divorce or separation, being raised in a single-parent home, lack of parental nurturing, and more.

A landmark study published in the *Australian and New Zealand Journal of Psychiatry* found that angry, cold and 'over-protective' parents are rearing a generation of children with significant risk factors that can (and likely will) impact their mental health as they grow, with effects lasting well into adulthood.[14] The study indicated that 20 per cent of our children are exposed to at least five 'risk factors' for mental illness by the age of eight or nine – risk factors that reduce resilience over the short term, and may have even greater influence over the long term. The study pointed to three central triggers for children's negative outcomes: parental anger, bullying and 'low parent warmth'. The researchers discovered that a little over 50 per cent of our children under three are experiencing risk factors that will undermine their resilience and wellbeing, from parental psychiatric problems through to divorce, alcoholism and drug abuse.

As children grow, these family-based challenges grow with them. One in six teenagers has a parent with a mental illness, 18 per cent of teens have parents who are separated and one in five adolescents has an alcoholic parent. One in three of our children aged 12 to 13 is on the receiving end of parental anger or hostility. This is not just the 'my dad got cranky at me' kind of anger or hostility, which of course we still prefer to reduce. Rather, this is anger and hostility that boil over into yelling, threats and even physical harm.

This means that if our children are struggling with their resilience, we need to hold the mirror up to our own parenting practices, and the way our family functions. Families are so critically important in child development and socialisation that any breakdown in family function has the potential to present a serious threat to optimal and adaptive outcomes in children.

A 30-year study published in 2016 that has followed 263 children from birth through to the age of 30 reports that children of depressed parents continue to have a three-fold increase in the risk of major depression or anxiety. The study began in 1982, and the last interviews were completed in 2015. There were six waves of interviews, at baseline and then at 2, 10, 20, 25 and 30 years. Children were assessed as either high or low risk for poor wellbeing outcomes, based on whether or not their parents had a history of depression. If parents possessed that history, children were rated as high risk. Although the high- and low-risk groups did not show differences in education, employment status or income at the 30-year follow-up, those in the high-risk group were more likely to be separated or divorced and have fewer children. They also received more treatment over a longer period of time, and had worse overall functioning than those in the low-risk group.[15] Other emerging recent research links parental depression to adolescent risk-taking and accompanying structural neurological change.[16] In an 18-month study, young people whose parents showed greater depressive symptoms took more risks, consumed more illicit substances, and experienced greater activation in their ventral striatum, a brain structure associated with rewards and risk-taking, and also with depression. The way *we* live our lives casts a long shadow over the lives of our children.

Of course, many children (and adults) function remarkably adaptively in spite of adversity, and this is resilience. However, this is not the norm. This is why family function is either a risk or a protective factor, depending on its quality. Just as they do with individual factors, family risk factors often pile up one atop the other in co-occurring fashion, elevating the risk of maladaptive outcomes. They also co-occur frequently with individual risk factors and community-based risk factors. Here is an example.

If a child is being maltreated, that child is experiencing a significant risk factor. In fact, child maltreatment may be the most dangerous of threats to optimal development.[17] Researchers have discovered that a child is most likely to be mistreated and abused in a *family* that is non-functioning and struggling to meet typical and basic responsibilities in other areas of childrearing or living, generally. Child abuse and neglect are most likely to co-occur with other risk factors like poverty, domestic violence, alcohol and illicit drug use and abuse, and more. These risk factors combine to undermine our children's resilience. And risk factors can work in the opposite direction as well. Rather than a family resilience problem impacting on a child's resilience, the challenges a child experiences or presents can become a risk to a family's overall resilience. A child who is stricken with a chronic illness, suffers bullying at school or experiences an accident may disrupt family functioning in significant ways.

Resilience and Chernobyl

A much less obviously impactful example relates to pre-natal stress in expectant mothers and the link that stress has to lasting post-traumatic stress disorder in the foetus. The Chernobyl disaster of 1986 occurred when a massive nuclear explosion occurred in the USSR, releasing radioactive particles into the environment and contaminating vast areas of atmosphere over Europe. A Finnish study examined twins who were in utero when the disaster occurred and compared them with twins born approximately one year later, once the fears related to radiation contamination were reduced. Stress hormones in both groups of children were measured several years later once the children reached adolescence, and researchers discovered that the twins who were conceived and born around the time of the nuclear disaster had significantly higher levels of cortisol (a stress hormone) and testosterone in saliva. The researchers suggested that pre-natal stress exposure may actually program a foetus to experience higher levels of stress and potentially lower their capacity for resilience.[18]

Neighbourhoods influence resilience?

Researchers at Duke University, North Carolina, USA, identified that the community a child is raised in can be predictive of psychotic symptoms – an obvious risk for reduced resilience. Researchers analysed outcomes related to four experiences children might be exposed to in their neighbourhoods to determine the cause of psychotic symptoms: supportiveness and cohesiveness between neighbours; the likelihood that neighbours would intervene if problems occurred in the neighbourhood; disorder in the neighbourhood, such as graffiti, vandalism, noisy neighbours and loud arguments; and crime victimisation. Even after statistically controlling for family history of psychosis, socio-economic status and other factors, the longitudinal research indicated that psychotic symptoms were more common in children who lived in areas with low social cohesion, low social control and high neighbourhood disorder and whose family had been the victim of a crime. But low social cohesion and crime victimisation seemed to have the largest impact. That combination of factors explained a quarter of the association between urban living and psychotic symptoms in children.[19] In terms of structural/community-based risk factors, the safety and security of a neighbourhood are powerfully predictive.

There are big differences between US neighbourhoods and Australian neighbourhoods, but the research highlights the impact community has on resilience.

The biggest risks

In short, risk factors encompass a significant percentage of children today. There is no doubt that some parts of the world present greater external, community-based structural threats to children's resilience than others. However, the greatest threats (or risks) to positive human development for those of us fortunate to live in safe, secure, developed nations (and safe, secure locations within those nations) are those that interfere with normal developmental processes like brain growth, secure relationships between caregiver and child, emotional and social development, learning to regulate behaviour, and a desire to learn and master the environment. If something interferes with relationships, with desire for autonomy, or with learning, it typically impacts on resilience.

One of the reasons that these risk factors are so consequential is the chronic nature of so many of them. Chronic risk increases something called *allostatic load*. A person becomes stressed to the point where their capacity to adapt to ongoing difficulty and challenge is reduced until they finally cease functioning and begin to shut down.[20]

A mother spoke to me following a parenting session. 'I'm worried for my second son. He is 11. My eldest boy is 17 and is much bigger than him. He's a real alpha-male. But my second son is quiet and sensitive, and physically quite small. My eldest son has had a lot of trouble at school and is now in a special school for challenging children, and he is really harsh towards his little brother. He taunts, calls names, hits and teases him, and just the other day I heard him yell at him and say, 'Get me my drink now, you bitch!' Is this a risk factor? Will my second son be okay? He just laughs it off and shrugs, but I've watched him and he kind of shrinks and makes himself smaller, or disappears into his bedroom. Is that normal?'

I had to tell this mother that her eldest son was definitely a risk factor. Her younger son may not become depressed or even clinically anxious because of this brother. He may continue eating and sleeping as she might expect, and perhaps he is even keeping up with his friends and his schooling. There may not be any perceived 'dysfunction'. This mum confirmed that at present this was a reasonable description of her 11-year-old. However, the absence of dysfunction does not mean that he is functioning optimally.

Resilience is not just being able to say, 'Phew. I survived my brother. I'm still all in one piece.' It is about achieving positive developmental outcomes. A resilient child continues to grow, thrive and develop in spite of setbacks. In this situation, this woman's son would need to *not* be negatively impacted by his brother, but he would also have to continue to grow in developmentally appropriate ways. That would be true resilience. And while possible, it would also be unusual under such circumstances.

Protective factors

Risk factors have a potentially negative impact on resilience, but protective factors bolster it. While resilience is not as simple as the balancing of risk factors vs protective factors present in a person's life, it is reasonable to suggest that the more protective factors are present, the greater the likelihood of increased resilience levels, avoidance of maladaptive or dysfunctional outcomes, and achievement of positive developmental outcomes. Resilience researchers distinguish between promotive factors (or processes) and protective factors (or processes) for resilience. In simple terms, promotive factors are those that are associated with optimal outcomes and adaptations *whether or not risk and adversity and challenge exist*. These are often called 'assets' or 'resources'. Examples might include internal resources such as self-control or problem-solving capacity, or external resources such as a functional, loving family, an engaged teacher, a thriving economy, or government policies that promote family and individual wellbeing. Protective factors are those that are particularly important *in a challenge, risk or adversity context*. These may sometimes be the same as promotive factors, but they play a specific role in a crisis that is different from their role when things are humming along smoothly. For example, engaged and involved parents are a promotive factor when things are positive, but when a threat arises, those same engaged and involved parents do more than simply promote optimal development. They actually become a crucial protector of optimal development. They rally around the child, provide support and comfort, and respond in a protective way to ensure safety, predictability and security. In spite of these differences, for the purposes of simplicity in this book (and because in much of the scientific literature minimal differentiation is made), I will combine discussion of both promotive and protective factors under the one banner of protective factors. Many of the factors and processes described in this book can be either/or depending on the context.[21]

Protective (and promotive) factors include participating in a family that functions well, having a strong relationship with at least one adult (usually a parent), having a strong support network beyond the family, avoiding alcohol and other drug use, and achieving educational benchmarks. Other protective factors include knowing that the adults in your life are capable, secure, predictable and interested in your welfare, belonging to social institutions (like a church or other community group), having traditions that bind you to family members in meaningful ways, and so on.

Up-to-the-minute research confirms and adds to this, indicating that while exposure to adverse childhood experiences (ACEs) dilutes resilience, healthy environments protect and promote resilience in spite of those ACEs. Among the most influential protective factors were having access to high-quality healthcare, parents and carers being in excellent mental health, and high-quality community support. Additional protective factors in this research pointed to parent education levels being high, and living in safe neighbourhoods with good facilities.[22] And a number of other studies point out that the more that dads are involved in their children's lives, the more resilient the child is, the more resilient mum is, and the more resilient the *family* is.

Take-home message

We give our children the best shot at developing in typical ways (and therefore overcoming adversity without maladaptive or dysfunctional outcomes) when we provide them with the following:

- Strong connections to adults who are both *competent* and *caring*. Relationships are the centrepiece of resilience – for better or for worse.
- Support for the development of social and emotional skills.
- Motivation to master their environment, or the things that interest them.
- Opportunities to develop autonomy, and to be responsible for their own decisions.

These resources for resilience are neither surprising, extraordinary nor difficult to develop.[23] Nor do these resources only appear during tough times. It may be that resilience is developed during the good times, but remains invisible, only appearing when difficulties arise.

Every family can provide its children with good relationships, opportunities to learn and grow, and the chance to choose (autonomy). The more information we have about how to do these things, the more strategies we have at our disposal to guide our children successfully.

Young children are resilient

We cannot train our babies not to need us. Whether it's the middle of the day or the middle of the night, their needs are real and valid, including the simple need for a human touch. A 'trained' baby may give up on his needs being met, but the need is still there, just not the trust.

LR Knost[24]

Are children *born* resilient? Or do we make them resilient by the way we raise them? The answer is still disputed among research scientists, but to me it seems that it's a bit of both. Inside each child – each person – is the capacity to adapt to challenge and overcome it positively. That's the 'nature' aspect of the debate and it is generally accepted among theorists from multiple perspectives. But it is undeniable that the attributes and characteristics we teach our children make a direct and significant contribution to how resilient they become. This is the 'nurture' component of resilience, and this is the focus of this book, because we *want* to do all we can to create and build more resilience in our children. There may be no time more important for building a foundation for resilience than the first two to three years of our child's life.

One of the distinct advantages to being the parent of six children is that you get a lot of chances to learn from previous errors, and improve your parenting. As a dad to six girls, I have had plenty of opportunities to improve on 'last time', and do better with the next one. My wife, Kylie, and I often joke that we're just going to keep on having more children until we get it right! (We're really hoping that we get it right with this one, because six feels like enough!) When our first baby was born, we did what we thought was normal, and right. We brought her home from the hospital and started 'training' her to fit in with our lifestyle. This was more difficult than we thought it would be. As each baby was born, and as we learned more about what babies really need, we discovered some important things that led to us shifting our focus from demanding our babies fit into our schedules to trying to make our schedules work better with our babies. We developed new sleeping and feeding patterns and habits, changed the way in which we responded to upsets and protests, and established a more child-centred environment. As most parents can attest, this is challenging. But from time to time, we got it just right.

Perhaps you have had a day like the following with one of your children. It happened many times more with our sixth daughter, Emilie, than it did with our first daughter, Chanel. I woke up to the sounds of a ten-week-old baby girl in the bassinet next to the bed. She was gurgling and singing, her arms waving in a gorgeously uncoordinated way. Her eyes were bright with delight as she amused herself touching her fingers together, laughing, and then waving her arms about some more. After a short while, she began to fuss. Kylie and I debated who would change her nappy. I lost the argument and when I removed the nappy I decided there was good reason to give her a bath! Once cleaned up, I held my little girl against my bare chest, skin to skin, before handing her to Kylie so that she could breastfeed her. This is one of those magic moments of pure connection between parent and child. Emilie stared into Kylie's face as she suckled, feeling skin-to-skin and eye-to-eye contact. Babies only have good vision to about 30–40 centimetres at this age, which is perfect for gazing up at Mum during feeding. We spent a few minutes playing together before I got myself ready for work. During the rest of the day, the baby slept, fed or had a few minutes of quiet time with mum. That night, I arrived home for more nappy duty and more cuddles before Emilie went to sleep beside our bed once more.

I don't want you to think I'm modelling perfection here. We have struggled in various ways with each of our children. Not everything has gone to plan. Kylie wanted to breastfeed for longer than she did with all of our children but was physically unable to do so. We found co-sleeping to be a genuine pain. Our kids were all 'wriggle-worms' and our sleep was disturbed if our kids didn't sleep in their own beds. Dealing with our own 'stuff' meant we were less patient than we meant to be. Work and other commitments meant we could not always be right there when they needed us. Sometimes it felt as though we couldn't be there at all when they needed us. Life can get in the way of our best laid plans. Our modern world is not designed to accede to the demands of a newborn baby or a toddler. In spite of our strongest instincts and desires, we easily find ourselves in all kinds of challenging circumstances that leave us potentially unavailable to a desperately needy infant or child. Work demands, outdated gendered ideas about who should be responsible for parenting, minimal government or business spend on parental leave – these and other factors can influence the parenting decisions we make. The additional challenge of being a single parent, and the seemingly endless clashing priorities we *all* experience, can affect our capacity to really be there all of the time in those first years. But these basic elements, consistently provided during the first years of life, create the building blocks for that sense of worth, self-esteem, and of mattering that is fundamental to the development of resilience.

There is a myth that our infant children must be trained to be self-reliant when young. The myth emphasises that babies become more independent and more resilient if we teach them while they are young that they must stand on their own two feet (before they can crawl), self-soothe, and regulate their emotions on their own. It is an inconvenient truth that our children do not have the developmental capacity to become independent at a young age. Like *all* mammals, humans are designed to be physically and emotionally connected to their parents from the moment they are born, and it takes a *long* time for them to develop the capacity and resilience needed for independent living. The push for children to become independent begins, for some Western families, too soon. It is the equivalent of a bird leaving her day-old hatchlings beside the nest and saying, 'Good luck. Off you go. Fly!' They need to develop certain attributes and characteristics before they're ready to do that. Exposing them to early hardship hurts rather than helps them.

Creating a safe nest

Dr Darcia Narvaez is a Professor of Psychology at the University of Notre Dame. Her central area of study is something she calls the Evolved Developmental Niche, or 'the nest for the young that matches up with the maturation schedule of the child, optimising development'.[25] For humans, our nest is the post-natal environment that surrounds and envelops children as soon as they're born. For the human nest to function optimally and lead to the best resilience, wellbeing and even moral outcomes in our children, the nest must be responsive to the changing needs of the child, thus allowing for optimal development. A nest such as this provides both promotive processes that aid in the building of resilience while adversity is absent, and protective processes that support resilience when challenge and adversity strike. That nest is the home and family.

As I described in the previous chapter, we are influenced by both our pre-natal and our post-natal environments in significant ways, shaping development, personality, morality, resilience and wellbeing.[26] Fortunately we have a sound research foundation on which to build a safe, supportive, secure nest as our baby enters the world. Anthropological, sociological and psychological data points to specific practices and processes which appear strongly linked to building resilience, morality and wellbeing.

Medicalised childbirth

For the past century we have had medicalised childbirth. This has improved survival rates of babies and mothers – an undeniably good thing. However, research suggests our current mainstream medical birthing practices are detrimental to our children's resilience *from the beginning* unless there are genuine health risks to mother or baby. For example, when a baby is born vaginally, an abundance of neurochemicals stream through the brains and bodies of both mother and baby. These neurochemicals are designed to facilitate physiological, social and emotional responses that foster optimised development in each of them.[27]

Research also shows that the long-term risks of caesarean births are substantial for the baby. A 2015 study conducted by Jan Blustein and her colleagues at New York University found that compared with children delivered vaginally, children born via C-section were at significantly greater risk of chronic long-term illness later in life. This is thought to be related to the neurochemical and hormonal rush that is contemporaneous with vaginal birth, but is also related to the baby's exposure to its mother's vaginal fluids while working its way through the birth canal.

The medical community is concerned with the risk factors for a child's long-term (and short-term) health and wellbeing and are trying to compensate in a variety of ways, yet caesarean rates are climbing.[28] Of course, in some instances intervention is entirely necessary, and should be utilised without guilt. (There is far too much 'mother-guilt' already.) But there are undeniable risks and impacts on children, the more we interfere with the natural birth process and medicalise it. The World Health Organization acknowledges that C-sections are often necessary, but that they carry risk for our children, stating 'there is no justification for any region to have higher caesarean rates than 10–15 per cent.'[29] Yet caesarean birth now accounts for approximately 32 per cent of all babies born in Australia.[30] This means about one-third of babies enter the post-natal nest missing out on specific and important exposure to processes that boost health and wellbeing, and potentially even resilience.

Extended breastfeeding

Not all mothers can breastfeed, for a range of important reasons. There are babies who wean themselves at four months, to the great disappointment of parents who imagined breastfeeding for years. In our experience, Kylie was simply not producing enough milk to sustain a growing child. A decision not to breastfeed or to shorten breastfeeding is rarely taken lightly, but when that decision is made, there are unfortunate risks for a child's resilience and wellbeing. Evidence is abundant that when breastfeeding is possible, it builds health and wellbeing. For example, breastfeeding acts as a protective factor from disease.[31] Breastfed infants are at a lower risk of being obese, in their early years and also in later childhood.[32] Breast milk improves digestive health. It contains unique nutrients, sustains healthy growth, and promotes the body's production of hormones, immunoglobulin and proteins that encourage healthy sleep, sustain balanced emotional wellbeing, and build brain and cognitive capacity, among dozens more benefits.[33] Beyond its many physiological benefits, breastfeeding is correlated longitudinally with less externalising (aggression) and internalising (depression) behaviour, even after the child has grown and is no longer on the breast.[34] Perhaps as important as anything else, breastfeeding is a time for bonding and love between mother and baby. It is this bond and sense of unconditional connection, compassion and love that establishes the beginning of a relationship that will be foundational to resilience and happiness throughout life. The more that connection can be built through touch, eye contact, and the literal giving of a life force from mother to child, the better.

From a baby's first moments, natural birth and breastfeeding are best for wellbeing and resilience. They build a strong nest for the baby to receive all of the physical, social and psychological nutrients it needs to maximise protective factors and health. Again, to be fair to all parents and children I must emphasise that children can be well and resilient *without* breastfeeding. Alternative experiences can be positive and allow beautiful bonding, wellbeing and health. If mothers cannot breastfeed, their children can still thrive. But breastfeeding will always remain a potent protective factor.

Touch and presence

From the very beginning, we know that positive (affectionate) touch affects the development of multiple systems: immune, digestive, respiratory, emotional regulation, cognitive growth and more. In people raised in safe, secure environments, touch increases oxytocin release.[35] Oxytocin is the bonding neurochemical – it makes us feel close to people. The more we touch our children in gentle skin-to-skin contact, the more oxytocin is released, which strengthens social bonds (among many other functions). And 'kangaroo care', or lots of close touching, snuggling and holding with skin-to-skin contact, is shown to enhance a baby's emotional regulation. It makes them feel safe. They relax, regulate and become easier, more contented, more resilient babies.

Because of ethical reasons, psychologists cannot conduct experiments where they expose some children to a parent's presence or touch, but not others. However, ethics boards are (rightly or wrongly) comfortable with this kind of experiment with other mammals, and results show presence and touch are crucial for resilience and wellbeing – from the start, in the 'nest'. In his now classic psychology studies, Harry Harlow noticed that monkeys reared in his nursery without their mothers behaved in strange, often anti-social ways (shy, reclusive, and hanging on to cloths for comfort), compared with monkeys raised by their mothers. Often they showed a lack of fear or they became aggressive. Noticing this, Harlow designed some 'surrogate mothers', made of wire and wood. He also designed mothers made of cloth. In some instances, he attached a bottle of milk to the wire and wood surrogate. In other cases, he added the milk bottle to the cloth surrogate.

Harlow found that the monkeys overwhelmingly clung to the warmth of the cloth surrogate, regardless of where food and nourishment was.[36] They intrinsically craved closeness and touch with a warm, soft surrogate. Ongoing studies by Harlow and those who have followed have shown a consistent lack of wellbeing and resilience in all mammals when reared without close and affectionate touch and warmth. Furthermore, those reared with parental absence and lack of touch often grow to be anxious, depressed, angry, aggressive and unable to effectively regulate themselves – all hallmarks of a lack of resilience.[37]

Of course, we touch, hug, caress and lovingly reach for our children, even if life demands that we see them far less each day than we would like. Does our partial absence and a limited lack of touch really undermine resilience that much? The answer is, frustratingly, a clear yes. Human studies investigating how mothers' touch relates to infant development in the first year of life show that children respond to parental affection as they grow, using it to regulate emotions and communicate with their parent.[38] When touch is lacking, resilience drops, as does wellbeing. The effect is long lasting, emotionally and psychologically.[39] Touch and presence matter for children's resilience and wellbeing as they get older too. In a study of nearly 400 students, researchers discovered that the more a child is touched, hugged and held by parents, through early years until Year 9, the lower their risk of depression.[40]

Responsiveness

Babies and young children learn to regulate their emotion and behaviour best through a coordinated interaction with a responsive mother, father or caregiver. Our baby cries or communicates with us and we respond softly and gently. The conversation sounds like this:

> **Baby:** Mum. Mum? Mum! Mumma!!
> **Mum:** Oh, precious baby. Are you upset? Do you need mum?
> **Baby:** Cuddle me, Mum. I need to know you're there.
> **Mum:** I'm here, bubba. I'm looking right into your eyes and touching your hand.
> **Baby:** Thanks. I think we should hang out and do this more. Can you stay with me?
> **Mum:** I'll be right here with you.

Of course our children aren't really going to be talking with basic words until they're about one year old, and they won't use stilted sentences until around eighteen months or two years. But the purpose of this illustration is to show that an infant develops a sense of mastery over emotions and coping when there is a match between communication attempts (through crying) and being responded to by a nurturing parent. When there is a mismatch (such as when the infant is ignored), stress levels in the baby increase. (They often increase in the parent too!)

When we don't give our baby our presence and that precious, vital touch, our child's emotional circuitry in the brain is rewired, stress hormones such as cortisol and adrenaline increase, and vagal tone suffers, which means that the major systems of the body become less resilient.[41] Vagal tone is related to the vagus nerve – the longest nerve of the autonomic nervous system which affects digestive, cardiac, respiratory, and immune as well as emotional systems. We build resilience in our child by responding to our child. When our child feels that we are attuned, they relax. They learn that they are safe. Their brain learns how to relax in response to stressful situations through repeated experience with parental availability, responsiveness, touch and soothing.

Though often well-meaning, strategies that turn parents *away* from their child's distress rather than towards it, such as ignoring a child's difficulty, are detrimental to the child's innate reservoir of resilience, and to the ability the child has to learn resilience from the surrounding environment. It communicates to the child that no one is coming, that they don't matter.

Professor Neal Halfon describes *parental benign neglect* as the accidental turning away from our child that we routinely demonstrate when other things become a priority.[42] It may be an email, or dinner. It could be another child. We turn away from our child to attend to something else and our child begins to feel isolated. In those first years of life, such unassuming and unintentional neglect transforms our child's difficulty into distress. Initially they protest. But then they turn inwards and become quiet. We think we have taught them to self settle. However, what actually happens is anything but soothing and settling. Instead, children begin to show the same kinds of behaviours we see in infants and toddlers whose parents are depressed, or who are drug addicts. When a parent is non-responsive, the baby becomes agitated. Without an attuned parent, the child feels lost and alone.

The baby's right prefrontal cortex, so vital for the regulation of empathy and relationships, starts to reduce in blood flow while the left prefrontal cortex lights up because of the adversity the baby is now experiencing. The baby sticks their hand in their mouth to provide some sort of stimulation and to act as a substitute calming mechanism, all the while feeling emotionally alone. This is what this mismatched communication looks like:

Baby: Mum. Mum? Mum! Mumma!!

Mum: Oh, seriously. Again? I just picked you up. I'm too busy. You're too needy. You're going to have to figure this out yourself this time.

Baby: Cuddle me, Mum. I need to know you're there.

Mum: I love you, but you're driving me mad. If I ignore you, you'll be able to work out how to settle yourself. It's important for both of us that I do this.

Baby: Mum! Mumma! I need you. Please pick me up. Please. Please!

Mum: I'm not listening. If I listen I'll get emotional and pick you up. I'm just going to ignore you until you get it.

Baby: Mum! Mum?

We probably don't consciously think those words. But when we turn away from our child, this is how they feel. And many of us have done precisely this type of thing with our child. It's a normal part of living in the 21st century. But normal does not equal ideal. We might argue that in these first two or three early years it is crucial that our children not suffer from PADD – parental attention deprivation disorder. In fact, it would be best if they never suffered from it. PADD is not a psychological illness, although maybe it should be. PADD is the result of these seemingly small, innocuous actions and events that compound over time to produce significant effects in our children's developmental processes, their wellbeing and their resilience – and it happens when we are seemingly benignly neglectful, by turning away.

When parents are calm and responsive, their children relax, and are more likely to be calm and contented. They regulate their levels of stress and arousal more effectively. Their brain releases oxytocin and serotonin, chemicals that increase feelings of trust, safety and contentment. Children are more cooperative. Responsive parenting increases children's vagal tone, diminishing psychological pain and enhancing happiness.[43] It tells them that we are there for them. It reminds them that everything is okay. Responsive parenting always has been, and remains, the rock on which resilience rests.

Before we wrap up this chapter, I want to point out one more important aspect of everything I have mentioned here: natural birth, breastfeeding, touch, presence and responsiveness. These may be ideal, but they are not always realistic. In the harried lives we live, we sometimes need to make choices that are theoretically and technically suboptimal. The birth plan may not work out. Breastfeeding may be a pipe dream. A parent may travel a lot or work long hours away from home, meaning their touch and presence are impossibilities. Responsiveness may be ideal, but if depression, stress, anxiety or some other challenge is hampering a parent's wellbeing, perhaps there needs to be an alternative strategy to help the child – and the parent. There are also times when a baby will not sleep, so a parent will not sleep. In these cases, we need to find some kind of middle road. We know what the ideal is but we also know that we can't get there. Rather than beating ourselves up with ongoing pain and guilt, we can only do what we can do. We can marshal resources, calling in family or friends to give us some respite. We can be creative in other ways.

Similarly, this idea of being responsive, particularly, should not mean that every time a baby whimpers or whines, we have to put down the baby monitor and race to their room to offer cuddles and comfort. Sometimes we're too exhausted. It's not realistic. But if a baby is hollering and showing genuine distress, they need us. There are times we can be flexible, and times when we need to be there, or to ask someone to help us. That bond and that security are too important to let go.

Take-home message

We give our children the best chance to 'thrive by five' when we encourage healthy and natural birth, a strong and long emphasis on breastfeeding, high levels of touch and parental presence, and responsiveness to any emotional or physical distress our young children experience. Decisions like this are sometimes out of our hands, and when they are, we cannot beat ourselves up. But where possible, these opportunities will give our children the best start to a resilient life.

Steeling our children: why 'Toughen up, Princess' damages resilience

It's not our job to toughen our children up to face a cruel and heartless world. It's our job to raise children who will make the world a little less cruel and heartless.

LR Knost[44]

The bell had just rung for the end of recess. Children were heading back to their classrooms, and Year 1 teacher Mrs Boonen was preparing to return to hers when she noticed one of her students stumbling across the playground towards her, fists clenched, rubbing her eyes, sobbing.

Mrs Boonen crouched to the ground and extended her arms to Amelia, and the six-year-old rushed into her teacher's embrace.

Mrs Boonen asked, 'Amelia, what happened? What's wrong?'

Amelia pulled away from her teacher and pointed to a group of girls leaving the playground and walking to Mrs Boonen's classroom. 'She ...' (sobbing) '... she ...' (more sobs) '... pointed at me.' The accusation was followed by more tears.

Heidi was confused. 'She pointed at you?' Compassion was quickly turning to incredulity.

Amelia nodded, feeling the change that had come over her teacher.

Imagine for a moment that you are Mrs Boonen. What do you say to Amelia?

After speaking about emotional intelligence and the power of positive relationships for two hours in a staff development session, I told Amelia's story and asked this question. 'What do you say to Amelia?' Without pausing, the school principal exhaled, 'Oh, come on. Toughen up, Princess!'

Nervous laughter rippled around the room. The response is not unusual. In my presentations to parents, educators and even in corporations, people respond, 'For goodness' sake! This is what happens when you cotton-wool children. They need to be ready for the real world. If she can't handle being pointed at by one of the children in the playground, how is she ever going to cope when life throws a really nasty obstacle in her path!'

There is a dominant belief – a powerful myth – that for our children to become resilient they need to experience hardship, fend for themselves, push through it and toughen up. We are consistently told that we are doing our children a disservice when we cotton-wool them. We are criticised for raising bubble-wrapped, spoon-fed kids; little emperors who believe they're entitled to their every whim being met. Gold stars for everyone! No one can come last.

Let's examine the evidence to see whether resilience is developed or diminished with tough love.

Steeling

The technical term is steeling. Resilience researchers suggest that experiencing adversity can lead to one of two responses: sensitising, or steeling (also called strengthening). Sensitising refers to a child becoming more sensitive, anxious and ultimately less resilient. And the simple concept behind steeling is that steel is strong, so steeling is representative of a 'toughening up' process, or a resiliency-boosting effect.[45] Vaccination is analogous. When we vaccinate a child, we provide a low dose of dead or weakened antigens. These antigens cannot cause an infection, but they are an enemy to the body's immune system. They act as an agonist, or an 'enemy' for the body to fight. The body produces antibodies to destroy the antigens and thereby strengthen the body. The body 'remembers' the antigen and develops a newfound, increased capacity to respond to it should it be exposed to it again. This facilitates faster, healthier responses to subsequent exposures to that disease, which allows antibodies to (typically) overcome it before it causes any harm. The immune system has been 'steeled' against subsequent infection.

The steeling principle appears to apply to resilience. Being able to deal with basic and mild stressors strengthens and steels our children (and even us adults), aiding optimal development and bolstering resilience. Overcoming minor challenges helps us to cope more effectively. We feel competent. We develop greater confidence. Then, when a new and tougher challenge arrives, we draw on our previous steeling to enhance our self-belief, and develop the perseverance and resilience to push through the new challenge. Our previous inoculation can help us become less stressed, anxious or emotionally overcome when we encounter obstacles. That's resilience!

Unfortunately, as we saw in the previous chapter, during infancy, childhood and (as we will see) even adolescence, our resilience 'immune' system is highly sensitive and surprisingly easily harmed. The idea that many behaviour experts (and parents) advocate, that we should allow a child to suffer because it's for 'their own good' and will help them toughen up, can quickly prove destructive. For example, controlled crying during infancy is supposed to toughen our children up and help them figure out how to regulate their own emotions. Similarly, leaving a four-year-old to cry in the corner after getting in trouble or squabbling with a sibling is an example of the 'what doesn't kill you makes you stronger' approach. This idea of steeling our kids by letting them suffer through simple challenges may be valid to a point. However, research shows that attempts at steeling must be mild and developmentally appropriate. Too much too soon creates sensitised children and adults, increasing helplessness and hopelessness – the opposite of resilience.

Resilient monkeys

David Lyons and his colleagues exposed some infant squirrel monkeys to normal separations from their mother, at around 17 weeks of age, when the mother left the 'nest' to forage for food just as would happen in nature.[46] Other mother/infant pairings were kept together all the time with no separations at all. At the conclusion of ten weeks, both groups were again reared in identical conditions – with their mothers present at all times. Lyons and his colleagues began collecting data on the young monkeys' behaviour, hormone levels and brain activity, and manipulating their environments to see how they would respond – how resilient they would be based on their prior experience with, or without, a mother at those separation times. Being placed into a novel situation can be stressful, so Lyons placed the young monkeys into new and sometimes challenging situations and observed what happened. Regardless of whether tests were for behaviour, cognition, curiosity, brain volume or stress hormones, the monkeys who had never experienced the moderate and developmentally appropriate separation from their mothers showed diminished outcomes. This was even the case in stress-free novel environments. The stress hormone cortisol was less present in monkeys that had been steeled. Lower stress hormone levels means lower stress and anxiety, and better coping. That mild, developmentally appropriate separation the young monkeys experienced reduced anxiety and bolstered resilience against subsequent novelty, stress and adversity when compared with the young monkeys that did not experience separations from their mother. Brain scans of the separated monkeys indicated greater brain development and capacity in the ventromedial cortex, part of the prefrontal cortex responsible for processing risk and fear. In other words, steeling was experimentally shown to foster brain growth that assisted the monkeys to identify novel situations, assess them for risk, and regulate emotion and behaviour accordingly.

This experiment seems to support the idea I'm calling a myth. My argument is that putting our children through stressful situations so they learn resilience is a bad idea. Yet the research points the other way. It argues that stress is good. It steels and builds resilience. But there are important caveats, which is why I hold the position I do. First, the stress experiences must be both brief and repeated. A one-off minor stressor is typically insufficient to create steeling. The second proviso is crucial: the stress experiences must be *minor*. There should be no other deprivation, pain, adversity or challenge. The monkeys (or rats in other experiments) are in warm, positive, nurturing environments. The only thing that is different between groups is the brief separation encounters. When the experiences are too strong, or there are too many other adversarial environmental stressors, the animal is sensitised rather than steeled. Third, the stress experience must be developmentally appropriate. If stressors occur too early, they create stress, anxiety, and later depression or aggression. There is sensitisation rather than steeling.

I was discussing these ideas with a mum, Kerryn, who wanted to 'toughen up' her two-year-old. The little girl was crying at night time, refusing to go to bed without an hour of cuddles and songs, being patted off to sleep, and requiring her parents to stay in the room as she drifted off. She was on high alert every time Kerryn or her husband, Derek, attempted to leave the room. Kerryn was concerned that her daughter had no resilience. And Derek felt that their little girl needed some tough love: some steeling. He was angry at the intrusive way that their daughter was impacting on his time with Kerryn. After songs and cuddles, Derek laid down the law to their little girl and left Kerryn to put her to sleep. (This was probably unhelpful. Think of a time that you've been told off, and then tried to relax and fall asleep!) Kerryn stayed to comfort her daughter, explaining to her that she was not allowed out of the room. 'It's bedtime. You stay here no matter what. I will not be coming back into the room to help you. It's time for you to be a big girl and to stop making night time so hard.'

On leaving the room, the predictable calls for help echoed down the corridor. Kerryn wanted to go to her little girl and comfort her, but Derek was immovable. 'She has to learn.' At each new burst of screaming, Kerryn would flinch and look to Derek who would reaffirm that their child had to toughen up and get used to it. Finally, after more than two hours of screaming and kicking the door, the toddler gave up and went to sleep. Both Kerryn and Derek felt relieved and settled in to some quality 'couple time'. The following morning, Kerryn was ready to celebrate her daughter's success, but, on opening the door, she was immediately overcome with guilt. Her little girl had become so worked up that she had vomited all over her bed, and remained in it all night. Moreover, this little girl did not adapt positively to the change. She instead became more clingy, more worried that her parents would leave her, and more afraid of the dark. The adversity Kerryn had created for her child was too great. Rather than steeling, she built damaging sensitivity.

Many children are developmentally capable of putting themselves to sleep from an early age. Some are not. There are individual differences based on children's biology and personality, and the environment in which they are raised. Kerryn and Derek's daughter was simply not developmentally ready to let go of being close to her parents at bedtime. Kerryn and I talked things over and determined that a new strategy that relied less on tough love and more on compassion might make her daughter more resilient and capable of overcoming challenges like bedtime. We created a gentle routine – a series of steps for her two-year-old that would help her feel safe and loved. We agreed that cuddles would continue without a time limit, and that pressure to go to sleep would be removed. Derek preferred to take a hard-line stance, so Kerryn took the responsibility on herself to stay with her daughter until she felt safe, or was asleep. The first few nights were long. Her daughter was afraid her mum would leave. Derek grumbled and complained that the parenting expert had no idea what he was doing, and that he was a soft touch who didn't know how to impose limits. But after about four or five nights of following their routine, Kerryn described her daughter as feeling more relaxed. At the end of two weeks, Kerryn would put her daughter to bed, spend a few minutes hugging, and then explain that she was going to do the dishes and then come back for more cuddles. At the end of about four weeks, Kerryn extended her time away a little more. By the end of three months, Kerryn was able to finalise the evening routine, gently tuck her little girl into bed, tell her 'I'll see you in the morning', and walk away, knowing her daughter would comfortably go to sleep feeling safe. Kerryn's unconditional support, compassion and love provided a foundation for resilience that tough love could not. It took time, because building a sense of security and resilience is not a quick fix. And importantly, Kerryn's persistence also helped Derek to see that a kind approach was better for their little girl's resilience than his tough approach.

The tipping point

Where is the tipping point? How do we know what is developmentally appropriate and what is not? How do we help to 'steel' our children, rather than increase their stress sensitivity?

There can be no easy or straightforward answers to these questions. Every child responds to stress differently because of genetic influences, personality and environmental factors, as well as the many variables described in previous chapters – from parental stress while pregnant through to exposure to illness, family violence or, at the extreme end of the scale, the displacement experienced as a refugee; even living through a war.

The critical role of a parent is knowing when to step in, and knowing when to step out. Our children do need steeling experiences, but they do not necessarily need to face them entirely alone. A choice to increase a child's distress and tell them to toughen up or the decision to prolong what is an obviously traumatic experience for a child may do more harm than good, however well-intentioned. Isolating a child in distress, for example, through time-out, will be similarly harmful. Counter to popular belief and the tough-love approach endorsed by some 'experts', researchers have discovered that the decision to support, comfort and coach a child through difficulty actually builds resources and resilience, acting as a protective factor.[47] That is, our support, perspective and compassion may assist more to steel our child than the act of leaving a child to work it out alone or attempting to steel the child through enhanced hardship. Getting the balance right between stepping in and stepping out is vital, as is the balance between our involvement and our support once we do step in.

Stepping out

What does stepping out look like? When we attempt to steel a child in order to bolster resilience by stepping out, we can do so in both negative and positive ways. If we step out negatively, we either dismiss or we disapprove.[48] We demonstrate dismissal in a range of ways. There's the kind-hearted stepping out with well-meaning but dismissive words such as, 'Oh come on. It's not that bad. You'll be right,' through to something more mean-spirited, such as, 'I'm not going to listen to you when you carry on like that.' At times, out of frustration, we step out and try to toughen our children up by saying, 'Would you just get over it?' Such statements are illustrative of a parent who is stepping out to steel a child, trying to promote independence and the ability to bounce back from difficulties without being ... well ... difficult. Dismissal demands that the person we are annoyed with must figure the issue out by themselves.

There are some instances where stepping out can be positive for a child. If a child is struggling to complete a task or activity we might intentionally keep our distance. But we can do so in a supportive way by acknowledging, 'I know it's tough. But I also know you can do it. I'm right here. Keep it up.' Similarly, we might have a child come to us in tears of exasperation or difficulty. A discerning parent may see an opportunity for their child to develop through this situation and gently indicate that, 'I know this is hard for you. But this is something I think you can work out on your own. If you get stuck, I'm here to encourage you, but this one is up to you.' They might also ask, 'What would you do if I wasn't here?' before encouraging their child to go for it alone. This stepping out is entirely different to the dismissive form of stepping out I indicated earlier. And this is the kind of stepping out that can, under the right circumstances, build a sense of competence and a sense of autonomy in our children that ultimately strengthens and builds resilience.

Then there's the disapproving approaches used to promote resilience by stepping out. These include statements like, 'Cut that out.' We might hear ourselves say in exasperation, 'You're being ridiculous.' Perhaps something a little less contemptuous, such as, 'I don't like it when you act like that.' When we disapprove, we are telling a child (or adult) that they don't measure up to our expectations. I once heard another 'expert' share an experience where a parent voiced strong disapproval by telling her child, 'I'm very, very disappointed in you.' While this may be appropriate to say in some significant and challenging circumstances, this form of stepping out via disapproval is typically only going to leave a child feeling worthless and hopeless. It is hardly motivating to be told that you are a disappointment, or that you're nothing but trouble. Indeed, it would be an unusual circumstance in which disapproval as a means of stepping out might lead to improvements in resilience. These critical statements tend to undermine perspective (ours and our children's), lack compassion and leave children feeling incompetent and unloved. Stepping out and away with disapproval is a generally unhelpful strategy.

Some may be wondering if I am suggesting that we should never provide correction, instruction, guidance or teaching. After all, if we can't disapprove or dismiss in case it undermines our little precious one's resilience, what can we do? My suggestion is that we do need to clearly develop limits and boundaries around behaviour that is inappropriate. It is essential for parents to socialise their children. And we do need to encourage our children to stretch further than they have before, even when it is hard. But there are ways to do so without breaking down our children's resilience through coercive and contemptuous disapproval, or detached dismissal.

Here's an example. Richie and Teejay were best buddies. Aged six, they played together in the street outside their neighbouring homes most afternoons. Richie's dad, Phillipe, spoke to me about a recent challenge between the boys and wanted to know how best to handle it. During the course of their playing, Teejay had called Richie an idiot. He had hurt him, and then called him stupid. Phillipe explained that 'those are words we don't use in our home'. He described Richie as a sensitive boy who was generally gentle. Richie had become upset by Teejay's behaviour and words, and began to cry. Teejay's mum had seen Richie's tears, asked Teejay what happened, and then told Richie he needed to 'toughen up', before sending him home to his dad.

'I don't want my son to have to toughen up,' Phillipe told me. 'I want him to stay sweet and soft and gentle. But I want him to be resilient.'

We discussed Richie's response. His feelings had been hurt, and he had been physically hurt by his friend. His emotional and tearful response was age-appropriate. Children struggle to regulate their emotions and behaviours while young, but they get better as they get older, usually from about age eight. (And we all know some adults who struggle with it too!) But he had moved past the hurt in a quick and effective way. Some cuddles and a listening ear from a dad who knew it was resilience-building to step in and be protective meant Richie had a few minutes of quiet time to work through his emotions safely, and then he was back playing with Teejay again.

Our children do need to get on with things when times are tough, but painful experiences can stop them in their tracks. When they experience those challenging moments, they do not need us to push them away, dismissively telling them to toughen up while disapprovingly chastening them for their 'silliness'. This doesn't steel them against adversity. As a result of our children's cognitive, neurological and emotional resources being much less developed than our own, they become increasingly sensitised by such treatment. Their immaturity and lack of resources limit their capacity to leave or alter a difficult or adversarial situation effectively, and they can do little in most cases to change their environment. Our children are far more reactive, far less likely to think logically and rationally, and far less nuanced in their understanding of the challenges life throws at them. They require us to act as scaffolding, supplying them with additional support to wade through the challenges they experience.

When a child faces difficulty, they are already dealing with adversity that may act as a steeling agent. The challenge is enough. They do not need to have a parent – the person in their lives who is supposed to be there for them unconditionally – to start adding more pressure to them to stand on their own two feet, toughen up and get on with it.

Let's return to the story from the beginning of this chapter. When Mrs Boonen knew she had heard correctly, and that Amelia really was upset because a girl had pointed at her, she had a choice. Do I tell Amelia to shrug it off? Or do I coach her through her feelings and see if she can work out a solution? Choosing the latter, Mrs Boonen talked a bit about Amelia's big emotion.

'You're feeling so upset about this. It's left you feeling like no one cares about you. It doesn't feel good when people point.' While not agreeing with Amelia (and while secretly thinking that it was all way over the top), she named Amelia's emotions and let her sit with them. There's a saying that teaches us, 'If you can name it, you can tame it.' Amelia was so emotionally flooded that she didn't know where to begin with describing how she felt or why. As she heard Mrs Boonen describe the emotions she was feeling, Amelia began to feel safe and understood. As she calmed down, her teacher stated, 'It's unusual for you to cry just because someone pointed at you. Are you having a horrible day?'

Amelia nodded.

'Would you like to tell me about it?'

Amelia slowly explained a little more to her teacher. 'At recess those girls were teasing me. Then they started stealing my food and throwing it to each other so I couldn't get it. And then they threw it all in the bin.'

Now things were starting to make more sense. 'Oh, that's why you were so upset. Because the girls have been teasing you and you lost your food.'

Amelia added, 'Yes, and when I told them to stop they just laughed at me and teased me and told me I'm in love with Jordan.'

As she listened, Mrs Boonen realised the teasing had reached a climax just before the recess bell rang. As Amelia had told her peers that she was going to tell the teacher, one of the girls had mocked her: 'Oh, she's going to tell the teacher.' Then she had pointed at Amelia and laughed as she had run away.

That's when Mrs Boonen had caught her, at the peak of her emotional distress. Had she chosen the tough love option, would that have helped Amelia become more resilient? Would telling Amelia to 'toughen up, Princess' or to 'drink some concrete and harden up' have steeled her against future challenges and difficulties? Or did having a caring adult who listened and understood make a positive difference? I suspect that the answer is the latter.

Take-home message

It is a myth that we need to toughen our children up, whether they are two days old, two months old, two years old, or twenty-two years old. The world will throw enough at them. Instead, we need to be a safe place for them to land and be supported when life gets tough. Children become resilient as a result of the patterns of stress and of nurturing that they experience early on in life. The stress does make them resilient, but only when they are developmentally capable of facing it. In the same way that working out in a gym is bad for developing bones and muscles in children, too much resistance via adversity and challenge at too young an age can incapacitate and sensitise our children.

Is helicopter parenting *really* ruining resilience?

We are so afraid of getting parenting wrong
that we overdo it getting it right.
Julie Lythcott-Haims[49]

Jai was a quiet boy. It wasn't that he had nothing to say. Instead, his mother spoke for him. Everywhere. All the time. Jai's mum would tell people, 'Jai is quite shy.' She would let them know, clearly, that she would speak for him. If someone asked him a question and he began to respond, his mum would speak over the top of him. Jai recalled being in his early teens and having his mother enter a room, see he was speaking with someone, and walk across the room and take over the conversation 'to help' him. He was in his late teens before she finally began to step back so that he could 'find his voice'.

Another young man I spent some time with, Sam, informed me that 'Mum won't let me do anything. I literally have to stay in the house. I can't have a job. I'm not allowed to get my driver's licence. I'm 17 and I'm still not allowed to ride my bike to the shops.' Sam's mum made all of his decisions from clothing to friends. Sam acknowledged, 'I know she's doing it because she loves me but I can't seem to make any decisions for myself.'

Media articles that point to over-parenting are common, and are usually followed by hundreds of comments decrying 'kids these days' who can't cross the street without their parents holding their hand, or who need mummy to sit with them at a job interview or their first day of university. Some universities are now providing guidelines to staff, giving direction on how best to interact with such parents.[50] My personal favourite example of 'helicopter parenting', as it's come to be known, is the parent who called an HR manager to negotiate a pay rise for her child.[51]

Not all helicopter parenting is so extreme. In some cases, parents might refuse to allow a child to ride their bike to school. Some parents install apps on their children's phones to be able to locate them, wherever they may be, with little more than a finger swipe. They may hover over their children's dietary choices, friendship decisions, school assessments and reports. They are forever at the ready. Is this a problem? Is this helicoptering leading to an unhealthy form of over-parenting?[52]

What does the data tell us? Tales like those above are parroted around parenting blogs and even popular books, but their authors never provide empirical data to point to a problem. One Australian research report that received global attention showed that 25 per cent of school psychologists, counsellors, teachers and mental health workers identified that they had seen 'many' instances of over-parenting. Nearly two-thirds said they had seen 'some' instances of this behaviour. Only 8 per cent had never witnessed it.[53] The media alarmists clamoured over a generation of needy, spoon-fed children with no resilience, being raised by Baby Boomer and Generation X mums and dads who try to do everything to protect their children. Yet the study did not indicate anything that could demonstrate ill effects in the lives of the children being spoken of – because neither the children nor the effects of over-parenting were being studied. It was a sample of school counsellors and associated staff being asked what they had seen. Further, only 25 per cent of participants indicated seeing 'many' instances. Perhaps helicopter parenting is not so much an 'epidemic' but something newsworthy purely because it is unusual? After all, normal is not newsworthy.

I was unable to uncover any studies examining the prevalence of helicopter parenting for parents of younger children, or sufficient studies on older children, to draw clear conclusions. Also, a study asking a convenience sample of counsellors about their exposure to helicopter parenting is answering a vastly different question. Because of a lack of meaningful data, a more helpful question we might examine is whether or not helicopter parenting is ruining resilience in our children.

What is helicopter parenting?

Helicopter – or over-involved – parenting is only just beginning to be studied scientifically, even though the term was first coined in the bestselling 1969 book by parenting guru Haim Ginott, *Between Parent and Teenager*,[54] and it became a 'thing' in the 1990s.[55] Helicopter parenting is named for the tendency of some parents to 'hover' over their children. Helicopter parenting is 'a form of over-parenting in which parents apply overly involved and developmentally inappropriate tactics to their children'.[56] These 'hyper-involved' strategies are *meant* to protect children from experiencing adversity and difficulty, and to maximise opportunities for success. This is why helicopter parents hold their children so close, whether on a swing or bike, or while completing schoolwork and assignments. With the very best intentions (usually), helicopter parents are involved to the point where they disallow their children from assuming responsibility for their own choices. They do not allow choice that is developmentally appropriate.

I believe that helicopter parenting is occurring for a number of reasons. First, we care so deeply about our children. We want the very best for them. We are trying to protect and guide them. In

51

many ways we can't help ourselves. And we think that by being so involved and using our wisdom and experience to guide them, we are helping them, unaware that in some cases we may actually be crippling them. Second, we are having fewer children. This means we have greater emotional, financial and time investment in our children, which only ups the ante. Third, our children's lives seem more pressured than they may have in the past. Every decision seems to count. The push for excellence in schooling, employment and extra-curricular activities is relentless. We want them to achieve so that they stand out and have the best opportunities, so we hover, help and do all we can to hasten their progress.

Another explanation is also possible in some circumstances. In examining Myth 1, we explored how we interfere with early processes, with the undermining of resilience being a possible result. If we are neglectful, or provide insufficient care during infancy and early childhood through practising 'cry-it-out' methods, or through a lack of presence, touch and nourishing habits, toxic stress can accumulate and compound in babies. This can create a dysregulated system because that beautiful give-and-take pattern of interaction between parent and child is not quite working. If our children are feeling this level of insufficient care, then they are at greater risk of both internalising (depression and stress) and externalising (aggression) issues, depending on the timing, the intensity and the duration of that stress in their life. When we see our children exhibiting these symptoms, we feel the need to helicopter them. We become over-involved, because we see a child that is unconfident, or unruly, or struggling in some other way. And of course, if we as parents experienced a level of under-care ourselves when we were children, we'll almost certainly be more anxious about our own children and lean towards over-control in order to satisfy our own anxieties.

Brigham Young University researchers Laura Padilla-Walker and Larry Nelson suggest that helicopter parents are high on warmth and support for their children, but also high on behavioural control. Traditionally this might be called 'authoritative' parenting – a little confusing because this warmth/strictness model is often described as the 'gold standard' of parenting,[57] so how can it also be problematic?

Current models of parenting add an important third dimension to the old warmth/strictness model to change our way of understanding parenting: autonomy.[58] Padilla-Walker and Nelson have discovered that while helicopter parents look like great parents with their limits and love, they actually go too far in their disallowance of their children's autonomy.[59] And it seems that children *feel* controlled too. When researchers ask children who have helicopter parents about their experience of their parents, they say their parents are very emotionally supportive, but they also identify that their parents are overprotective and oversolicitous. They are inappropriately intrusive and controlling. Helicopter parents' intentions are good. The trouble is that helicopter parents are so concerned about getting it wrong, they overdo it in terms of getting it right and ultimately undermine what they are trying to achieve.[60] Helicopter parents are, to paraphrase Julie Lythcott-Haims, not trying to be psychologically controlling. They are not trying to change the way their children feel or think – in fact, they are often supportive of feelings and thoughts. But motivation aside, they actually are overly controlling, over-involved, and get in the way of their children's development.

So is helicopter parenting actually a problem?

Some researchers don't use the term 'helicopter parenting'. They prefer to speak of over-solicitous parenting, over-involved parenting or over-controlling parenting. For simplicity, I'll refer to helicopter parenting as over-involved parenting. Again, research in this area is limited, but those studies that do exist suggest there are problems with being *over*-involved in our children's lives. The message to parents seems fairly clear: back off a bit. Stop being so intrusive and controlling. It will be better for your child's resilience and wellbeing if you do.

How do we get this balance right? Our children need to know that we care deeply for them and want to be involved in their lives, but when we over-involve ourselves we may inhibit their ability to develop the skills and abilities that they require to act independently. Instead, because of our over-involvement we teach them to keep relying on external sources of support (us) to get through life.[61] This is inconsistent with the principles of resilience. If we always carry our children, they may never develop the leg strength to carry themselves. If we carry them emotionally, they will not develop the resilience to support themselves as they encounter emotional hurdles in life. While independence is not an explicit attribute of resilient people, an overly heavy reliance on others is unhealthy. For example, researchers have found that parental over-involvement overrides some preschoolers' ability to learn how to regulate emotions.[62] When we swoop in too quickly to soothe every symptom, children may struggle to develop the capacity to work through their 'stuff'. So we must find the balance between stepping in and stepping out. We want to be responsive and supportive, but not fix everything before our child has learned to experience, process and respond to their challenges. Helicopter parenting may harm children by limiting opportunities to practice important skills and abilities.[63]

When Kya and Annabel have a disagreement at the age of eight, they should be given time to work things out with our support, but not our correction, direction or instruction. If we solve our children's challenges before they can experience them and work through their options, they do not develop skills, abilities and competencies that will steel them for later life. Because competence lifts confidence, they may also either struggle to develop confidence in their own ability to figure things out because we keep doing it for them, or alternatively they may develop a hollow confidence, easily crushed, when we undermine their skill development by swooping in to fix things.

All of this leads to another significant drawback of over-involvement. Research has shown a positive relationship between over-involved parenting and something that psychologists call *internalising* difficulties (things like anxiety, depression and low self-esteem) in children aged just two and four.[64] A positive relationship means that as one variable goes up (over-parenting), so too does the other one (internalising). The more we over-involve ourselves in parenting, the more our children internalise, and increase their risk of depression, anxiety, stress or sadness. Such outcomes are clearly linked with decreased resilience. Similar results have been identified in a mid-childhood-aged sample.[65]

These issues are not just impactful on young children. As children move into the school years there is evidence that the more parents are involved in the daily lives of their children, the less engaged they are in school.[66] The evidence tells us clearly that it is vital that we are involved in our children's education, but over-involvement is associated with diminished school engagement. These educational impediments continue into early adulthood too. Emerging adults with intrusive parents appear to be less proactive and less personally invested in pursuing an education or career. A study of over 500 parent–young adult pairs pointed to the dreaded *entitlement* issues. Young adults with over-involved parents felt that others should solve their problems, including their education and career difficulties.[67]

The sins of the parents

A mother complained to me that her seven-year-old daughter was highly anxious, and she wanted to know whether her child needed to be medicated. I had the opportunity to observe the mother interacting with her daughter as they participated in a range of everyday tasks in their home, including tidying the bedroom and kitchen, doing some schoolwork and playing a game. As I watched I was struck by two things. First, the mother was exceptionally edgy and highly strung. She exhibited clear perfectionist tendencies that led her to appear endlessly and disproportionately anxious as she carried out her basic tasks and interactions with her daughter. Second, the mother was highly controlling. She persistently pointed out what her daughter should be doing and *how* she should do it. The mother told me that she believed she was being on her best behaviour and downplaying what she might normally do. This mother's behaviour led to a high degree of anxiety in her otherwise content and happy seven-year-old as the child attempted to pre-empt her mother's correction and direction, and to minimise her anxiety and control. While there may have been a genetic component to this little girl's anxiety and reduced resilience, the way this mother tried to help was pushing the control too far and affecting her daughter's wellbeing.

In many cases, it makes sense that we try to over-parent. Our intrusiveness may be a reaction to children's anxiety or other challenging behaviour. As an example, parents of children who have low self-esteem offer higher levels of praise than they do for children who feel good about themselves: the parents attempt to compensate.[68] We become protective, almost instinctively, when our children struggle. We want to step in. But doing so can often undermine rather than support their resilience.

One father told me he completes his son's homework for him so he doesn't have to struggle like *he* did when he was younger. I asked him how he felt his son would fare once he was in the workplace or at university, when he came up against something unknown or challenging. The father replied that he would help him then too. While not only unrealistic, these maladaptive over-parenting behaviours, according to research, are likely to lead to poor outcomes. Studies indicate that children who report higher levels of over-parenting are more likely to endorse solutions that rely on others rather than taking responsibility themselves.[69] The researchers suggested this result was particularly damning because the students were able to identify that their parents were too involved, yet even with that insight they still demonstrated dependence, due to low self-efficacy. Even if these individuals possess the technical abilities to accomplish their work – which they often will not because their parents are the ones with the skills – their lack of self-efficacy hinders soft skills, such as responsibility and conscientiousness, that employers value.

Children in late adolescence really do want to have their parents engaged and involved in their lives. Two-thirds of students confirmed that heightened levels of parental involvement was normal, and they were positive about the significant part their parents played in their lives.[70] They want us close. They want our input. Studies with adolescents have demonstrated that relationships *are* more positive, parents *are* viewed more warmly, and children experience *more* positive outcomes when parents are highly involved – but not overly involved. Parents who are involved in guiding their children when dealing with moral or prudential domains (alcohol, drugs, sex) but are less involved in personal domains (music, hair, clothing) have children who stay close to them, and who make better choices that are ultimately beneficial for their resilience.[71] But – and it's a big but – *their clear preference is that parents be neither behaviourally nor psychologically controlling.* Interestingly, better relationships lead to more latitude around this issue of control. That is, when the relationship feels good, kids accept more control. Trust is present. Influence is allowed. But when the relationship feels lousy, children resist control, show a lack of trust in their parents, and become impervious to influence. When we look at research with younger children, once again we see that if high levels of parental involvement lead to a *positive* parent–child relationship, then children give increased latitude to their parents for their controlling behaviour. Conversely, a negative relationship would lead to a certain parental behaviour being perceived as controlling.[72]

Ultimately, there are behaviours that are controlling regardless of the quality of the relationship. Developmentally inappropriate controls (such as those described at the start of this chapter) will almost universally undermine our relationships with our child (eventually), and are a clear risk factor for low resilience. Knowing when to step in and when to step out is where the difference lies.

Parental involvement vs over-parenting

The top-line summary of all of this research is that children *need* their parents to be involved in their lives. They need consistent presence, predictable routines, clear limits and boundaries, and the sense that they *matter*, which they gain through our interest, engagement and involvement. They feel safe and secure. High levels of involvement are predictive of children flourishing.[73] There is a mountain of data from decades of research demonstrating that young children whose parents are highly involved in their lives and who also provide developmentally appropriate structure have better academic, emotional and social outcomes. They enjoy more positive peer relationships and exhibit fewer behaviour problems at school. And for parents who are struggling with adolescents, research highlights the importance of staying close to them at this challenging time. One of many studies describes that when mothers are highly involved in their teenagers' lives, their teens behave more pro-socially and have higher levels of hope.[74]

And note that these studies *do* point to involvement being *high*. This is where the best outcomes exist for our children. Where do we draw the line between high levels of parental involvement and over-parenting? After all, the evidence clearly says that over-parenting leads to suboptimal outcomes. While we can't say it undermines resilience because that hasn't been explicitly studied, it certainly reduces a range of attributes strongly related to resilience. The answer to where to draw the line is: it depends. The clearest differentiator between parental involvement and over-involved parenting may be this: Ask your child!

When we ask a child, 'Can you do it?' and they say, 'Yes,' they are demonstrating self-efficacy. They believe that their action will lead to a desired outcome. We should only become involved in doing things for our children that they can do for themselves if they genuinely *need* help – such as if they are tired or stressed. When we go beyond involvement and become over-involved, we reduce self-efficacy.[75]

Parental involvement offers support – scaffolding – to give children the confidence to try things, knowing that if they fail, someone will be there for them. But over-parenting does the opposite. It reduces the feeling a child has that they can do something on their own. An involved parent is concerned enough to ask, 'Can you do it?' Then that parent will either leave a capable child to their own devices if they say 'yes', or they will coach and guide their child if they say 'no'. An over-involved parent assumes that whether the child can do it or not, they, the parent, should do it for them. Not coach. Not guide. But do it. This may be anything from making decisions for their child, to taking responsibility for them, or completing tasks and activities for them.

Take-home message

It is a myth that we make our children more resilient by saving them from themselves, and from everything else around them. Our children value high levels of parental involvement. They want us in their lives. They want to be in ours. They require it. Parental involvement is related to positive life experiences in our children. They experience elevated feelings of worth, wellbeing and, by default, resilience. What they do *not* require is developmentally inappropriate levels of control. Clearly, when taken to extremes, evidence demonstrates that too much helicoptering is unhelpful and unhealthy, and may be harmful.

To build resilience, we need to trust that our children can do things on their own. Then we must give them the space to try. By all means, stand close and support. But don't 'do'. Don't control. And when they fail, don't fix. Instead, console and then ask, 'What do you think you should do now?'

The dark side of grit, and how being too gritty might reduce resilience

Nothing in the world can take the place of persistence. Talent will not. Nothing is more common than unsuccessful men with talent. Genius will not. Unrewarded genius is almost a proverb. Education will not. The world is full of educated derelicts. Persistence and determination alone are omnipotent.

Calvin Coolidge

Joanne was a failure. At least, that's what the letter she held in her hand told her. Like so many other letters, this one was polite but devoid of hope. Her book had taken years to write. She had found an agent who thought it was worthy of publication, but the publishers were consistently saying no.

Joanne had lived a relatively quiet and ordinary life. She had never been a standout student. Her teen years were particularly unhappy. In a little less than ten years since leaving high school Joanne had obtained a degree, lost her mum to disease, travelled, taught overseas, married, had a child, divorced, moved home, suffered from clinical depression, found herself unemployed; yet she had also been working on a novel. It had taken six years, but finally, the book was done.

After a dozen rejection letters, a London publisher agreed that there might be something in Joanne's book, and they decided to give it a go. Joanne was obviously elated. But she was given a stern reality check by the editor working on her book, who told her that while her book was good, she should not expect to make money. After all, not many authors gain any real financial rewards from their books.

The book was finally published. The first print run was fairly standard for a book that no one held high hopes for: 1000 copies. And then ... nothing much. Some books sold. Some people said some nice things. And all was quiet. Five months later, however, Joanne's little children's book won a major award. Two months later, it was named the British Book of the Year for children, and then it won another major award. Then the US rights were sold.

Joanne was thrilled. She was already working on a sequel, and a year after the first book was released, she watched the new book take off. It won more awards, as did the third book in her series, just twelve months later.

When Joanne released her fourth book, sales records were smashed all over the world. The momentum continued when, a few years later, book six sold nine million copies on day one. Finally, book seven, the last book in the Harry Potter series, became the fastest selling book of all time.

JK Rowling showed the kind of resilience that may, when you think about it, seem rather ordinary. After all, resilience is showing up each time you fall and being able to achieve great outcomes in spite of those setbacks. And that's about all Joanne did. She was persistent. Determined. Hopeful. But at times she was despondent. Despairing. Hopeless. Yet day after day, she showed up, tried a little more, did something extra and, like Dory in *Finding Nemo*, she just kept swimming.

Defining grit

I call grit 'stick-to-it-ness'. That's not particularly scientific, but you probably get the picture. Grit is *the* buzz-word in education and organisation circles. The topic has spawned bestsellers on the promise that grit is the secret to success, and the cure-all for our children.[76] Grit is the tendency a person has to maintain their effort and keep on going on a long-term goal.[77] People with high grit are more likely to succeed than those with high 'talent' or 'intelligence'.[78] They are also less likely to change their careers repeatedly, and less likely to divorce.[79] And while there is no research investigating the relationship between grit and resilience, it makes sense that the two concepts might be related. Someone who persists and persists, even when things are tough, would be considered resilient – though resilient people are not necessarily always going to be gritty. More on that idea shortly.

If grit is associated with so many optimal outcomes, and is at least theoretically associated with resilience, surely we want it for our children. Young children appear single-minded in their determination to achieve what they want to, and they need to be. Whether it's learning to crawl and walk, figuring out how to communicate, or doing whatever is necessary to get that goal, our children need to be persistent. And they are! But as they mature, some children lose that 'go get 'em' attitude and become disengaged or apathetic when the going gets tough. Is this a problem? Does it demonstrate a lack of resilience? Will they be able to thrive?

Angela Duckworth, the positive psychology grit guru, suggests that a child with true grit is one who:

- is not easily distracted by new ideas and projects
- bounces back from setbacks
- works hard
- doesn't flit from project to project but stays focused
- holds on to an idea and finishes whatever they begin.[80]

The key theme to grit is a single-minded focus on achieving a goal or outcome that matters to the individual. Once again, that sounds at least similar to resilience, and it sounds like it's what we want our children to have and be. But if that does *not* sound like your child, does that mean that you're in trouble? Maybe. But maybe not.

There is little doubt that grit is a key part of success. We need to stick with a relationship with dogged determination to make it work over the long term. The same might be said in the pursuit of career or financial success. But do those with grit ever quit? And if they do, does this mean they are not resilient?

On the contrary, sometimes being gritty might be unhealthy. To persist in doing something when you cannot succeed, or when it is causing pain, upset and is ultimately stopping you from progressing as a person, may be less healthy and functional than just stopping. Here are some scenarios we may experience with our children:

- Your son desperately wants to play soccer. But after three weeks of running around on the field barely kicking the ball he wants to stop. Should you let him? Would it be different if it were three years? What if he was quite good but just lacked desire?

- Your daughter begs to be allowed to learn a musical instrument. You agree and purchase a second-hand piano, have it moved into your lounge room, get it tuned and commence lessons. After 16 weeks, she can play a few basic tunes and decides she is more interested in the clarinet. Or the guitar. She definitely wants to play music, but the piano isn't what she had hoped. Is that okay? What if she has worked hard, played for four years, passed her Grade 3 assessment and now wishes to start a new instrument?

- Your child performs worse than expected on a school exam or test. The score or the feedback leaves her feeling like a failure, and she begins to tell you that she hates

maths – and she is only in Year 2. In fact, she decides
that she would like to quit school altogether!

The correct answer for what you should do in each of these
scenarios is: 'It depends.' In some instances, you might hear a
child's complaint and respect their judgement. In other cases
you may suggest that you recognise your child's preference, but
feel that perhaps some more time, effort and learning might be
worthwhile before decisions are made. Your child might, at that
point, throw a fit. It may be overwhelming. When this happens,
calm things down, and reconsider the decision when emotions are
less heightened. This buys you some time, helps your child think
things over, and allows everyone to exercise better judgement
when emotions are calmer.

Failing and getting back up again is an essential part of grit, and
of resilience. Sticking at something for the long haul is likewise.
But that doesn't mean that every failure *should* be bounced back
from. Nor does it mean that every path chosen *must* be followed
to the end. It's okay to take counsel from life. There are times
when life gives clear signals that 'this isn't working'. There should
be no shame in accepting an honourable defeat when you've given
what seems reasonable – or beyond. This is, of course, a little
different from trying something briefly and changing your mind
on a whim. But even giving something a go and deciding it's not
for you should be okay. Yes, it can be inconvenient – and costly.
Sometimes it may mean letting someone down. But if a productive
alternative choice appears and it matters more to you (or your
child), then why not try it?

And researchers from Harvard University have recently begun
to question the pre-eminence of grit as *the* secret to success.[81] While
steely determination is valuable, they discovered that in many
cases successful people do not clench their teeth and work hard
at something for a long time with painstaking commitment to the

cause, come hell or high water. Instead, their research showed that success is entirely individual. For some, it's all about the hours and the commitment. For others, it's about following a natural strength or passion. In some cases, it's nothing more than luck, knowing the right person, or being in the right place at the right time.

At what point do we say a child (or adult) is, or is not, gritty – or resilient? The child who wants to quit may not be quitting because of setbacks or a lack of ability. They may simply not have known what would be enjoyable. They might wish to experience new ideas. Or perhaps they feel self-conscious because of immediate failures in a new venture.

Grit and persistence can help us achieve things we may never have believed were possible. This book has identified some of the most remarkable stories of grit and persistence – stories that would be impossible to achieve without remarkable resilience, pushing on and adapting to setbacks. But once again, we need to consider the way we view grit.

Grit for the sake of grit

While ever we are emphasising someone's need to develop grit or persistence we are not stepping back and asking about the actual value of the task itself. Most of our children are not pursuing Olympic glory or elite athleticism. Sometimes, they have tried something and don't want to do it any more. Perhaps it was a failure. Maybe it's of no interest. But we should be careful that we don't prescribe sticking at something for the sake of grit, and grit alone. Yes, persistence will help us achieve more than we ever could imagine when compared with the alternative – giving up. But is that achievement really what our children want? Will they truly be grateful that they achieved it? Doing something for the sake of doing it makes a given task inherently less valuable than doing it because we want to do it. When we talk about a person's grittiness, we focus on the person rather than the position that they are in or the preferences they hold.

Some years ago one of my children expressed an interest in racing bikes at the velodrome. I was riding in a local competition on Friday nights and she loved the atmosphere, so she asked if she could participate. This meant buying a second-hand track bike and a used pair of racing shoes, Lycra kit, a helmet and a few other bits and pieces. As I was a full-time student, this was a burdensome commitment. We made some challenging choices, decided to forego some necessities, and dug deep into our pockets. The financial sacrifice was significant, but we gave our little girl the chance. And she loved it ... for about three weeks. Then came the night where she complained, 'I don't want to go.' She wasn't just being beaten. She was being decimated. The other children were stronger, more experienced, and were competing well together. My little girl was barely even an also-ran. And it was demoralising her.

We talked it over together; mum, dad and daughter. We discussed her enthusiasm. We considered the costs that were recoverable through selling equipment and those that were a pure loss. And then we shrugged our shoulders and let her decide for herself. Surprisingly, that support and autonomy led her to show some grit. She kept going for a little while. Eventually, however, we could all see that it was not enjoyable and, after a couple of months, she quit.

Demanding unthinking grit ignores the value of the task. In my daughter's case, fitness mattered. But this was not the only way for her to be healthy and fit. Sometimes we ask our children (and even ourselves) to participate in, and complete, tasks that have no value, or tasks where the same value can be obtained elsewhere. And sometimes value is subjective. For example, while we value health and fitness tremendously in our home, I do not value my children's performance in a school athletics carnival at all! Their performance is entirely irrelevant to me, except to the extent that it matters to them. Some of my children feel the same way I do. Others care deeply about their sporting ability and want to be as good as they can be. Little is to be gained by forcing a child to run full pace around a grass oval and persist with grit until the end of the race if it doesn't mean anything to them.

Of course, there are some tasks that really do have objective value. Persisting with an education is almost universally necessary for success in the society in which we live. However, even in this, *demanding* persistence may not be what we need if we wish to achieve optimal outcomes. A strong argument can be made that our education system challenges students, not by stimulating a love of learning, but by disengaging them or making content seem irrelevant. In fact, much of it is for most students. One of my children complained as she did her Year 9 maths homework and struggled to understand surds, 'Dad, why am I even learning this? Every adult I know except my maths teacher has forgotten what this is, and no one can tell me why surds matter or where I would use them in real life.' For me to tell her to knuckle down and learn it anyway ignores the singular point that for her and her goals this content was entirely irrelevant. Grit and determination are necessary only because of a system that demands it. We can hardly blame our children for lacking resilience when they are stuck completing work that means so little. Some people will argue that our children need to 'learn how to learn', and that is the purpose of grit. They just have to get through it. Life requires all of us to do things that we do not wish to do at some point. I reject this for the following reasons: first, our children are already learning, and they do so quite grittily and willingly from the moment they are born if they have the inner drive to develop a certain capability or attribute. Second, our children are already pushing through hard things they'd rather not do on a regular basis anyway. Life simply demands that we all do this.

68

Putting horrible, hard, ugly things in front of them just to teach them to 'learn, dammit', does nothing to encourage grit or other admirable characteristics, never mind resilience.

The role of autonomy and motivation in being gritty

One of the basic human requirements for resilience – and motivation – is autonomy.[82] Many people, regardless of their age, fail to persist (and achieve) because they are not choosing what they do. Whether it is school, extra-curricular activities or even a career, a lack of choice reduces the motivation to persist, particularly following challenges and setbacks.[83] It's hard to be gritty when you don't really want to do something, intrinsically. Stress and burnout result. However, when intrinsic motivation is high and an activity is entirely volitional, there are rarely any problems with grit – or resilience. In other words, when a child is motivated to do something simply for the sake of doing it, such as during play, we would say that they are intrinsically motivated. When they are choosing to act for themselves without parental (or other external) pressure, their actions are volitional and freely chosen. They are using their 'agency'. And there is a surplus of gritty persistence.

In seminars I run with educators, a common complaint is, 'Kids these days have no resilience. They've got no willingness to persevere. I give them a C, and they tell me they hate writing essays and they don't want to get any better.' The same principle might apply in the workplace when an employee receives performance appraisals from a manager. I suspect that wherever evaluation exists, determination, grit and resilience will be undermined. This is because there is so much focus on outcome and not enough focus on process.

My suggestion to educators: where possible, give results that are either an A or an incomplete. If a student receives an A they know they are performing at a high level. If they receive an incomplete there is an implicit suggestion that more work – or focus on process and learning – is required. This should lead to useful feedback and another opportunity to demonstrate capability. It should also increase rather than deplete grit and resilience. Feedback that is less about evaluation and more about 'where to from here?' means we are focusing less on *how well* children are doing something, and instead emphasising *how* they are doing it. A focus on *how well* a child is doing leaves them deciding, 'I'm no good at this. What's the point?' But a focus on *how* a child is doing something allows them to think less about their ego and more about the task, thus building the persistence so integral to resilience.

It is usually at this point that someone will say, 'Well, it's just the system and we need to accept it.' I disagree. In fact, I think that we need to resist a system that is designed in such a way that it actively undermines the very attributes we wish to build up in our children. Such brutality harms children's educational, career and lifetime aspirations. It demotivates and demoralises kids who have tremendous capacity but don't quite fit in the system as it stands. Surely in a world so rich with opportunity our children should be able to learn and engage with material they see as relevant, interesting and meaningful to them. Information is at our fingertips. We have the resources. We just don't seem to have the political will to question the structures that demand persisting at tasks that all too often seem pointless. Our politicians appeal to ideals such as accountability and transparency with high-stakes standardised tests and internet-based school comparison tables that are designed to apply pressure to school systems and teachers. This pressure trickles down to our children, who are required to sit high-pressure tests that provide them with a number or a ranking to highlight how they've performed. Too many children discover their ranking and feel despondent. They decide it's all too hard. And their resilience is dented – or even decimated. They lose motivation, and grit goes south.

My friend Wally told me that his son Andy wanted to be a pilot. To become a pilot would require gritty determination over a long period so he could raise the money, take the lessons, go to school and eventually graduate. Wally wanted Andy to have those opportunities but needed to balance this with an understanding of the relevant costs and investment Andy would need. Together, they read a book about gliding. The thrill of flight seemed more exciting than ever. Wally purchased a gliding experience for Andy so that he could experience flying. Andy was ecstatic. The day arrived, and he boarded the glider. He flew up into the air with an instructor and had the opportunity to fly and glide through the afternoon. The experience led to a change of heart. This was due to two reasons: first, the discomfort of the cockpit on a sunny day was more than he had imagined it might be. Second, he had overeaten on his way to the airport. Andy shifted his energy towards art and graphic design, something that was another passion. This was something that he could stick at. His office could be air-conditioned, and overeating was not an occupational hazard.

To continue to work hard but find no satisfaction suggests that, as Covey put it, 'The ladder is up against the wrong wall.'[84] We should not demand this of our children, nor is it inspiring to expect it of ourselves. But if an activity creates a sense of flow (where our ability is neatly matched with the difficulty of the task), or deep engagement, then it may be worth pursuing. Those activities that are enriching and life-enhancing will still be difficult at times. But the positive energy that comes from flow will offset the pain of pushing through the hard times.

Sometimes our children lack grit – they have no stick-to-it-iveness. They lack motivation and will. Sometimes they need us to help them to persist at useful, meaningful, worthwhile, purposeful tasks because that persistence will endow them with attributes that will be a blessing to them and to others throughout their lives. Sometimes, developing grit will bolster resilience. But at other times the problem is not with our children (or with us). Sometimes the problem is with the structures and systems, the policies and practices, that demand a certain level of compliance or completion at tremendous cost but with limited, if any, gain and in areas that may be irrelevant to the child. Does everyone really need calculus? Is it essential that all children learn to program?

The answer to these questions is that it depends. Sometimes, as in the case of JK Rowling, grit and determination are all-powerful, all-conquering attributes. And then there are the cases like those of Andy, the almost-pilot who became a fine artist.

In Thailand, there is a story that is a bit like the classic 'little engine that could'. But instead of repeating the mantra, 'I think I can', this character repeated, 'Maybe I can and maybe I can't, and either way is okay.' This Taoist philosophy may seem defeatist to some, but it makes a curious cultural counterpoint to the overpowering and intoxicating demands of our culture for more grit, more determination, more perseverance and more success.

Take-home message

As a society, we tend to elevate a particular attribute or quality as *sine quo non* – without which not, the absolute essential and complete truth. It's the single quality that makes *all* the difference. But everything has its tension. Grit is valuable, but it doesn't stand alone. It requires the travelling companions of good judgement mixed with experience.

Good praising: why praise is a problem in promoting resilience

Most of us would rather be ruined by praise than saved by criticism.

Norman Vincent Peale

You walk into a psychology laboratory to participate in an experiment about problem-solving. The researcher greets you, invites you to sit at a desk, and after providing you with a brief overview of the study he hands you a booklet with a series of ten puzzles.

Each puzzle contains a table set up with three rows and three columns. A shape is in each of eight of the nine squares, and the shapes follow a pattern. There is nothing in the ninth square at the bottom right. Your job is to work out what the missing shape should look like, based on eight possible answers to the puzzle, displayed on the page underneath the table. One puzzle looks a little like the one on the following page.

You are the only person participating in the experiment, so it is just you and the researcher in the room. He explains that you will have a total of five minutes to complete all ten puzzles. As you work through the matrices you think to yourself, 'Wow, these are incredibly easy.' And you're right. The ten puzzles are the ten easiest in the book. Instead of taking five minutes to complete them, you take about two minutes, and as you watch the researcher mark your responses you feel very, very smart. You get all of them correct.

He looks at you, smiles and states, 'Wow, you're really smart at these. You got ten out of ten.' At least, that's what he says if you're in the experimental group. The experimental group is being praised for excellent performance. The researcher is trying to make you feel smart for doing well. He's praising your intelligence. There is also a control group who get different feedback, of the neutral variety. If you were in the control group you would have been told, 'You got ten out of ten.' That's it. No praise. No smiles. Just a neutral reporting of your score.

Next the researcher hands you a second set of ten matrices. Once again you have five minutes to complete all ten puzzles. This time, however, you struggle. These ones are almost impossible! Your five minutes is up before you have attempted more than a few, and you discover you only achieved a score of one out of ten.

Ugh. You feel deflated – and defeated.

Regardless of whether you are in the experimental group (where praise was previously given) or the control group (where neutral feedback was delivered), the researcher states, 'You got one out of ten on that set.' Then he explains, 'There's just one more set of puzzles to complete. This time, you get to choose. Would you prefer to do another ten puzzles like the first ones you completed, or ten like the second set you completed?'

You know it's a psychology experiment. You know that this is the moment of truth. But you really don't know what he's getting at or why he's giving you a choice. And you don't know how your choice will relate to any psychology theory. So, after pausing, you choose. And whether or not you were praised has a significant impact on the choice you make.

The 'smart' choice – or more accurately, the choice that smart people should make – is to take on the more challenging puzzles again. Scoring one out of ten offers tremendous opportunities for future learning and mastery. The 'dumb' choice is to request another ten simple puzzles where a high score is assured.

In 2003 I conducted this experiment at the University of Queensland. More than 100 participants from highly competitive university degrees came through my lab, one at a time. To ensure random allocation to the praise and the control groups, I praised every second person for their intelligence after the first set of matrices, while offering neutral feedback to every other person.

Consistent with previous research on young children, I discovered that praise changed participants' mindsets. When people received praise for their intelligence, they were significantly more likely to choose the easy set of matrices when given a choice. Those who had been given neutral feedback consistently opted for the harder puzzles. Moreover, those who were praised scored significantly worse the second time they did their puzzles, regardless of which set they chose. It was as though my simple 'Wow, you're really smart' statement placed a load of pressure on them that sabotaged their capacity to perform.

Participants who were not praised but who instead received neutral feedback typically embraced the opportunity to take on the extra challenge of the harder puzzles when given the option. I recall one young man looking at me and enthusiastically requesting, 'I want to try more of those hard ones. There's no point doing the easy ones. I'm not learning anything from them. I want to figure out those tough ones. They were challenging.'

Pumping up tyres

One of the most persistent myths in parenting generally, and specifically related to resilience, is that to boost wellbeing, self-esteem and resilience, we need to pump up our children's tyres. We need to praise them. Parenting experts consistently push praise as a permanent part of their platform for raising resilient children.[85] If you look up 'praise' on the internet you will be inundated with well-meaning advice describing how many times we ought to praise children to help them to be resilient. The argument is that praise provides important scaffolding that helps children believe they are capable and competent. Praise is said to be a resilience booster because when children experience the all-too-certain setbacks of life, they can rely on our praise to sustain them and help them bounce back.

However, the idea that we should be catching our children doing something right and praising them for it may be less useful for resilience than we think. The research literature is far less effusive in its praise of praise. In fact, many studies just like mine point to praise as ineffective, or even downright dysfunctional.

What are the arguments for praise?

The first argument for praise is pretty simple. Ask just about any parent and they'll tell you that praise is a reinforcer. It is designed to motivate children, and to show them that we appreciate them. As adults, we know that when we are praised, we generally feel good (although this is not always the case ... I'll address that shortly). And we have watched our children respond with added enthusiasm when they hear us praise them. So it makes them feel good too.

Secondly, one of the world's most celebrated psychology researchers found that praise can boost self-efficacy. This is a person's self-belief, or sense that they *can* accomplish what they set out to accomplish.[86] Another two of the world's esteemed psychology researchers acknowledge that praise can enhance feelings of competence and motivation – in the short term.[87] Other scientists have identified that praise can increase the level of motivation a child feels and make them want to behave a certain way so they get a certain outcome.[88] It can also act as an incentive to increase engagement in a task,[89] and it can make a child believe they are as good as the person praising them says they are.[90] Many of these studies that offer support for praise are old, with more recent research becoming increasingly nuanced, and increasingly critical of praise.

That said, praise is broadly accepted as important.

What are the arguments against praise?

The detrimental effects of praise are surprising, and have been studied for several decades now. One of the most interesting findings applies to children around age five, six or seven.

These children, when praised, will often decide that the reason they are being praised is not because they are great, but because they are not very good at all.[91] The thinking goes: 'If I've done well and I'm not getting praised, it's because they expect it of me. They must think I'm smart. But if I've done well and I *am* getting praised, it's because they were surprised, so they must think I'm dumb.'

While little children accept most of what they hear as gospel truth, when slightly older children hear us telling them how kind they are, or how smart, or how good at drawing or sharing they are, they feel judged, evaluated. This is particularly the case for children with low self-esteem. We give more effusive praise to the kids who 'need it most', and they seem to understand this. Kids with high self-esteem and resilience accept the praise with a shrug and a 'Yep, I know.' It doesn't impact them at all. But those with low self-esteem and resilience have an internal argument. 'Mum just told me I'm really smart. But she doesn't know I just fluked that word on the spelling test.'

The more evaluative and inflated the praise, the more judged children feel, and the greater the negative impact.[92] In one recent study, researchers considered the impact of *inflated praise*, as opposed to normal praise. Inflated praise is the kind of praise that goes over and above 'good drawing' or 'nice picture'. Inflated praise is 'Wow, that's not just beautiful. It's incredibly beautiful. You have a gift!' Once again, parents give inflated praise because they think that their praise will elevate their child's self-esteem. And it seems logical that children with lower self-esteem would likely receive more praise – particularly of the inflated variety. The data shows that inflated praise is given about twice as much as regular praise when parents are working with a child who has low self-esteem. In this case, the praise is actually causing harm because the child is actively arguing against it and reinforcing negative self-beliefs. Inferences of low ability are bad for resilience and motivation.

The second way that praise might reduce our children's resilience and wellbeing is that it can be seen as controlling. Whether we mean it or not, there can sometimes be an element of control or even manipulation as we try to socialise our children through positive feedback. This can create resistance on the one hand, or pressure on the other. This was shown in a study where people were praised for their performance of a task, and their performance on subsequent tasks suffered as a result of being praised. They felt they had to live up to the performance expectation that had earned them the praise, and they also became self-conscious.[93]

Praise can also leave children feeling that we are usurping their autonomy, perhaps because we don't have the belief that they'll do the right thing without our reinforcement. I overheard a school teacher say to her students, 'I love the way that everyone is sitting so quietly and working so well.' But several students were not doing that at all. She was using praise as a cover for coercion and manipulation. When we hear ourselves saying things like 'Wow, good sharing' or 'Gee, great helping,' there is a possibility that our comments could be interpreted as a gentle, sugar-coated form of control – not praise. This is a theme I'll return to at the end of the chapter, because obviously much of our praise is not meant to be controlling, and often our children will not interpret it as such. The point here, however, is that sometimes it can be, and in these instances, praise is problematic.

Third, many researchers (and parents) have discovered that praise does lead to increased effort and motivation sometimes. But many studies have identified that once setbacks or failures arrive, children wonder whether the praise was a mistake. They feel they can't live up to the expectation. The bar is too high. Praise sets up a label that creates pressure and leads to self-doubt. Children think, 'I have to live up to that ... but I can't.' Then they might take shortcuts, perhaps making themselves look foolish and incapable while trying to look smart or able. Praise creates a belief in self that is contingent on performance or on the evaluations of others, and it decreases self-worth either in the moment (when self-esteem is low) or following setbacks and failures.[94] I recall praising my children for sitting so nicely in the back seat of the car on a long trip. I was genuinely pleased, and was sincere. But I was also thinking that if I praised them and pointed out that I'd caught them doing something good they would feel reinforced for their behaviour. Instead, about 90 seconds later, they began bickering and hurting one another! Praising the positive backfired almost instantly in that case, and soon they were getting my attention for all the wrong reasons.

Fourth, psychologists use the term *over-justification of performance* to describe what happens when a person does something because of the promise of a reward, rather than for the activity itself.[95] It means that when children do something simply to get the praise, they're not thinking about the activity. Thus, some children turn into praise junkies.[96] And if the praise is not forthcoming, they wonder what is wrong with them – and they lose motivation to do things that might otherwise be worthwhile.

Fifth, and particularly concerning from a resilience perspective, praise shifts children's (and adults') locus of control from internal to external. Instead of feeling that they are capable and competent and are making good decisions for themselves, they begin looking to external sources for confirmation of their competence.[97] They become unsure of themselves and seek external approval before they do things.

And sixth, praise can promote competition and comparison.[98] The next chapter will describe why this is not what we want if we hope to have resilient children. Clearly, the evidence suggests we must rethink our ideas about praise being good for our children's resilience and wellbeing.[99]

What's the intention?

But let's get out of the theory and look at praise in practice. Most of the praise I hear comes from parents who are honestly trying to reinforce ideal behaviour. They are sincere. And they certainly do not mean anything bad by their praise. They're often genuinely enthusiastic and excited about their child's accomplishment. I recall one young, well-intentioned, attentive mother exclaiming, 'Great sharing' when her three-year-old son offered a toy to a playmate. But there was something about her tone. She meant well. She was proud of her son – and she was being sincere and enthusiastic. But underlying this, there was a (potentially unconscious) attempt at control. This was reinforced a few moments later when she cried, 'Great running' as he chased a ball his playmate had kicked. Shortly after, she exclaimed he was 'such a good boy' and was doing some 'great eating' with his morning tea. This mum's enthusiastic praise was sincere, but examined in light of the research there may have been an unintentional dark side to her praise – not from her, but in the way that her son interpreted and internalised it. Evidence suggests he could receive that praise as controlling and even manipulative.

The issue here is that praise may mask that a parent is (perhaps unintentionally) attempting to exert control over or manipulate a child to influence behaviour. When our intentions are sincere and our desire is to genuinely express our enthusiasm for our child's accomplishment, then our meaningful descriptions of what we're witnessing can be reinforcing. This is particularly the case with young children. But some parents cross a line. Their praise is less about their thrill at a child's accomplishment, and more an overt statement designed to reinforce a desired behaviour. As I pointed out earlier, this praise can be received as controlling, and feel like an imposition on a child's autonomy. It may leave the child feeling that he can't sustain all of the great running, sharing, eating or whatever else he is praised for. And ultimately, it could turn the child into a praise junkie.

Praise the process, not the person.

Professor Carol Dweck, of Stanford University, published two highly influential articles in the late 1990s that impacted the way praise is viewed.[100] These studies examined the way different forms of praise affect children's motivation to work on challenging problems when they make mistakes. The 'person praise' groups were praised explicitly for their intelligence: 'You must *be smart* at these problems.' The 'process praise' groups were praised for their effort: 'You must have *worked hard* at these problems.' The remaining children were in the control group and received no additional feedback. When praised for being smart, the kids were far more worried about their performance and how smart they seemed than when they were praised for process. This underscores several of the key concerns researchers have with praise. But process praise led to the children becoming interested in the activities themselves rather than the outcomes. When given free choice, the person-praised children showed clear preferences for easy, rather than challenging, problems. And they persisted less on the tasks, particularly after failure. To add insult to injury, they also enjoyed the tasks less. This led to them feeling like they actually weren't any good at the task, despite the earlier praise. And some actually decided that they just weren't very smart after all.

Other studies have clouded the picture somewhat, as children of different ages have been given different forms of praise. Most often, short-term benefits have been found, but the longer-term is what matters here. The outcomes for resilience are critical, and the weight of evidence seems to be accumulating *against* praising our children when we keep the long-term view in mind.[101]

Is praise good or bad for resilience?

So where does that leave us in relation to whether praise is good or bad for resilience?

Like most things that people claim are good for resilience, there is no good-quality research available where resilience is actually used as a measure. That is, no one has done a study to see whether praise actually affects resilience. The best we have are measures of the impact of praise on motivation, self-esteem and mindsets. In each case, the long-term outcomes of praise are neutral at best, and negative as a general rule.

Some people still feel that even though praise is said to be bad for kids in the research, it can't really be that bad. After all, it feels good and we *want* to shower praise on our children. Being puritanical about not praising may seem too much for some. Therefore, drawing on the many studies that are on offer, if we want to get our praise *right*, so that we are not undermining resilience, motivation and wellbeing, we should keep the following five principles in mind:

First, don't praise children for winning or being the best or being awesome. This is outcome-driven and 'person praise'. This has been shown to lead to less effort and less perseverance, and ultimately this lowers resilience. Instead, focus on process, effort or learning. This builds intrinsic motivation and perseverance. Saying things like 'I saw how hard you worked on that' is much more positive than saying, 'You're the best!'

Second, non-controlling praise builds intrinsic motivation. It is an expression of delight and excitement. This is wonderful! It encourages autonomy and intrinsic motivation. When our praise is manipulative or agenda-driven, our children can sense that we are attempting to control them, and we reduce positive outcomes associated with resilience. Positive feedback that tells a child, 'You look so excited' is far less controlling than, 'It makes me so happy when you do well', or 'You're such a good boy.'

Third, when our praise provides positive information about how our children are doing then we may, in some circumstances, build our children's sense of self-belief, which is great for resilience. Saying things like 'I saw you practising and contentrating so hard in that recital' is not controlling or comparison-focused. But if our praise conveys competence through social comparison, such as, 'Great, you beat everyone in the class!' we are likely to ultimately undermine competence, self-efficacy, self-worth and motivation. Resilience will suffer.

Fourth, praise that conveys high but realistic expectations or standards and that is descriptive can provide helpful guidance and assist in promoting task engagement. However, praise that promotes impossible standards, or that is given too easily (such as 'Good running' or 'Good helping') will ultimately backfire.[102] Even when our child deserves it and has worked hard for it, there may be better ways to convey our feelings.

Fifth, and most importantly, praise *has* to be perceived as sincere if it is to be beneficial.

Putting it together

So how do we consolidate all of this? Praise is a tough form of feedback to get right. We want to be process-focused, non-controlling, non-comparing, descriptive and sincere! We can get it right, but it's complicated. The price of getting it wrong can be steep, with our children's resilience being a potential casualty.

Rather than praising, I recommend the following forms of feedback as ultimately superior:

1. Use gratitude instead of praise where possible.
   Of course, gratitude can be coercive and agenda-driven,
   but it is less likely to be when compared with praise.
   We are unlikely to excitedly say to our two-year-old,

'Thanks for being such a good boy' or 'Thanks for running!' Instead, we might say, 'I really appreciated it when you shared with your sister (or friend). It made me grateful for you.' Or 'It makes me smile to see how much energy you have! And I'm grateful to see you enjoying yourself.'

2. When you feel the urge to praise, lean towards describing what you see rather than making big, sweeping, effusive statements about your child's ability. Don't say, 'You're a natural musician'. Instead try 'I loved listening to the way you played that piece. You really seemed to be focused on feeling the music.' Or 'I've really noticed a big change in the way you played that song over the past week.' This is aligned with the idea of process praise, and the evidence supports this approach.

3. Perhaps the best response to our children's successes and efforts is to invite them to praise themselves. If a child asks, 'Do you like my picture?' you could say, 'Yes, I do.' But this may make them reliant on *your* evaluations and judgements to determine whether they're doing fine or not. Alternatively you could thank them for it, or you might describe the effort you guess they've put into it. These responses might feel forced or contrived. The optimal response could be, 'Why don't you tell me what you like the most?' Or 'How do you like it?'

   If a child aces a test, the temptation might be to say, 'Wow, you're such a braniac! I knew we had a future Nobel Prize winner in the family.' But it might be more effective for our children's motivation and resilience to invite them to do their own reinforcing. We could say, 'How did you feel when you saw that result?' Or 'Wow. That must have been exciting. I remember you were really worried. How did you get an A on that test?' These responses allow our children to tell us how excited they are, to emphasise the process they went through to achieve their outcomes, and to reinforce the principles that will help them succeed again in the future. And the responses will also help them through the tough times and setbacks.

After our child has made his own assessment, we can add ours: 'I was really excited about that too!' or 'You did an amazing job. I'm glad you can see that.'

Take-home message

The bottom line is that our intentions are critical, and to understand our intentions we must be deeply honest with ourselves. When our intentions are to control, then praise will typically have undermining effects that lead to negative outcomes. When our intentions are to sincerely and honestly express delight and celebrate our child's achievement, that praise is unlikely to have resilience-reducing results. It's a myth that praise boosts resilience though. On the contrary, much of our praise will do precisely the opposite. There are better ways to provide feedback, and these will foster motivation, wellbeing and resilience far more effectively.

Winners are grinners, but what does that make everyone else? How competition undermines resilience

Competition has been shown to be useful up to a certain point and no further, but cooperation, which is the thing we must strive for today, begins where competition leaves off.

Franklin D Roosevelt

Steven lay on the ice and willed himself to keep his eyes open. He had to stay awake. If he closed his eyes, he might never wake up. Blood was pooling around him – fast. He could feel its life force leaving him via a vicious wound in his quadriceps. Moments before, he had been racing over the ice at full speed, his heart pumping at around 200 beats per minute. But another competitor in his race had fallen, and as a result, a carefully sharpened skate blade had sliced into Steven's leg. His thoughts were slowing. 'If I lose consciousness, I'm going to die,' he told himself. Somehow he hung on.

Steven found out later he had lost around four litres of blood following his accident. The surgeon repaired his leg with more than

100 stitches. And the surgeon's advice? 'Don't skate any more.' Never one to let go of a dream, Steven duly ignored the advice of his specialist and returned to competitive sprint skating as soon as he could. The next 18 months were spent in painful rehabilitation, strengthening and rebuilding, and he made a seemingly successful return to the ice rink. Six years later, however, Steven was injured again. Badly. It was another life-threatening accident, this time in training. Another skater fell in front of him. Steven tried to jump him, but clipped him with his skate and slid head first into a wall, breaking his neck in two places. Pins in his neck and screws in his skull, combined with plates bolted into his back and chest, repaired the damage, and again Steven was told by his doctors that he should get off – and stay off – the ice.

With a level of persistence bordering on insanity, Steven returned to training, and at 28 years of age he was selected for his fourth Olympics in 2002 – in Salt Lake City. Steven had spent the best part of the previous decade hovering in and around the top ten speed skaters in the world, but he was past his prime, and was never considered a real chance at a medal in Salt Lake City.

Speed skating is as unpredictable as it is dangerous. Skaters fall fast and hard as they fight for position, their sharpened blades promising potentially lethal damage when they contact skin. And winning a race is often as much about staying upright as it is about speed and skill. Steven knew this as he entered his semi-final and created a strategy he hoped would see him through to the gold medal race. Let the front skaters fight and potentially fall, and maybe ... just maybe, skate through to the final.

The strategy worked. Steven made it to the gold medal race, not by being the fastest, but by allowing others to make mistakes and by capitalising on their falls. As the final began, Steven was immediately in trouble. The other four skaters tore around the rink while he chased, attempting to stay in their slipstream but falling further and further behind. As they entered the final corner of the 1000 metre race, he was at least 10 or 15 metres behind the four bunched-up leaders. Fifth and final place was assured. He would have to be proud of that. Then, the unlikeliest of incidents occurred with only 50 metres to go. The second-placed skater fell, taking out the legs of the skater in front of him. The skater behind could not avoid the crash, and the skater in fourth place was caught with nowhere to go. All four skaters collapsed across the ice and into the barriers. Steven Bradbury skated around the others and raised his arms in shock and amazement as he crossed the finish line victorious, becoming the first southern hemisphere Olympian to win a gold medal at the Winter Olympics. Steven was the last man standing, and his success has become the stuff of legend.[103] His resilient, never-give-up attitude helped him to accomplish his dreams.

When we hear stories like that, we are entitled to think that surely competition is good for resilience. Sport and competition provide hope, exhilaration and inspiration for children, adults, communities and even countries. Some of the most inspiring and exciting moments of our lives are shaped by competition. Every year we see displays of excellence in the sporting arena borne of remarkable resilience, gritty determination and pure talent. Competition is given credit for boosting performance, character, productivity, creativity and excellence. So surely competition is good for resilience – or is this another sacred cow to be slain? Is it a myth that competition boosts resilience?

Is competition bad for resilience?

First, we should acknowledge that there is a difference between competition and competitiveness. Competition is just *one* process that governs how we share rewards and other resources. Sometimes resources are limited, such as positions in medical school. Competition is the process by which certain resources are allocated. Do well in the competition, and get into the school. Competitiveness is the desire to be better than others. Of course, competition promotes competitiveness, but one can be competitive without competition.

As with so many of the myths we have explored, the answer to whether competition and competitiveness are bad for resilience is that 'it depends'. This may be a generous assessment, though. Indeed, many studies indicate that competition may be particularly detrimental to our children's resilience, whether they're winning or losing. As with most of the topics covered so far in this book, the positives and negatives come down to a number of factors, but to argue that competition is good for kids because it teaches them resilience and how to bounce back from failure – well, that is not supported by the evidence.

Winning isn't everything: it's the only thing

As parents, we want to think of ourselves as good sports. We want our children to be good sports too. We repeat, over and over, that in competition, 'It doesn't matter if you win or lose. It's how you play the game.' Part of the myth that competition can boost children's self-esteem and resilience relies on the presumption that the child must win, or learn to lose 'well'. That's the essence of 'healthy' competition, and the implication is therefore that it is a good thing.

But when they lose, do we point out our children's need for improvement, their deficits and their mistakes? We blame the coach, the weather, the other team or the referee. Sometimes we even get mad. There are regular stories in the news about parents behaving badly on the sidelines of children's sport.[104] One such example was reported in the media recently: a father allegedly punching a teenage referee who was running a junior game of football. While this is an extreme example, many of us have been watching our children play and felt those instincts arise as the ref made calls with his or her two eyes that we could see with perfect vision in our one-eyed view were wrong.

On the flipside, when our children are winning, let's face it ... most of us go nuts! We're thrilled. We glory in their triumph. We praise their ability, tell them they're champions, give them treats and other rewards, and we say things like, 'Winners are grinners!' Attributed to legendary American football coach Vince Lombardi but actually spoken by another coach, Henry Sanders, is the quote, 'Winning isn't everything. It's the only thing.' There are times when even the least competitive among us might begin to care greatly about who wins a game and what is necessary to win it. This is especially the case with parents who want their children to succeed. Winning is a clear metric of 'success'.

Many parents remain aloof, but some are less reserved in their advice and ideas following a competition. In our earnest desire to help our children be the best they can, many of us offer our guidance, our tips and our ideas to motivate them more. So even though it doesn't matter when they win or lose, everyone prefers winners.

Failing hurts

Science has shown that as much as we might like to think that a defeated child will 'get back on the horse' and try again and again until they finally succeed, failure wears most kids down. Their resilience drops. Their motivation is muted. They develop an avoidance mentality for those activities in which they fail, and an approach mentality for those in which they succeed. Moreover, kids who experience failure pervasively begin to believe they really *are* failures, and if they happen to win, it is a fluke, dumb luck or the result of some kind of external cause. This vicious circle is devastating for resilience. Our feedback can contribute to that belief as well as we point out all the ways they can improve and all the things that they did wrong.

Children's responses to competition – and failure – exist on a continuum. Some children will be so intrinsically drawn to an activity that they will persist in spite of failure. And there are some who are so drawn to winning that they will be persistent simply to savour the special feeling winning produces as often as possible. But given enough failure, most children (and adults) will walk away, defeated.

Sore losers/sore winners

As with losing well, when they win, children usually need to be taught to win well, with character, and with empathy for those they have defeated. To be sure, this is an opportunity for us to teach our children important lessons around compassion, kindness and helping out those less fortunate than ourselves. We can teach them a level of humility and modesty that few winners exhibit. But experience shows that typically, when our children are victors they don't give a thought to the other team or competitors! In some cases they actively ridicule them. Indeed, research shows they may even seek opportunities to take further advantage.

Amos Schurr and Ilana Ritov at Ben-Gurion University showed that not just competition, but the actual act of *winning* a competition, led to subsequent unethical behaviour – and the lack of ethics was not confined just to future competitions. It spread well beyond the competitive arena into unrelated areas of life.[105] In their research, participants were pitted against one another in a competition. Following the competition, they were invited to participate in two other 'unrelated' activities/studies and the researchers watched what happened. They found that winners lied in subsequent activities and did so significantly more and at significantly higher rates than those who had lost. They actually cheated their opponents out of extra money! But the unethical behaviour only occurred in competitive situations. It wasn't actually about winning something, but it *was* about beating someone. The unethical behaviour didn't occur when winning was down to chance (such as when they 'won' a lottery they were unaware was rigged). In fact, in those situations participants were generous and collaborative with others involved in the activity. Nor did it occur after they were successful in an activity that was non-competitive. Setting goals and achieving them (without needing to be a victor over a 'loser') was associated with ethical, honest, egalitarian behaviour. It was only after competition that the winners were dishonest or unethical.[106]

This theme becomes even darker in a 2016 UK study that found that high-achieving adolescents in sport are being pushed to cheat by parents who demand perfection.[107] Parental involvement in pushing kids to cheat must undermine the relationship they share, *and* ultimately the resilience and wellbeing of the child. A Belgian up-and-coming cycling superstar was driven to be exceptional. Her parents were deeply involved in her sporting achievements. Femke van den Driessche's brother was already serving a ban for doping when Femke was caught during an international competition with a bicycle that had a hidden motor inside it! She was kicked out of her sport for a minimum six years, though some might argue there is no coming back from such an incident.[108]

If competition – and specifically the act of winning – elevates the likelihood of cheating and builds entitlement, what does this mean for *resilience*? Obviously those who cheated at such high levels suffered. But the same goes at the individual level, even down to our kids. Competition with others is all about social comparison and a feeling that 'I'm better than them.' If a competitor believes this about themselves, then that person now has to maintain that sense that they are superior – by winning! So now they become fearful of situations where they may lose. This is not good for resilience, motivation, development or wellbeing. To avoid challenges because you might lose, or to go into challenges knowing cheating is a viable way to win, are not hallmarks of a resilient (or moral) human.

Competition when the stakes are high

If it can happen in an innocuous experiment, imagine what happens when the stakes are high. We glorify and glamorise those who win in competition, but one does not need to dig very deep to find horribly unethical behaviour in all of its varieties in all competitive spheres. In the sports arena there are the well-known doping stories in everything from cycling to tennis, football in all its varieties, running, swimming and athletics. The business world, too, is ultra-competitive. When Turing Pharmaceuticals increased the US retail price for a life-saving drug from $13.50 a tablet to $750, it caused a worldwide outcry. (They later backed down.)[109] Then there's Volkswagen and the 'diesel dupe', in which emissions were technologically hidden in order to make the car look better for the environment.[110] Consider the global economic downturn of 2007–08, dubbed the Global Financial Crisis, in large part caused by banks' unethical and dishonest lending practices.[111] Enron, HIH, Bernie Madoff: each of these examples are very public, embarrassing and extreme. And there may be other explanations – at least in part – for the willingness to cheat. But ultimately, the behaviour of individuals and organisations is consistent with what research suggests: winning, and the desire to win, can lead to unethical, dishonest behaviour.

This is not to say that every winner is an unethical, amoral, entitled, unempathic rapscallion, but that competition increases the likelihood of this kind of behaviour. It guarantees inequality, entrenches an egocentric perspective, and decreases pro-social behaviour. And research proves those with higher social status (meaning those who have typically won the game of life in terms of education, wealth and opportunity) behave in a more entitled way, and are less pro-social or charitable, when compared to those with lower social status.[112] Competition may also be harmful for resilience because it is inherently about comparisons. Losers feel lousy (and may be more inclined to cheat or behave anti-socially), and winners may become unethical (as described above) or entitled.[113] Researchers have shown that lack of ethics is even *more* likely to be demonstrated when egos are on the line. No one wants to lose. It hurts. Resilience suffers. And many will do whatever it takes to make sure it doesn't happen.[114] And in any competition, there is generally only one winner. Everyone else loses. In fact, from time to time we have all heard the person who came second complain that they were the 'first loser'.

Competition promotes a fixed mindset

But how about when children (or adults) are in the midst of competition? For two years I stood on the sidelines of netball courts as my daughter was defeated in game after game. Her team was learning. The coaches were learning. Mistakes were common. Losing was the norm. Unfortunately, some of the children, including my daughter, saw their court time and game losses as a reflection on themselves as people. They saw their competitive failures as personal failing. Each week girls would despondently leave the netball court, heads bowed low, defeated. The following week as they took to the court, parents would encourage them, 'Just go out there and have fun.' Many girls lost interest, feeling like failures. Some children responded to losing with a 'mastery' mindset as described in Chapter 5, There's no such thing as smart. They just wanted to improve and get better. But competition reduces the likelihood of that happening. Competition shifts children's focus too far towards performance and away from learning the process and developing skill.

As Dweck and many of her colleagues discovered in dozens of studies,[115] when children experience subsequent setbacks following their winning ways, defeats can crush confidence and leave some children questioning their identity, competence and character. Winning pushes some kids into a 'fixed' mindset. The consequences include losing motivation for the activity, or, as competence and achievement increase, becoming fixated, unbalanced, and obsessively and unhealthily passionate.[116]

Competition affects self-esteem

Losing pushes self-esteem down. But winning impacts self-esteem too. Self-esteem stays high whenever winning is occurring. But win or lose, both successes and failures can become reflections of identity and self-worth. Big failures in competition may devastate resilience because of the powerful way that the failure 'reveals' character and identity. In some cases, our children (or even we, as adults) may become depressed because of poor performance, or suffer unhealthy anxiety while awaiting their next competitive experience.[117] Resilience is partly about being adaptive in the face of adversity and setback. Highly resilient children and adults will respond positively to their losses. Research suggests this is not the norm.

Winning is an exclusive event. Only one student can be dux. Only one team can win the premiership. Only one child can reign supreme in the spelling bee. When unsuccessful children place their feelings of worth in their performance and then fail, they can feel crushed. Their sense of identity may be questioned. In some tragic cases, they suffer a crisis that can have catastrophic consequences.

Competition reduces motivation

The cruelty of competition is far too often glossed over, but it is a real contributor to an unwillingness to try in too many children. The ongoing focus on extrinsic rewards that competition promotes wears down interest and motivation in the actual activity. This has been shown in numerous studies, but perhaps it's best to look at a real world example:

Nick Kyrgios, Australia's number 1 tennis player, has been described as *the* future of tennis. He has beaten the world's best players, but struggles with consistency and also has a reputation of being the new superbrat on the tennis circuit. At only 21 years of age, his future looks sensational. There's only one thing. Kyrgios is on the record as stating, 'I definitely don't love the sport.' He added (speaking in the third person about himself), 'There is zero chance that Nick Kyrgios will be playing tennis when he's 30 years old. There's absolutely no chance. I don't know how long my career will be but God help me if I am playing tennis at 30. There are so many more things to this world than tennis for me. Not tennis at 30. Please.'

He revealed that 'When I was 14 I had to pick. My parents were pretty strong pushing me into tennis. They probably thought it was easier to make it in tennis. I definitely liked basketball a lot better. But it didn't work out too badly, I guess.'[118] The extent to which Kyrgios's career was influenced by his parents may have combined with competition to undermine his resilience and wellbeing. His motivation may have been affected, and if he feels controlled and imprisoned in a sport that he does not love, it suggests that an alternative path may have led to a higher level of wellbeing.

Reduced creativity

A winning mindset can limit curiosity, creativity and exploration. Writer Alfie Kohn, in his book *No Contest,* cites a well-known study by Teresa Amabile, and states:

> In [the] study, seven to eleven-year-old girls were asked to make 'silly' collages, some competing for prizes and some not. Seven artists then independently rated their works on each of 23 dimensions. The result: 'Those children who competed for prizes made collages that were significantly less creative than those made by children in the control group.' Children in the competitive condition produced works thought to be less spontaneous, less complex, and less varied.[119]

Competition can devastate relationships

Again, this is a variable that can go either way. However, it would seem that competition is more likely to hurt, rather than help, relationships. 'That kid is a real competitor' may be meant in a complimentary way, but we generally do not encourage friendships with overly competitive people. We know that if our child is in a relationship with someone who always has to win, there will be conflict, and that can impact on resilience and wellbeing.

Relationships can be ruptured in a team context when one person is not performing as expected – or when everyone is failing to perform. But even when it's individual people in a setting such as a workplace, classroom or family, competition turns people against one another. Competition undercuts an openness to collaborate with others. If children see everyone as a competitor, they are unlikely to work with them, share ideas, build them up, or promote the idea of 'team'. If it's a race to achieve sales targets in the office so someone can win the holiday to Fiji, there will be little sense of 'team'.

Competition reduces cooperation

Competition means defeating others. Helping others is counter to the purpose of competition. Yet cooperation and collaboration may be at the heart of many of the most remarkable advances and successes of our world. When Michael J Fox began the process of creating a foundation to combat Parkinson's Disease he witnessed the destructive effects of competition on collaboration. In speaking with the director of one organisation he was told, 'Well, if you don't help us, then, at least don't help *them*.'[120]

Is competition always bad?

It would be disingenuous to argue that competition is always bad. Sometimes it can be good for producing remarkable results, and even producing a resilient human. We live in a competitive society, and it is typically argued that competition allows us to make full use of our abilities and elevates standards. This may be true, but in competition, there will always be casualties. Others suffer regardless of whether the competition is individual vs individual, or team against team. Others experience diminished capacity, wellbeing or resilience. But there is evidence for some benefits to competition in some situations.

Four studies by leading motivation researcher Judith Harackiewicz evaluated how competition and cooperation might impact on performance and the extent to which participants enjoyed the task they were involved in. The 'pure cooperation' grouping was a team of two that had to work together to achieve the highest possible number of points in a basketball shooting contest. The 'pure competition' grouping was two players who had to see who could score the most points against each other rather than a combined score. The 'combination of the two' grouping pitted a team of two against another team of two to see who could

99

score the most in teams, so there was a collaborative element to what was ultimately a contest. Competition played in a cooperative way (one team vs another) led to significantly higher enjoyment than either a purely collaborative or purely competitive game. Performance was generally better in the combined competitive environment as well.[121] So at least in the short term with an essentially meaningless but fun game, competition enhanced the experience when played in a team. This probably resonates with our own life experiences when the stakes are low and we are competing 'for fun'. But for some people, the stakes are always higher, and that element of fun diminishes. And studies like this tell us little about resilience.

What's the alternative?

One of the most famous psychology experiments of the past several decades is the Robbers Cave experiment. It was the 1950s, and a researcher named Muzafer Sherif was interested in why groups often experienced tension. He pitted two groups of 11–12-year-old boys against each other on a camp. During the first week the boys were separated into two groups. Neither group knew about the other group. The intention was to create a strong bond between the boys within each group. In the second stage of research, the boys were brought together to participate in competitions where prizes of resources were offered. The intense and unexpected rivalry led to cabins being ransacked, flags being burned, and fights breaking out. The competition was unhealthy in every way.

Stage three of the experiment occurred once the rivalries and group hostilities were reaching a peak. Now the researchers created situations that required both groups of boys to work together to solve major problems. For example, the water stopped working at camp. The researchers blamed vandals, but they had rigged it themselves. The boys had to problem-solve together and identify how to fix the issue. Another activity that was 'set up' without their knowledge was the vehicle they were travelling in breaking down, and the boys had to work together to pull it off the road with a rope. These team-building activities continued until the competition was forgotten. Collaboration and working together united the boys and helped them achieve more than any of their previous competitions.[122]

Is success really about beating others?

We have been trained to believe that success is found in victory, in beating someone else. And we have been indoctrinated with the idea that successfully defeating others – or learning to accept that defeat – is a necessary ingredient in a diet that determines resilience.

It isn't.

Superior performance and building resilience does not *require* competitiveness. As humans, we seem equally predisposed to cooperate, to collaborate and to coexist as we do to compete. In fact, enormous successes are often (or usually) achieved in the absence of competition. While companies may be in competition with one another, amazing advances are as likely to occur just because someone is passionately interested in solving a problem as when someone else is motivated by wanting to beat another person to a solution.

The simplest way to understand this is to consider the following: will a child achieve excellence in trying to do well, or in trying to beat others? While it is possible that trying to beat others can lead to excellence, trying to do well, to learn and to master something appears optimal. And if not optimal from an overall performance perspective, it is certainly optimal in terms of character, ethics and the development of healthy relationships. What will a competitive focus do to children's resilience? If they grow into adults who walk into every situation wondering whether they are better than others, or stronger, or more athletic, or smarter or wealthier, they will become insecure about their competence, their relationships will rupture, and their resilience will suffer.

One of the biggest studies of its kind underscores the main points this chapter is making about how extrinsic motivators (like competition) affect intrinsic motivation – or the desire to do something just for the sake of doing it. The research showed that competition undermines intrinsic motivation (and by association, wellbeing and even resilience) by essentially saying, 'If you do this, you'll get THAT,' where 'that' is a trophy, or a prize, or the knowledge that you're better than someone else. The emphasis in competition is not on doing something for its own sake; instead, it's about doing something better than someone else. The researchers found that these external motivators, such as competition, leave people essentially saying, 'What do I get if I do it?' Further, the research showed that competition damages relationships through the need to defeat another person. On the flipside, the researchers also acknowledged that competition can be good for intrinsic motivation (which would typically enhance wellbeing and resilience) when the competition is more about providing feedback and developing skills and mastery than about beating others.[123]

A central reason that researchers believe that competition is harmful to resilience but that *some* may be beneficial, therefore, comes down to relationships and the experience of mastery. Think about your own life experience. Perhaps you used to (or still do) love to play sport or other games with a friend. You would go at it pretty hard: you were aiming to vanquish your friend. But it was also an activity you both enjoyed, and one that strengthened your relationship. Thus, you acted as sharpening stones that enabled improved mastery and performance. This competitive activity, therefore, made you feel connected and competent. This is called *constructive competition*. But if our opponent is trying to tear us down through annihilation, taunts and sledging, or mean-spirited play, or even if we are just feeling incompetent or disconnected from others, the competition will likely be *destructive* and undermine our wellbeing and resilience.

Take-home message

Ultimately, competition pushes us down the negative side of the continuum when we want to foster resilience in our children. Competition *can* be great in some circumstances. Much depends on the mindset of the kids and their motivations for competing. If they're competing because they love the activity, they'll do their best and be intrinsically motivated. Defeat will hurt a little, but they'll be back for more, and will eventually grow and develop. But if they tie their worth to winning, they are at risk of making poor choices, losing motivation, damaging relationships, working against rather than with others, becoming less engaged in creativity and curiosity, and ultimately losing out in the resilience stakes.

Sports and other competitive pursuits can be fun. However, someone always loses, and the benefits of losing are tremendously over-exaggerated. Resilient responses are far more likely when a person has had more experiences with success than with failure. The more experience a child has with failure (which is the most likely outcome for most kids in most competitive exchanges), the more likely it is they'll be motivated to *avoid* rather than approach that situation again. Repeated failure experiences lead to children inferring low ability in themselves, thus damaging resilience further.

The alternative is that we shift the paradigm and move to collaboration rather than competition. By changing *opponents* into *partners* and pursuing cooperative activities with others, our children are able to play, have fun and enjoy relationships without the psychologically destructive elements of competition – and without the risk of stealing, cheating, lying and other morally bereft behaviours interfering.

One of my daughters was invited to participate in a writing competition. She told me, 'Dad, I don't want to go in the story-writing competition because I know if I lose I'll feel bad about myself and think I'm a lousy writer. I'd much rather just write a story because I want to than to have someone judging me.' Doing something for the sheer joy of it will always lead to superior resilience outcomes.

PART TWO

BUILDING RESILIENCE

The second part of this book considers ways we can support our children through their sadnesses and challenges to allow them the growth they need to be truly resilient. As our children develop through the everyday adversity they experience, with our support, but without our over-involvement, the invisible process of resilience steels them, improves them, increases their perspective and empathy, and helps them to become more whole.

There are three 'environments' that contribute to our children's (and our own) resilience and wellbeing – or lack thereof. The first environment is within them: their thinking, their cognitive processes and their personal way of being. The second key environment that affects resilience is the quality and experience of the relationships our children share with those who are close to them – usually their family. Parents (or guardians and carers) have profound influence. Finally, the third environment that contributes to resilience in our children is the extended, broader environment. When our children can find purpose and meaning in their contribution to (or place in) society, when school is a place that is supportive and positive, and when their devices don't dictate their lives, resilience is supported and life is full. This part of the book will briefly explore these three environments, with a core focus on the individual and the family.

CHAPTER 1

Who am I? And why does it matter for resilience?

When I discover who I am, then I'll be free.
Ralph Ellison[124]

This chapter begins with a confession. I love to sing ... but I am not very good at it. Yet in the early 2000s, when 'reality' talent programs hit our screens, I dreamed of auditioning. Wisdom, and a deep belief that I had something else to offer the world, ensured I never did try out for anything resembling a singing career. But that's probably because I had begun to develop a strong sense of who I am – and a singer I am not.

Conversely, a young Hawaiian named Peter Hernandez Jr knew he *was* a singer. His dad had music in him, his mum was a singer, his uncle was an Elvis impersonator, and by the age of three, Peter Jr was performing with the family band on a daily basis. At four, he was the world's youngest Elvis impersonator, following in his uncle's footsteps. Peter could play instruments, sing, dance, and he had the looks!

Peter was successful at the local level but that didn't pay the bills, and it left him wanting more. So Peter took a gamble. He flew to California and hit the jackpot instantly. Motown Records said 'Yes'. But there were conditions: Enrique Iglesias was the big Latino success hit at the time, and Motown wanted Peter to be their Latino guy. He had the looks, the voice and the moves. Plus, he was a Hernandez! With a surname like that, the Latino pathway was obvious, and he was set. Initially he said yes, but the decision never felt right, and the more that Motown pushed him into a box that he didn't feel was really him, the more he resisted until he knew he had to leave the company, and try again.

For the next few years Peter worked the LA music scene. With the Hernandez name, Peter still felt pushed into the Latino box, so he adopted his childhood nickname – a name he'd been given as a two-year-old because he resembled his father's favourite wrestler. And he added what he called an out-of-this-world surname because, 'I felt like I didn't have [any] pizzazz, and a lot of girls say I'm out of this world.'

Peter's heritage was an important part of who he was, but the music in him was more central to who he was than even his name. He was a singer. He was a performer. And he was going to be successful.

Within a short time of adopting this new name, he had a new deal. This time Atlantic Records was willing to give him a go, and he was encouraged to be himself. The following year (2010) he released his first album. It was a smash. He was nominated for *ten* Grammy Awards. And that was only the start. In 2014, he ended up in front of the biggest crowd on earth performing for 115 million viewers at the American Super Bowl and this time, he wasn't impersonating anyone, and he wasn't in a box. He was himself – Bruno Mars.[125]

Who am I anyway?

The development of identity is a lifelong process. Even as adults, we continue to refine and shift aspects of our identity. While some people, perhaps like Peter Hernandez Jr, have a clear sense of who they are from a very young age, most of us usually begin to work it out through our teen years as we try on a range of different identities and ideas, eventually adopting a fairly stable view of ourselves and who we are by the time we are reaching the end of our adolescence (which is increasingly being seen as some time in our early- to mid-twenties[126]). Developing a clear sense of self – an identity – is a critical piece of the resilience puzzle.

How to help your child's identity development

Since identity is central to the development of resilience, we need to know what it is and how it develops, as well as whether we can do anything to help our children *know who they are.*

Young children are typically content to accept life as it comes. They tend away from contemplating questions like 'Who am I?' and 'Where do I belong?' Instead, most children tend to accept, adapt and internalise the norms, values and behaviours of their parents or caregivers. But as they grow, our children become increasingly aware that they are at least somewhat unique. They begin to want to fit in, yet stand alone. And they also begin to identify consistent patterns in themselves and those around them that make up 'identity'. As children begin to describe themselves, they are identifying who they are to others. I asked a four-year-old boy to tell me who he was. After he gave me his name and I prodded for a bit more information, he said, 'I'm a boy.' More prodding about what he does led to, 'I run fast.' I asked what he likes to do. He said, 'I like to play with my trucks.' When I asked about what he loves to eat, his response: 'I love lollies and chocolate.'

An eight-year-old girl I asked about herself shifted away from 'things' and towards relationships as she described her identity to me: 'I'm a girl. I love my friends. I like playing netball – and Club Penguin. And I love chocolate.'

A confident ten-year-old boy described himself by saying, 'I'm a soccer player. I love Minecraft. I like riding my bike with my friends. And I'm tall like my dad.'

These simple statements are the beginnings of identity development. As our children grow, they begin thinking more about who they are, particularly as they enter adolescence. As they do so, their descriptions change, becoming more nuanced and more about internal rather than external characteristics (though both will still be mentioned in some conversations). In a heartbreaking conversation I had with a 14-year-old girl with low self-esteem and resilience, she described her identity to me: 'I'm shy and quiet. I'm not very smart or very sporty. I don't think I'm very important or have much worth to other people.' That is a direct quote. This girl's identity is becoming clear, detailed and, sadly, defined in the negative. It describes all of the things that she is not, or it identifies qualities or attributes that might not be seen as positive – at least in her eyes.

I asked a 14-year-old girl who has high self-esteem and resilience about her identity. She told me, 'I'm beautiful, intelligent, and I'm happy with who I am because I am a good person. I know I'm honest, and a good friend, and if I stay true to who I am I'll do well in my life.' Once again, a direct quote, and again a clear and detailed overview of who she is. This time, though, her description is inspiring, positive and elevating.

A 15-year-old boy who lacked resilience shrugged his shoulders when I asked him about his identity. He mumbled something like, 'I dunno.' When I gently encouraged him to give me a little more he divulged that he didn't care and he didn't think about it much. I asked him about his interests and he indicated that hanging out with friends was all he was into. Slowly he opened up a little more, telling me he didn't know who he was or who he wanted to be. He was confused about his values and was engaging in some serious rule-breaking. He wanted to do what he wanted without his parent's involvement, and then he disclosed that he 'hated' his dad. When I asked why, he told me that his dad treated his mum 'like scum', and that he was a 'liar'. 'So long as I don't end up like him, I don't care who I become.' As the compounding effect of his difficulties with his father has built, and his anger and sadness (and fear) have grown, his identity development has almost been put on hold, in moratorium. Again, lacking resilience and hope, he defines himself in the negative. He is not sure who he is or who he is becoming. He just knows what he doesn't want to be.

The development of identity is not usually a conscious process. Instead, identity occurs as children either do or do not feel security in early childhood, and then identify personal attributes that feel consistent, stable and unique – or if not unique, attributes that are shared with others that are important.

Identity appears to be related to resilience in interesting and important ways. When our children have a strong sense of who they are and what they value, they are willing to make unpopular decisions, stand apart from the crowd and be themselves – whatever or whoever that is. This sense of self helps them to respond more positively to adversarial or challenging situations. This enhanced resilience helps them become psychologically healthier than those who lack a clear sense of identity.

Family stories, identity and resilience

In what has become a well-known piece of research, Dr Marshall Duke and Robyn Fivush of Emory University conducted a study. Their research was prompted by Duke's psychologist wife, Sara, who reported to him that in her work with children with learning disabilities, those who knew a lot about their families and their family *stories* seemed more resilient.[127]

From the time our children are born, we have the opportunity to completely immerse them in stories. We share stories, even before our children can understand them, as a way of helping to make sense of the world, to pass along information, promote creativity and teach children about who they are. There is a strong consensus in psychology that knowing stories about yourself and your world teaches you a lot about identity and helps you work out who you actually are. Children who know these stories do better in life. Duke's much publicised study described the creation of a 20-item questionnaire called the 'Do You Know' (DYK) scale. His analysis showed that children (aged 9–12) who had the highest scores on the DYK scale lived in homes where families have more dinnertime conversation. Even more important, the DYK scale was related to children's *locus of control*. This refers to whether we believe we are in control, or whether outside forces are controlling us. We have much less control than we think, but researchers have found that wellbeing is higher when we feel in control. Duke and Fivush discovered that children who were told – and who recalled – family stories believed they were responsible, and that they were capable of controlling things rather than being at the mercy of external or environmental elements. They had an internal locus of control, and it built their wellbeing. As scores on the DYK scale increased, so too did self-esteem. And higher DYK scores were related to children having lower anxiety and lower internalising and externalising behaviours. (Internalising behaviours are things like depression and other unhealthy ways of being that stay inside a person; externalising behaviours are things like acting out, being delinquent or oppositional, or using alcohol and other drugs.) Lastly, family functioning and participation in family traditions also increased with higher scores on the DYK scale.[128] This finding has significant resilience implications. Children who know their family identity tend to come from better-functioning families, and tend to also have higher levels of resilience. They're doing well.

This research is correlational, not causational. This means that if you sit your children down in the living room tonight and begin telling them all of the family stories you know, they are not going to suddenly become resilient! Their challenges won't necessarily disappear overnight, nor will they stop being oppositional if they have been previously. And something else may be causing these great results – like families enjoying time together. Knowing family stories may not *cause* resilience. And there may be plenty of highly resilient people who were never told family stories at all. Instead, this research shows that when one of these elements is high, so too is the other.

But while knowing about your family is helpful, does it make a difference to who you are as a person? With his colleagues, Marshall Duke recently extended this research to children aged 14–16 to determine how knowing family history might relate to adolescent identity development, and whether teens who had a better-established sense of identity did better in life. He found that the better teens knew their family stories, the better adjusted they were. They possessed a general sense of self-worth and the ability to plan for the future, and they felt good about who they were. They had begun to achieve a sense of identity. As with younger children in the previous study, they also showed fewer internalising and externalising problems, although more advanced statistical analysis showed this latter finding was less to do with knowing family stories and more related to positive family functioning.[129]

The Do You Know (DKY) scale

So what are the 20 questions that comprise the DYK scale, and can they really elevate resilience in our children and teens? Or even in us as adults? Professor Duke was kind enough to share them with me so I could share them with you.

Each of the following questions should be answered with either a Y for Yes, or an N for No. Here they are:

1. Do you know how your parents met?
2. Do you know where your mother grew up?
3. Do you know where your father grew up?
4. Do you know where some of your grandparents grew up?
5. Do you know where some of your grandparents met?
6. Do you know where your parents were married?
7. Do you know what went on when you were being born?
8. Do you know the source of your name?
9. Do you know some things about what happened when your brothers or sisters were being born?
10. Do you know which person in your family you look most like?
11. Do you know which person in the family you act most like?
12. Do you know some of the illnesses and injuries that your parents experienced when they were younger?
13. Do you know some of the lessons that your parents learned from good or bad experiences?
14. Do you know some things that happened to your mum or dad when they were in school?
15. Do you know the national background of your family (such as English, German, Russian, etc)?
16. Do you know some of the jobs that your parents had when they were young?
17. Do you know some awards that your parents received when they were young?
18. Do you know the names of the schools that your mum went to?
19. Do you know the names of the schools that your dad went to?
20. Do you know about a relative whose face 'froze' in a grumpy position because he or she did not smile enough?[130]

Score: Total number answered Y = ____

Important Note: In their study, 15 per cent of respondents actually answered yes to the final question! Obviously such a story is untrue, but those stories may have been told and laughed about in fun family conversations and remained a part of the family folklore.

What matters most is not that your child can answer these particular questions, but that you are having conversations that relate to who you are, who your family is, where your family came from and what your family is about. Marshall Duke's questionnaire is clearly written for the traditional, intact nuclear family, and we know there are many other forms that families take today. That does not mean it is irrelevant to children in families that do not conform to this structure. Some families have alternative parenting arrangements, or a child may not have siblings. In some families, parents may not be married, or a child may have been adopted. These are usually important details for you and your family identity, but they are unimportant in the context of this questionnaire. You can swap items around to fit your family. And there are more than 20 possible questions you might ask. The central issue is that we talk, we create a narrative and we allow that narrative to shape an identity – our children's identity. And when that identity is achieved, or even under construction via a positive and supportive process, our children make better decisions in their lives and they become more resilient in dealing with the challenges and adversities that they face.

Remember who you are

When we know our family history and have a sense of that identity, it can provide a map to follow. May was 13 years old when her best friend lost her mum to cancer. Deeply moved, May decided to do whatever she could to help her friend through her grief. She came from a home where her parents regularly looked for opportunities to carry out anonymous acts of service. The family would often make a batch of treats for a neighbour or friend, or randomly wash someone's car or mow their lawn. Service was a part of their identity, so when May's friend was suffering, May automatically felt that because of who she was, she should help. May discovered that in a few months' time a charity was holding its annual 'Shave for a Cure' fundraiser. People sign up to raise funds, and seek sponsors to donate. And they shave their heads.

May's parents were grateful to see May's compassion and desire to help. But they were also mindful that early adolescents are not always kind – particularly towards people who stand out. May had recently moved to a new school and barely knew any students. Her friendship group was very, very small. May's parents knew that if May shaved her head, there was a strong chance that she would bear the brunt of bullies who might call her names, misunderstanding her motives. They cautioned against the decision, but agreed to support May if she felt strongly about it. May proceeded.

May's little sister, Gracie, was inspired by her big sister's decision to help a friend and make a personal sacrifice. In the weeks leading up to the shave, eight-year-old Gracie begged permission to shave her head as well. Again, the girls' parents were reluctant to agree but ultimately acquiesced after again explaining that sometimes people can be cruel to people who look different. When the day to shave her head arrived, May sat in the hairdresser's chair and smiled as her long hair was cut off at the scalp. Then her young sister climbed into the chair and smiled as her hair was also shaved. The girls' fundraising efforts brought in over $5000.

Over subsequent months, both May and Gracie experienced name-calling and bullying. May was called a lesbian – ongoingly – by several of the girls at her school, teased incessantly by the boys and told she looked 'like a boy', and even had things thrown at her because she 'looked gay'. Little Gracie was subjected to even more teasing at school by the boys who could not understand why a girl would shave her head. Gracie's teacher explained Gracie's motivation to the boys, but the teasing continued for some time before finally ceasing.

I spoke to the children's parents, and then to the girls themselves and asked how they coped with the teasing. The girls' responses were powerful. They told me, 'We know why we did this. It doesn't matter how we look. Our hair grows back after a while and things will be normal again. But our friend won't get her mum back. Things won't be normal for her again. But doing this helped people. So we don't care whether people tease us. They just don't understand.' May was particularly insightful. She told me, 'I've gotten a better understanding of how it is to be one of the people who stand out. And I've also realised that for people who are gay, they get this type of bullying all the time. It's horrible and now I know what it's like so I can help make things better.'

The sense of meaning and purpose that these two girls derived from making this sacrifice gave them a sense of who they were – their identity. They were people willing to help others. They were people who understood that some things matter more than the petty judgements of others. This sense of identity made them resilient. They were able to withstand and move beyond the teasing and personal attacks they experienced, and enjoy the feeling of knowing who they were and what they stood for.

Take-home message

We can help our children develop a strong sense of identity by literally *teaching them who they are* – or at least by teaching them about who we are and where *they* came from. By talking to them about stories from our family history and helping them create a narrative about their own life experiences, we can help them feel consistent, unique and a part of something bigger than themselves. Become the family who does hard stuff, or who creates things, or who helps, or ... whatever it is that develops identity for your family. Teasing out principles and values from their personal life experiences will consolidate our children's sense of self. These understandings shape their identity and help them to create positive patterns for living their lives, enhancing their wellbeing and resilience.

CHAPTER 2

Building resilience by being psychologically flexible

Psychological flexibility is the ability to adapt to a
situation with awareness, openness and focus and
to take effective action, guided by your values.

Russ Harris[131]

One of the reasons we love movies so much is that they make us feel something. Our emotions are piqued. We can place ourselves into completely unreal situations and live certain experiences vicariously through the actors and their circumstances. Those movies can move us emotionally – and the emotions aren't always warm and fuzzy.

Years ago, Sylvester Stallone starred in a film called *Cliffhanger*. The opening scene of the film is filled with intensity and emotion as an actor fails to rescue a woman, high above a chasm between two peaks. It is one of several mood-inducing clips that participants were invited to watch as part of a series of experiments conducted by psychology professor Barbara Fredrickson at the University of Michigan. Participants were shown one of five videotaped film clips. Two clips were designed to elicit two distinct positive emotions and two were designed to elicit two distinct negative emotions. There was a fifth clip that was designed to induce no emotion at all – the control clip.

When Fredrickson carried out this experiment, she discovered something crucial for our understanding of psychological flexibility (we'll explore what that is later in this chapter), and for the way our ability to think positively and broadly bolsters our resilience – and the implications are as important for our children as they are for us. She found that seeing something that induces positive emotion leads us to expand and broaden our perspective and thinking. We see the big picture. We can create and consider possibilities. We can find the opportunity in the challenge. When viewing something that induces negative emotion, our thinking and perspective are narrowed and become rigidly inflexible.[132] We only see what is right in front of us. We struggle to consider options. We find the problem in every possibility.

Think about the last time that you dealt with an unhappy child who was behaving in a way that resembled anything but resilience. Perhaps he was being obstinate or stubborn, refusing to answer you. Maybe he was sobbing, unable to control those big emotions that had welled up inside. If this is the case, your child's *thought-action repertoire* would have been extremely limited. That is to say, he would have struggled to develop any real sense of his options, or of positive, effective ways to respond to the cause of his challenge. His thinking would likely have been narrow. His possible actions in the moment would have been limited. His ideas about how to manage the situation would have been rigid. All in all, he would have been psychologically inflexible.

As a father of six children, I have had many conversations with upset, frustrated and unhappy children. If you've been there, you know they're not really conversations as much as monologues, with you as a parent trying ever so hard to stay calm and discuss a challenge with a child who is non-responsive. I recall one such instance with one of my girls. Her day at school had been traumatic.

Her best friend was no longer talking to her. Cruel things had been said by both girls, and the relationship was in tatters. Her response to my understanding and empathy was limited. My attempts to invite discussion were fruitless. She gave monosyllabic nopes or disinterested grunts to my questions about how the relationship might be restored. My daughter had one solution, and only one. She was never going to talk to her friend again.

No doubt other parents have sought solutions to their children's inflexible, unyielding attitudes to a variety of challenges and had similar experiences. Stalemates within the family over whether a room had to be tidied, shoes put away, or regular contributions to family life should be made. Dealing with bad attitudes, screen-time squabbles, sibling fights and more. All these scenarios have led to both parents and children becoming increasingly determined and firm in their opinions, and increasingly closed to the idea that they might work with one another to solve the issue productively and positively. These challenges become even greater when a child experiences mood disorders such as depression or anxiety, or behavioural challenges such as attention deficit hyperactivity disorder (ADHD) or oppositional defiance disorder (ODD), and particularly Asperger's syndrome or autism. Children's thinking becomes entrenched in negativity, and their coping strategies become repetitive, unhelpful and fixed.

Psychological flexibility

What these children (and many of us as parents) lack is psychological flexibility. Being psychologically flexible is critically related to resilience. The greater our psychological flexibility, the more resilient we are likely to be. But what does it mean to be psychologically flexible? And how can we teach our children (and ourselves) a psychologically flexible – and thus a resilient – mindset?

At the outset, it may be easier to define psychological flexibility in the negative. Being psychologically flexible means *not* being psychologically rigid. Once we start seeing things only one way, we become rigid in our thinking and incapacitated in our efforts to see beyond our current situation. We tend to see our options as restricted and restrictive. The same things happen with our kids. It's as I described with the example of my angry child. When they become psychologically inflexible, they have no answers to the problems that vex them, or if they do develop a solution it becomes the *only* answer. For example, a child struggling with friendships might be convinced that the only thing to do is to move schools. If anxiety or depression are co-occurring then more drastic and harmful solutions such as running away, self-harming or even taking their own life may be the only options they can see. And if our child is younger, perhaps the only solution to the drama unfolding with a sibling is aggression and violence. With limited language skills, and even more limited problem-solving skills, fighting, biting, scratching, pinching, pulling hair or kicking might be the only solution a child can fix on. They also become entrenched in rigid, repetitive and less effective stress-handling strategies, express their emotions in socially inappropriate ways and struggle in novel environments. Psychological rigidity can be easy to spot in the short-term reactions we see in ourselves and our children. However, the longer-term outcomes of such a mindset can be concerning.

Being psychologically flexible, therefore, is the ability to adjust our behaviour and thinking so that we can pursue goals based on an authentic understanding of the moment, and in line with what we truly value. (It should be noted that because young children tend to not truly value much other than whatever they desire in the moment, we have a tremendous opportunity to teach values when these challenging moments of psychological inflexibility/rigidity arise. More on that soon.)

Because the definition of psychological flexibility is a bit of a mouthful, let's break it down. A person who is psychologically flexible does the following four things:

1. They recognise that some situations require certain behaviour and others require something different. For example, they know it's fine to shout in the playground, but shouting in the classroom is not okay. Or they recognise that jumping on Dad is fine in the lounge room but not appropriate while he is driving the car. They know it's fine to be noisy and energetic at the family Christmas party, but a family funeral requires a different response. They can be flexible and adapt to different situations based on context.

2. They prioritise, based on the situation. This requires that they pay attention to what *really* requires attention in the moment. A child may want to play outside, but recognises that finishing reading or piano practice or a chore is where her attention needs to be at this moment in time. As adults, we may feel under pressure from a child who is struggling with something when our sister calls us. If we are psychologically flexibile, we prioritise and either choose to ignore the call or we quickly answer and explain our mental resources are required elsewhere right now.

3. They shift perspective. This means that our children move away from the natural tendency to see everything through their own eyes and the way it affects them, and they instead see the world through others' eyes. Research indicates this is unlikely to happen in any meaningful and consistent way until around age five, and it takes ongoing effort for us to help our children consider others' needs and perspectives. (Again, many adults struggle with this

too.) Psychological flexibility means we recognise our perspective and feelings are not the only way of seeing a situation.

4. They balance competing desires and needs so they can be responsive in a values-based way, prioritising what matters most.[133]

In short, psychological flexibility means separating ourselves from our own thoughts and emotions a bit more than we typically might, and then choosing to act based on longer-term values rather than short-term impulses, thoughts and feelings. The reason it may seem tough is because being psychologically flexible requires that we be *mindful*. It means we need to be aware of what is happening in the moment, and then make judgements about our actions based on our deeply held values rather than on what we might want right there and then. In essence, we act with integrity, and that's no small feat – particularly for a child.

It sounds a little too perfect – perhaps even unreachable – for our children to be entirely psychologically flexible. It takes a lot of time, effort and guidance to help our children get there. We need to teach them to step away from a situation and evaluate it, regulate their emotions, consider their values and the perspective of others, and then act accordingly. Suffice to say, it's unlikely that our toddlers are going to be doing this with any real consistency. Nor will many of our under eights or tens. But by the time our children are entering and progressing through adolescence, we can guide them towards this type of living in a relatively consistent way.

Developing psychological flexibility

Some simple steps we can take to encourage this psychological flexibility in ourselves and our children include focusing on the ability to:

- **Be comfortable with all emotions.** We prefer it when our children are happy and bubbly, or at least content and peaceful. But sadness, anger, fear and frustration are also part of the human condition. Often we focus on helping our children (and ourselves) feel comfortable with some emotions and then we discount or devalue others. This is not a recipe for resilience or wellbeing. There is a solid body of research showing that the ability to be comfortable with our emotions, including our so-called 'negative' emotions, is critical to our ability to move forward effectively and productively in our lives. It allows us to be flexible and responsive to a variety of situations regardless of what we are confronted with. When our children can be at least somewhat comfortable with emotions that we typically call 'negative', they can be more flexible and broad-thinking in the manner in which they respond to situations that generate those emotions. This openness, curiosity and broader thinking increases their capacity to be resilient.

- **Recognise that our emotions – both 'happy' and not so happy – often signal things that are of value to us.** For example, when a child feels frustration, it can signal that access to something they value is being thwarted and this may create a desire to change the environment. Guilt can signal the need to make amends or recalibrate goals. When we ignore or deny these difficult emotions in ourselves or our children we lose a key piece of information about what we value, eroding the capacity to be flexible. A psychologically flexible response promotes a sense of curiosity about that negative emotion, and can highlight a need to change in order to live consistently with our values.

- **Not focus on happiness as an end goal.** There are
  two reasons for this. First, evidence is accumulating
  that **people who value the idea of being happy or who
  make happiness a goal actually become less happy over
  time.** This is not suggesting that happiness is wrong.
  Of course we all want happiness, but often the way
  happiness is pursued is counter to the actual attainment
  of happiness. If a person who has happiness as an end
  goal is not happy, they will become frustrated, angry or
  challenged in some other way, which can bring with it
  a corresponding level of inflexibility, undermining their
  capacity to think broadly and flexibly, and improve their
  situation. This reduces resilience.

  Second, **happiness pursued as a goal can result in
  emotion suppression** (for example, 'Think positive' or
  'I just need to be happy') or emotion rumination (for
  example, 'Why aren't I happy?'). When these ways of
  navigating our emotions are used as a default tendency,
  they paradoxically result in *less* happiness and resilience,
  not more.

The benefits of psychological flexibility

Those who are psychologically flexible not only have a stronger
sense of personal identity (see the preceding chapter), but research
shows they also enjoy raised resilience. Two separate studies
have identified that acting with psychological flexibility increases
resilience and lifts children's vitality, curiosity, self-reliance,
confidence, creativity, meaningful experiences and ability to
master challenges, and even speeds up recovery from stressful
events.[134] So children can do it, and it does make a difference.

Researchers have found that when people lack psychological
flexibility (or score low), they experience higher levels of

anxiety, more depression, more overall pathology, poorer work performance, reduced ability to learn, substance abuse, a lower quality of life and other negative outcomes. In other words, it can affect *almost everything*![135] High scores mean high flexibility, and high resilience.

One father proudly told me of his son's psychological flexibility when confronted with a challenging situation. Ben was in a bind. He had been invited to his friend's ninth birthday party, which was being held on the same day and at the same time as an important family event. Ben's big sister was performing in a production that she had been preparing for all year. The entire family was going to attend, and a function was to be held after the production with grandparents, aunts, uncles and cousins. Dad had explained to Ben that the decision about which event to attend was his, and asked him to work through the various scenarios so he could make a good choice. With his dad, Ben talked about how his mate would feel if he could not attend the party. Then he explored how the family would feel if Ben was not with them – particularly his sister and his grandparents. They talked about Ben's preferences: he wanted to go to the party a little more than he wanted to be at the production and the dinner. And then, together, they sifted through the various feelings and priorities Ben was wrestling with. Eventually Ben elected to forego the party and spend time with his family. This decision was autonomously chosen, and in alignment with his values of family before friendships. Because he made the decision himself, Ben was able to feel good about his time with family in spite of his sadness at missing another priority.

Michele told me of her son, Noah, and his psychological flexibility at a school sports carnival. Noah, a Year 9 boy, had been competing in a teams event with children of all ages. Some of the younger children in the team were struggling, and as a result, their team was losing. Some of the other boys in the team were screaming at their younger teammates, accusing them of being hopeless and not trying. Noah had interrupted the boys and reminded them that, 'It's just a game.' He had asked them to relax and suggested that yelling at the younger students was not going to make them feel better or perform at a higher level. It would only leave them feeling bad about themselves. Noah was one of the school's better athletes and wanted to win as much as anyone else, but he also recognised that in the scheme of things, the wellbeing of the younger students needed to be a higher priority than the immature win-at-all-costs mentality of his teammates. His ability to assess the situation, take on the perspective of others, and prioritise values of kindness and humanity higher than winning gave him the ability to be psychologically flexible and act in accordance with his highest values. It also made his mum proud.

My family encountered psychological flexibility and rigidity in our children when we made a decision to relocate interstate. With six children of all ages, you can imagine that we had a range of responses to our decision. But the move was necessary, and we did all we could to support our children and soften the experience. One child was deeply affected. To be clear, she was devastated. She cried quietly to herself as we held and hugged her. Over the subsequent days she had spells of deep sadness and grief. But throughout the experience she remained flexible. She could see the reasons, the benefits and the opportunities. She acted and communicated openly with us and bounced back from the hard news in a surprisingly short time. Another daughter, however, became instantly rigid in her response and refused to talk for days. She wept, threatened not to move house, and became insular and angry. We gave her space, and after a few days began to spend time in conversation with her. We talked about flexibility and rigidity, and worked through some of the ideas that you'll find in subsequent chapters of this book. It took a week or two, but acceptance seeped into her thinking, and her responses and interactions warmed up. Rigidity was replaced with reluctant acceptance. Then ideas started to flow, opportunities became obvious, and her anger abated.

The power of acceptance

An integral part of being able to be psychologically flexible is the capacity to accept things as they are. It is a paradox that when a person or child is incapable of *acceptance*, they are likely to respond to challenging situations with inflexibility. The frustration and negativity of a situation become too much. As a result, their ability to pay attention to the situation is reduced and they see fewer decision-making opportunities. They become rigid in their lack of acceptance! But when we accept situations for what they are, even when we do not like them, we then have a greater capacity to be flexible in the way that we respond to them, and we can draw on our deeply held values to guide our subsequent action. This ties in with Fredrickson's idea that we need to feel positive emotions so we can think broadly and develop ideas that will allow us to respond to situations with a range of options. The difficulty of coming up with positive solutions is increased by inflexibility and negativity. Instead of actively responding based on values, a person who is upset at or trying to avoid a difficult situation becomes psychologically unavailable and cannot adapt to what is right in front of them. Such an approach would be an entirely *mindless* response to a situation that requires *mindfulness*. When we are mindless we are essentially passive and inactive in our minds. While we may be forming judgements, we are forming them based on previous experience, allowing what has happened to us in the past to override what is happening now. This prevents us from being open to multiple perspectives and, instead, traps us into seeing things only one way. Thus we become insensitive to context and rely on rules or routines to govern our decision-making and behaviour.[136]

Here's a simple example of how we easily behave mindlessly towards our children. You walk into your child's bedroom and see they are on a device of some sort. This is a constant bugbear of yours, and previous experience has shown you that your child is unlikely to want to get off that screen. Besides, it was bedtime at least 20 minutes ago, and you thought that when you had sent them off to bed, they were actually going to bed. To top it all off, the room is a mess the likes of which you haven't seen since you last tried to find your way in there. The floor has become the floordrobe! The moment you see your child playing, all your past experiences play across your mind and you react immediately and forcefully. 'Get off that thing right now. Your room is a mess. You haven't done any reading or homework. It is past your bedtime. I specifically told you to go to bed. And I am *tired* of constantly badgering you about your screen use. You have five seconds or I'm taking it off you until the end of the week!'

Everything you have felt and that led to your response may be right. Everything you have experienced previously is feeding your emotion and your action, and there are clear justifications for what is going through your mind, and for your response. You know that you're right. Your child looks at you and responds, 'But I'm doing my homework. My teacher asked me to look this up for my project. See!' Or perhaps they say, 'I know I'm on Facebook ...' (or Snapchat, or whatever messaging app they're using) '... and I know you thought I was in bed. But my friend is in trouble and he needed someone to talk to.'

A mindless, psychologically inflexible response would be one where all that matters are the rules. While it is true that in *some* instances all that matters *are* the rules, most parenting situations are more flexible than we readily acknowledge in the heat of our emotions. And so we hear this response from our child and we up the ante. We become enraged, demanding better behaviour 'or so help me you won't know what hit you'. We get stuck in rigid thinking.

Psychological flexibility allows us to respond differently. We respond mindfully and in line with our deepest-held values. When we enter that bedroom and see our child staring at a screen, we pause and consider what we value most in life. Is it clean bedrooms? Sleeping children? A life devoid of screens after a particular hour of the night? Or is it loving relationships? For the sake of the argument, let's say that our desire for loving relationships in our home transcends those other things we value so we pick that and adjust our response to the situation accordingly. We have an active state of mind and remain right there in the moment rather than allowing past experiences to intrude on what is occurring now. We recognise the rules and routines that are important, and we bring them up in our conversation, but we are only *guided*, rather than governed, by them. Perhaps the interaction might proceed like this:

> **Parent:** I'm surprised to see you on your screen. You told me you were going to bed.
>
> **Child:** I was going to bed, but I forgot about Mr Nibali's homework assignment. I thought I'd do a quick bit of research before I turned out the light.
>
> **Parent:** Hmm. I'm worried you're not going to get enough sleep. You know what mornings are like when you're over-tired from staying up too late.'
>
> **Child:** Yeah I know. I won't be much longer.
>
> **Parent:** What time will you be asleep? I need a time so this doesn't drag on too long.

The same process could be followed for any situation where flexibility can be offered. When we are flexible we can do what author Alfie Kohn suggests and *work with* our children. When we are rigid we are more likely to *do things to* them. Sometimes we become preconditioned to behave in a certain way towards a child (or perhaps another relative, like a mother-in-law or *that* uncle). They merely have to enter the room and we find ourselves prejudging them. We are on edge, ready to attack, or feeling we must tread lightly to avoid confrontations. Our children can experience the same thing with us, with their siblings, or with friends in the playground at school. And once these impressions of others have formed, we tend to respond mindlessly to those people. We become resistant to reconsidering the kind of person they are, or changing our perspective. This makes it hard for us to be flexible with our children, or for them to be flexible towards others, because we tend to be closed to new or additional information about others, and we prioritise what we already 'know' about them over going to the trouble of considering who or how they might be in a different context. While it can be handy to have these mental shortcuts, the flipside is that they can make us rigid and inflexible, jeopardising important relationships – and even resilience.

You will, of course, note that the last example I shared is one where a parent is being psychologically flexible towards a child. Such an approach will typically make you and your family happier and more resilient. It will also make things a little more challenging because those hard, fast rules we can lean on need to be discarded. We instead adopt a more versatile and expansive style that allows for spontaneity where context allows, or a more stringent approach where required. A psychologically flexible parent recognises that *context is everything*, and then teaches this to their children, along with values, to aid in more responsive and adaptive decision-making.

Seven steps to psychological flexibility

There are times, though, when we need our children to be psychologically flexible too. Here are seven steps to help teach psychological flexibility to our children.

Step one – respond to emotions

When our children become highly emotional, or when their emotions are 'negative', they tend towards rigidity and inflexibility. They may despair, feel all is hopeless, be angry, or be set on the *One and Only Way*. For our children to respond flexibly, they need distance between themselves and their emotions. This broadens their thinking and creates the conditions necessary to facilitate psychological flexibility.[137] Help your child really be aware of how they feel as a result of the challenge they are facing.

Step two – increase awareness of the present

If your child will allow you to, sit and talk with them. Because they feel understood and emotions are decreasing somewhat (step one), it's time to invite them to tell you about what is happening in the present moment, both inside and around them. As they describe what they are experiencing with their five senses and in their heart, you can both empathise ('It feels so lonely for you when it seems as though you have no friends!') and contrast what they are experiencing with what their sometimes unreliable (or mindless) mind is *telling them* is happening. You might experiment with some mindful breathing to help your child step back from those distressing, resilience-reducing thoughts and become both calm and open to being flexible.

Step three – emphasise choice

Remind your child that even though it is hard, and even though they are struggling with this issue, they still have a choice. They can choose how they will respond to this challenge. While they might have some rigid, strong ideas, there could be other ideas or pathways to resolving things in a way that will help them and everyone else feel good.

Step four – teach curiosity

One of the most interesting things about being psychologically flexible is that it invites perspective, empathy and understanding. Scientists have used brain scanners to watch what happens when people experience something challenging and, instead of responding mindlessly with anger or frustration, respond with 'Hmmm, that's really interesting.' They found that in people who show reduced openness and receptivity to their thoughts and feelings (that is, low mindfulness and high inflexibility) the brain's limbic system, which is one of the brain's central structures for processing emotion, becomes highly active.[138] But those who are mindful and curious about their thoughts show a different neurological response. Their prefrontal cortex becomes active. This is the executive centre of the brain and is responsible for planning and decision-making. At the same time, the limbic system shows a much lower response, suggesting that a mindful, open, curious, flexible approach keeps emotions in check and allows broad, more flexible thinking![139] Scientists call this process *cognitive defusion* and it means that we change our relationship to our thoughts. Rather than our child believing everything his mind tells him about his situation, his friends or himself, we teach him to say, 'Hmm, that's interesting,' and then to ask 'Why?' This distance and curiosity about emotions allows children to avoid rumination, depression, anxiety or repetitive, unhelpful, rigid coping strategies. Instead, they stand back and say, 'Huh? I'm getting really angry about my brother and I feel like I want to hit him. I wonder why?' The answer may be obvious, and hitting may still be the clear solution, which is why the next steps are vital.

Step five – shift perspective

Now that emotions have reduced, we have an opportunity to talk with our children about how this situation impacts on them, and on others. We can ask questions that promote insight and understanding:

> 'How does it feel when this happens?'
> 'Who does it affect?'
> 'What are they thinking?'
> 'How are they feeling?'
> 'What do they want to do about it?'
> 'Where does this lead?'

Some other questions that can alter your child's perspective of the situation, themselves and others who may be involved include:

> 'What are some other ways I can view this situation?'
> 'How can I learn something from this?'
> 'Can this make me a stronger, better person?'
> 'Is there a hidden blessing or opportunity for me here?'

Step six – take values-based action

Psychological flexibility is ultimately about focusing attention on what it is we really want to achieve. Now we have responded to our child's emotions, become mindful and present, become curious and shifted perspective, it is time to ask, 'What is the best thing to do right now based on what's most important?' When working with our children, we can focus on asking, 'What do you think is the most important thing here?' This question focuses them on their values, and helps them determine what to do in order to act honestly and with personal integrity.

Step seven – reappraise

Once we're through the process, we take stock of what has happened and talk with our child about how the experience has been beneficial and meaningful. In other words, we look for the benefit in the problem. This approach is associated with lower stress, improved mental health outcomes and a sense of accomplishment. Each of these feeds resilience, strengthening our children and helping them to feel capable of responding to difficulties in constructive, positive ways.[140]

Take-home message

This is not a simple process where we pat our child on the back, say 'You'll be okay,' and leave them to it. Psychological flexibility is something our children will almost certainly need help with. They need us to help them be calm, think broadly, be curious, take the perspective of others, recognise they have choices, and then move towards values-based actions. It sounds complicated – perhaps it is, a little. But the results are important: children develop resilience. Why? Being psychologically flexible means acting in positive, constructive ways when times are tough. It is a process that builds self-efficacy and self-control. It leaves a child feeling that they have choice and autonomy, can behave in competent ways and build relationships. These are the building blocks of motivation and serve as crucial foundations for resilience.

In time, the processes involved in being psychologically flexible will become intrinsic. Your child will begin to develop the capacity to step back from their emotions, look at all perspectives and make good choices about how to act – all without your input! It will become the way they do things. And they will feel capable and resilient because of it.

CHAPTER 3

Self-control: the secret to success?

He who controls others may be powerful, but he
who has mastered himself is mightier still.

Lao Tzu

I tried to avoid it, but honestly, if we are going to talk about self-control there is no better, more captivating and more interesting story to tell than the story of Walter Mischel and the marshmallow experiment. Whenever self-control comes up, so does this story. It is arguably the most well-known psychology study of all time.[141] If you need a quick refresher, here's how it worked.

In the late 1960s, Walter Mischel, a psychology researcher at Stanford University, invited children aged around four years old to participate in a study to test an idea he had about willpower and self-control. Over a handful of years, over 600 children were brought into a room, one at a time, and were left alone, but covertly observed, and told they weren't to eat the marshmallow in front of them. If they abstained, they would get *two* marshmallows. Footage shows them distracting themselves by drumming on the desk, twisting their hair around their fingers, covering their eyes, spinning around in their chair so that their back is to the food, and more. Kids smelled the treat, held it to their lips or pinched tiny pieces. You can see delightful re-creation videos on the internet.

This marshmallow test has become celebrated as a test that has tremendous implications in our lives. Mischel discovered that children who were able to control their impulses went on to be more successful in life. They made more money, were healthier, were less likely to go to prison, they were happier and enjoyed better relationships.[142]

Unfortunately for all of the many people who have read this story and believed their child's future success (or resilience) is discoverable within a marshmallow, the typical interpretation of the experiment is around the wrong way. I'll explain more shortly.

First, let's quickly get clear what self-control is. According to Wilhelm Hoffman and his colleagues,[143] self-control is the ability to override or even to change our inner responses, and to stop ourselves from acting on impulses. You know that moment where you want to say something unkind to one of your children because they are driving you bonkers? Self-control means you override, and thus change, that impulse. You stop yourself, remember that you love your child deeply, and you hug and make things right instead. Self-control is getting out of bed when you'd rather sleep in. It is completing your work by your deadline when there are so many things you would rather be doing. And, as we shall see, self-control is critical to success, wellbeing and resilience.

Self-control makes us happy

At least some evidence suggests that not only does self-control increase resilience, but it also makes us happier. This may be at least a little bit counterintuitive. After all, if you don't control yourself, surely you get to have lots of fun. Kids who don't control themselves get to eat the marshmallow! They go to bed late, skip out on school, eat dessert first and more. And grown-ups who exercise limited self-control get to enjoy the pleasures that are so enticing too! But with a little bit of perspective and a long-term view, we can easily see that the short-term pleasures that come from a lack of self-control often bring with them negative consequences, while those who exercise self-control are far better able to achieve long-term goals, and with those goals, long-term wellbeing.

So how would you go in a self-control situation? Are you the kind of person who would eat dessert first? Would you agree or disagree with the following statement:

- I do certain things that are bad for me if they are fun.

Those with high levels of self-control are significantly less likely to agree with that statement than those with low levels of self-control. In a recent study, 414 participants responded to a questionnaire that asked a range of questions like this one. In another study conducted by the same researchers, just over 200 participants had been responding to smartphone messages (which may or may not have required self-control!) at random moments, asking whether or not they had been experiencing any desires, the effort they had gone to in order to resist those desires, and whether or not they had been successful in resisting. And in both studies, participants had also rated their mood and life satisfaction. The results were clear: higher levels of life satisfaction were associated with higher levels of self-control. Surprisingly, this was both in the short and long term.[144]

So, there we have it. We, and our children, *need* self-control to be happy, resilient, successful humans – and, according to the 32-year Dunedin study, we need it to stay healthy, wealthy and out of prison. Is it really that simple? Is that all that counts – having self-control or not? Or having as much of it as we can get? Should we be sitting our children in front of marshmallows and testing them? If you want to have an entertaining night and teach a somewhat valuable lesson, perhaps. One good friend of mine had his children participate in a marshmallow study re-enactment. He said, 'When my kids did the marshmallow test they put the marshmallows in their mouths and sucked them, and then put them back on the table when the person came back in, to qualify for their second one.'

But really, this is not a good idea. Why? For two reasons. First, trying to force someone to have self-control means that we are the ones doing the controlling. If we have to *make* a child show restraint, is it them or us in control? Self-control requires our absence to be the real deal. But there's more to it than that. This is the second central reason we shouldn't be trying to demand self-control from our children. We are treating it as if it is something where quantity is all that matters. Yes, it is important that our children possess self-control. But there's more to resilience and wellbeing than the mere presence and possession of this capacity to say no when it counts. It is also the quality of the self-control that is key, and that assists with and predicts resilience outcomes. As author Alfie Kohn indicated: *how much* tends to matter less than *what kind*.[145] And there are different kinds of self-control.

Self-control is enacted in different ways. Ed Deci and Richard Ryan, two psychologists from the University of Rochester, in New York, USA, have argued that just because a person is exercising self-control doesn't make that person healthy, happy or resilient. In fact, a heavily controlled form of self-control, even when that control comes from within, may be particularly unhealthy and lead to poorer wellbeing, motivational and resiliency outcomes.[146] Think of a person who really, really does not want to do something but they're doing it because they 'have' to. No one is standing over them, making them do it. Instead, they just know they have to. Maybe it is the decision to forego dessert because of your diet. This form of self-control is called *introjection*. There is no sense of autonomy or freedom. It is not a natural extension or expression of who we are and what we want. We just have to do it or we'll feel guilty. Or anxious. Or something else horrible.

The Dunedin study and many others have highlighted a correlation between low self-control/introjection and low socio-economic status (income). And by extension, children in poverty are, on average, less resilient than those from economically stable homes. But research also suggests that this may be underscored by that very low self-control, perhaps the inherited cyclical repercussion of intergenerational poverty and disadvantage. Parents – and eventually children – make choices that exacerbate their negative outcomes, and those choices relate to low self-control. The liberal argument is that better policies, government support and structures would change these people's lives for the better. The conservative argument is that if those in such circumstances showed more control, they'd keep jobs, be healthier and lift themselves out of poverty. A more balanced view would suggest that neither extreme is accurate, but that both improving systems *and* retraining the people those systems have already disadvantaged could help.

As a result of the many studies highlighting these facts, some schools in low socio-economic areas have begun addressing both the system and structure, as well as the learned characteristics of their students, by providing extra levels of intervention to promote self-control, grit and character strengths.

A ground-breaking research project published in the *Proceedings of the National Academy of Science* emphasises just how important the quality of self-control is when considering resilience for those in challenging financial circumstances. In this American study, conducted across several years, 292 young men aged 17–20 were followed to better understand the relationship between socio-economic status and self-control. The students had experienced this increased level of guidance at school related to self-control, grit and character strengths. They discovered that the participants in the study had developed high levels of self-control and other character strengths. They seemed resilient. Many of them had completed school and were attending college. They were also less likely to use tobacco, alcohol or other drugs. Their self-control was yielding dividends. But it came at a cost. The researchers found that these study participants were also aging faster and more unhealthily than their peers. They showed *poorer cardiometabolic health*, meaning they were more likely to be overweight, have high levels of stress hormones in their bodies, and have unhealthily high blood pressure. Self-control was leading to a form of resilience the researchers called *skin-deep*. These people's lives showed the outward appearance of resiliency, but their cells were showing a deep physical cost to the extent that they had to be controlled in order to succeed against the odds. By definition, they were resilient. They were thriving beyond what would be assumed by their circumstances. Yet their bodies were indicating that this was stressful and challenging.[147] Perhaps the self-control these teens and young adults were exhibiting was an *introjected* form of self-control that was more effortful, more taxing, and ultimately less healthy than an autonomous, self-determined form of self-control – and perhaps their circumstances and the broader social policies that affected them made it so. Or maybe their circumstances were such that trying to make those changes was extra stressful in spite of it being freely chosen. And while it was found that there was stress and challenge, they were still resilient, and were almost certainly improving their life circumstances over and above what they might otherwise have experienced.

The kind of self-control that is ideal is the type that comes from within and almost doesn't feel like self-control. Instead, it is a natural, authentic extension or desire of the person. It is this *intrinsic* form of self-control that is ideal for resilience. The further along the continuum towards forced forms of control, the poorer the outcomes for resilience and wellbeing. Once our children have internalised an idea, they will be far more likely to regulate their behaviour around it – and will do so without internal conflict. This will help them to consolidate their sense of identity, allow them the capacity to be psychologically flexible, and ultimately enhance their self-confidence and competence, building their resilience as a byproduct.

Back to the marshmallows

How much self-control does your child show? Would you agree with the following statements about your child?

- My child is persistent in activities.
- My child thinks ahead.
- My child is attentive and able to concentrate.
- My child thinks before speaking or acting.
- My child responds to reason.

If you have answered 'yes' to these statements then your child is probably already high on self-control. What about these statements?

- My child is stubborn.
- My child is unable to delay gratification.
- My child tends to go to pieces under stress.
- My child overreacts to minor frustrations.
- My child becomes anxious when the environment is unpredictable.

If you have answered 'yes' to these statements then your child is likely to be lower on self-control. Now for the good news.

We now know, from decades of studies, that self-control is malleable. Some people have high self-control from an early age. Some people become more self-controlled as they mature. And most importantly, most people, regardless of their baseline level of self-control, can be taught to exercise greater control. Mischel found that by teaching children basic skills to reframe their situation, their self-control could be massively extended. A child who couldn't wait 30 seconds before biting into the marshmallow or eating some cookie was able to wait the entire 15 minutes on a subsequent occasion after being coached to pretend that the marshmallow wasn't really there, or that it was a picture and to imagine a frame around it. The child with no self-control suddenly possessed maximal self-control with just a subtle shift in thinking. This enhanced psychological flexibility is really just a process of *reframing*. The vast majority of children were able to delay gratification after they reframed the situation based on Mischel's training. But that's not the story we hear when we read about the marshmallow study. It's not as sexy. It doesn't generate the same reaction because it doesn't create the same fear, uncertainty and anxiety. To be told that your child's destiny is in a marshmallow creates a sense of inevitability about the future that can be as comforting as it is disconcerting.

Mischel followed up with some children once they were adolescents and found that those children who showed limited or no self-control in the early preschool experiments had significantly lower SAT scores. (The SAT is a standardised American test that is used as a college admission benchmark in the USA.[148]) This seems to confirm all the scary things I have just argued against – the things we so easily believe as a result of the dominant narrative about those darned marshmallows. 'See, if my kids eat a marshmallow, they'll never do *anything* right at school!' But the point of the marshmallow experiment was *not* to work out which children had a lack of self-control and then predict their unhappy futures. Rather, it was to show how self-control can be changed and outcomes altered. It was to demonstrate how flexible people can be – even children – by helping them to understand that if they were to reinterpret the situation around them (mindfully), they could increase the extent to which they showed self-control.

When self-control was 'work', because it was introjected or barely internalised, it was depleting and hard and generally unsuccessful. When it became internalised because it was fun, desired or simply understood as a part of the individual's identity, self-control was easy, enjoyable and worthwhile.

Sometimes it is best to postpone and delay gratification by showing self-control. And with minimal effort we can actually teach our children how to do that. If it is done autonomously, it will be easier for them to do it, and they'll feel good about it. If it is controlled, it is less likely to be successful, and even if it is successful, it may not be an overall positive. But in other cases, a bird in the hand is worth two in the bush. Our children need to know that sometimes it's okay to eat dessert first. Importantly, our children need to be able to wait for something when it matters to them. If there is something that they value, then exercising self-control to obtain that thing should be easier than if it is something they do not value. If they cannot exercise self-control, then *that* lack of self-control may mean that the choice to wait or not wait was never a choice in the first place. And *that* is when resilience suffers.

Boosting self-control

There are a handful of simple strategies that can enhance your child's self-control from a young age.

1. **Talk – lots.** By communicating with your child about the importance of patience, values, hard work, setting goals and being present, your child will learn about self-control from you.
2. **Make decisions when emotions are cold rather than hot.** This means we decide that we will *not* be eating dessert at breakfast or lunchtime, rather than as we finish our

main meal and see the chocolate cake with fresh cream and raspberries. It means we help our children make decisions about kindness to siblings, social media, gaming or any other issue when emotions are cool rather than during the heat of battle.

3. **Stay the course when it counts.** There will be times when we need to compassionately and patiently do all we can as an external controller to help our children through challenges. Encouraging a growth mindset (covered in the next chapter) can help with this.

4. **Encourage autonomy.** It's rarely ideal to be the one doing the controlling. But we can offer support and encouragement as our children move from introjected forms of self-control to identified control, and then to internalised forms of control. The less controlling we are, the easier it is for them to make that progress.

5. **Get your child to wait ten minutes.** Whether it's sneaking a treat, checking social media or hitting a sibling (!), encourage your child to wait ten minutes and see if it's still something he feels he must do.

6. **Get curious and mindful.** Encourage curiosity, mindfulness and psychological flexibility when a child wants to show a lack of self-control. Get them to ask, 'Why does this matter so much to me?' That gentle curiosity can help them move away from the emotion of the moment and make a decision based more on values. This boosts self-control, making a child feel more competent and more resilient.

7. **Be an example.** If you're lacking in self-discipline, self-control or restraint, or if you are consistently behaving in controlled ways that you resent (introjected forms of control), your child will learn from you and act accordingly.

My last suggestion comes from Homer's *Odyssey*. On his epic journey, Ulysses received instructions that he must pass the Sirens – mythical women of the water – and he was warned that their enchanting song might lead his boat and crew to ruin. Ulysses wanted to hear the song, so he commanded his crew to stop their ears with wax and bind him to the mast of the ship. If he begged for release due to the enchanting song, the crew were to bind him tighter. While this is never ideal, there are times when we need to get others to exercise the control that otherwise evades us. At times this is essential for survival, let alone wellbeing and resilience. We should always minimise the use of external controls, but ... if a child (or partner) *needs* extra help and requests it, that level of support may be a tremendous lift and help them achieve a degree of success in their journey they may otherwise not experience.

Take-home message

Self-control matters for resilience. The most important thing about self-control that we need to know is that it can be developed. And simply because a child lacks self-control early in life, it is no indication that they are doomed! There is resilience that self-control offers, and a sense of confidence that comes when our children realise that they can say 'no' to what they need to, and 'yes' to what they know matters. The seeds of self-control are sown in the early years, and the fruits are consumed throughout the rest of life.

CHAPTER 4

Stinking thinking: overcoming a negative attribution style

If you want to build a ship, don't drum up the people to gather wood, divide the work and give orders. Instead, teach them to yearn for the vast and endless sea.

Antoine de Saint-Exupéry

One of the most remarkable things about resilience is that it appears to be the *natural* state for most humans. Unless life serves up such punishment that we cannot conceive of continuing to 'try', we seem to be a resilient, optimistic, positive species. This is not the case for everyone. Those with clinical depression or anxiety do not feel optimistic. But evidence suggests that a default optimism setting is standard for most. Scientists believe that humans possess an *optimism bias*.[149] For example, studies have shown that people believe they are less at risk of being a crime victim compared to others.[150] They believe they're at less risk of contracting cancer than others, or being divorced, or losing a job. In short, we massively overestimate the likelihood of positive events occurring to us, such as having a long life, getting 'that' job or mark, or having especially talented children. And we significantly underestimate the likelihood of negative things happening (like divorce, cancer or car accidents).[151] This bias is great for our resilience. Being hopeful and optimistic is a major predictor of wellbeing.[152] Life's buffetings can of course diminish hope and reduce the power of that natural disposition, and this is when we, as parents, can start to challenge our children's stinking thinking before it begins to pervade their psyches.

Thinking something doesn't make it true

The stoic philosopher Epictetus said, 'People are not disturbed by things, but by the view they take of them.' This profound insight suggests that it is our perceptions that determine the extent to which something affects us, and how. The ABC model[153] is our modern equivalent of Epictetus's statement, and it is one of the foundational models of modern-day cognitive behavioural therapy. It is simple to teach to children to boost their resilience mindset.[154] Here is an example how:

My 11-year-old daughter came home from school in a sobbing mess. She crumpled into our arms and cried. We held her and waited for her to calm down enough to talk. It took a while, but eventually she told us that she didn't want to go to school *ever again*. The reason? The children were playing sport and her best friend was the first girl chosen to be on one of the teams – before our daughter. A combination of envy, self-doubt and anger had exploded within her, and while she had put on a brave face at school, the pressure of not being perceived as the best had built up during the course of the afternoon, erupting as she reached the safety of our living room.

We sat with our daughter and spent some time labelling her emotions, describing how we thought she must feel. 'When you're not picked first, you feel like you're not good enough.' 'You feel jealous when you see other people being recognised as good at things that matter to you.' 'You hate feeling like this because it's your friend and you want to be happy for her, but you also feel like it should have been you that was picked first.'

Once she knew we understood how she was feeling, she became calm and we walked through the ABC model of stinking thinking. We explained, 'When bad things happen, we call those things adversities. An adversity is something challenging, horrible or difficult. Today you have experienced an adversity. It was not getting picked first for the team when you really wanted to and thought you deserved it.' We explained that we were going to skip the B for a moment and go straight to the C. 'C stands for consequences. In your case, the consequence of you not getting picked as the first girl on the team is that you became upset and jealous, and have come home hating school and never wanting to go there again. Is that correct?' Our daughter nodded, confirming that she felt understood and that she was still with us.

We asked, 'So what is it that the B might stand for? What made those consequences happen? Was it that you were not picked on the team first, or could it be something else?'

(At this point our daughter looked lost. And it is worth mentioning that this idea is quite challenging for children under about age seven. But kids from about four or five can get the hang of it with practice, so start early – just don't expect instant results.)

We explained to our daughter, 'It's not actually the adversity that leads to the horrible consequences you have experienced. Instead, it is the beliefs that you created when the adversity occurred. B is for beliefs. So let's talk about what you believed when you were not picked first.'

Her reply was insightful. 'I believed I must not be good at sport, and that makes me feel bad because I want to be the best sportsperson in my school.' We asked her if she had any other beliefs when she was not picked for the team. 'I believed I wasn't popular. And I believed I was just no good at anything.'

'Uh huh. And when you believe those kinds of things about yourself, what are the consequences?'

Our daughter calmly nodded, recognising that her beliefs were the creative force behind her horrible afternoon and her lack of resilience in the face of her challenge.

Then came the most important part of the conversation. 'What alternative beliefs could you have about this situation?' She stared at us blankly. This is not an easy leap for a child to make. So we chatted for a while and developed a few alternative beliefs.

- I'm great at lots of sports but my friend is probably better at this one, and that's okay.
- It feels nice to be picked first, and that's usually me. Now my friend knows how good it feels.
- At least I got picked early.

We also asked her how some of the other children who were picked much later may have felt. This helped her develop a sense of perspective and empathy for them, and a desire to encourage her friends to pick some of those people sooner than usual.

Lastly, we told her, 'Just because you think something, it doesn't make it true. We have lots of thoughts about ourselves that are wrong.' If we can help our children question and even attack their unconscious, unhealthy beliefs, we can raise their resilience.

Here is another simple situation that children struggle with. Steele fails a maths test. He is devastated and never wants to do maths again. So the adversity (A) is the failed test. The consequence (C) is his lack of resilience and a desire to avoid maths from now on. But what is the belief? In this case, Steele's belief (B) is that he is hopeless at maths. Or that he must get good marks or he has no hope. This is obviously an unhealthy belief that will undermine his resilience, and his resolve to improve. It will lead to defeatist thinking and the belief he is a victim of his maths teacher's craftiness or lack of attention, or his own poor intellect. If escapism becomes his default coping strategy, he will not be able to finish his schooling or pursue the various career options that might be important to him in later life.

Some children experience a lifetime of this kind of thinking in school. Yet thousands of others face adversity with much more equanimity. The difference is the beliefs they hold about that adversity. When the beliefs are rational, constructive and resilient, the consequences are positive, given time. There will almost always be a natural mourning process when bad things happen. But when we teach our children that their beliefs determine the consquences of those bad events, the adversity they experience is more likely to eventually be seen as an opportunity to grow and develop, to improve and master.

Attribution styles

Before becoming the modern-day patriarch of positive psychology, Professor Martin Seligman studied helplessness and depression. In his work with another extraordinary thinker, Professor Christopher Peterson, Seligman developed a theory about our attribution styles – or the way we think about positive and negative events in our lives, or *attribute* meaning to those events – that expands on Epictetus's philosophy and Albert Ellis's ABC model.

We know resilient people still feel lousy about life from time to time. Events can and do get them down. But the view they take of those events seems to be different from the view that someone who is less resilient holds. Perhaps while dealing with the initial disappointment of a negative event, they feel frustrated, let down and upset – just like anyone else. But the way they explain the event, even amid disappointment, is entirely different from those who lack resilience and feel they are victims of an unfair life. According to Seligman, it is this difference that is crucial in explaining who is resilient and who is not.

Those who are not resilient experience a negative event and make three attributions, or judgements, about themselves and their lives.

1. I caused this bad thing. It's intrinsic to who I am. (This is called an *internal attribution*.)
2. Bad things like this are typical for me. (This is called an *attribution of stability*.)
3. No matter what I do, this bad stuff always happens to me. (This is a *global attribution*.)[155]

This 'triple P' attribution model is a simple way to remember what stinking thinking looks like, and it is easy to teach to our children. It is seeing negative situations as Personal, Permanent, and Pervasive. Those with low resilience, depression, pessimism and a generally negative view of life have a pervasive sense that when bad things happen to them, it's normal, it's common, and it happens in all sorts of situations, from school or work through to relationships, money, physical health and so on. And our children are not immune from this form of stinking thinking. Here are some simple examples:

> Your child calls three friends on Saturday morning to see if they would like to play. One is busy with family commitments, another has sport, and the third one does not answer. Your child falls in a heap and cries, stating, 'No one ever wants to play with me. I've got no friends.'

In this situation, our child is showing a negative attribution style. The event is leading to a belief that they have caused the problem (personal), it's the way it always is (permanent), and this happens in many situations (pervasive).

Your child is lying across the dining table, books spread everywhere, sobbing. You recognise they are struggling with a school assignment and comment, 'Wow. This must be a really tough assignment.' Then you wait and listen as they tell you how much they hate school, can't understand anything their teachers say, and they never want to go there again.

Once again we see a child who has a personal, permanent and pervasive problem caused by a negative attribution style.

As a general rule, those with low resilience attribute negative events in their lives to personal, permanent, pervasive flaws or issues with themselves. When they suffer a failure or setback, when they experience a challenge, or when they endure a conflict or difficulty, their attribution style leads them to believe it's all their fault, there's something intrinsically wrong with them, these things always happen to them, and there's little they can do. They become psychologically inflexible and accept that life will always be like this for them. Few of us would want this for our children.

What is most interesting about these three Ps is that when our children experience a positive event, if they have a negative attribution style and they lack optimism and resilience, they will attribute the positive event to temporary (rather than permanent), specific (rather than pervasive) and impersonal (rather than personal) circumstances. In short, good things are a fluke while bad things are to be expected. And the reverse is true when optimism and resilience are high.

Let's go back to those scenarios on the previous page and give your child a positive attribution style. When they can't contact friends on a Saturday morning for a playdate, instead of thinking there is something wrong with themselves, they shrug and say, 'Oh well. I guess they're busy today. I'll have to come up with something else to do.' They may feel a little disappointed and glum, but they know it has nothing to do with them and that there will be other Saturdays, or other friends. For a child struggling with a school assignment, a positive attribution style does not take away the struggle that the schoolwork has created. Nor does it minimise the horrible and challenging feelings and frustrations the task engenders in the child. Instead, it shows up like this: 'I don't get it. Usually I can figure out what the teacher is talking about but in this case I have no idea.' Note the problem is not solved, but rather than blaming school, the teacher and life, they recognise that it is neither permanent nor personal, and it is not normal for them either. Because of this kind of thinking, they will be more flexible in their response to parental input, and able to think more broadly about possibilities.

Some research indicates that children really understand permanence well, and they relate easily to the personal aspect of the attribution style. But they do not particularly understand the pervasive, global component.[156] If that's the case, don't worry about teaching them that, and focus on what they can get their head around. Our task is to help our children challenge negative attributions when difficulties arise. We can do this by reminding them that 'This time, things didn't go so well. What can we do to help things go better next time?' This reduces the permanence mindset that undermines optimism, hope and resilience. It emphasises the temporary nature of the negative instead. We can do this by making it *not* about them: 'Your friends couldn't play today, which is frustrating. Wouldn't it be great if they didn't have those other activities planned?'

There may be some cases that are a lot less benign. Perhaps your child is being picked on. It could be that all of the children were invited to a party *except* your child. These are the big adversities that can lead to crushing consequences. And this means that we have the opportunity to work really hard with our children to help them see an alternative view, or to interpret the event in other ways.

One mother told me her daughter was the only child not invited to a party of a classmate. She rang the mother of the birthday girl to ask if there had been a mistake and was told, 'No, no mistake. My daughter doesn't like your daughter.'

Ouch.

That afternoon, this mum sat with her daughter and said, 'You feel awful you weren't invited to the party and everyone else was. Do you know what this means?' Her daughter shook her head. 'It means that for some reason that girl doesn't like you. Does that make you a bad or a worthless person?'

Mum explained that of course it still hurt. And then she asked if this was a reflection of her daughter, or of the girl having the party. She asked whether there were other parties her daughter had been invited to or might be invited to in the future. She asked about whether there was a way (or a desire) to build a friendship with the girl who had not invited her to the party (and there was no desire, for which the mother was grateful). At the end of the conversation, this mother reported that her daughter was comfortable that she had not been invited as the two girls did not get along. She still felt hurt that she would not be with her friends, but she had a plan to strengthen other friendships with playdates and activities. Plus, Mum was going to have a special day with her on the day of the party so they could have their own celebration.

Becoming optimistic

Can our children become more optimistic? Yes, they can. Will being more optimistic and eradicating negative, stinking thinking impact on resilience? Without doubt. When we change our thoughts we change our beliefs and ultimately our behaviours. Let's take a look at a handful of simple ideas for promoting an optimistic, positive mindset for our children, and in the next chapter we will explore one of the most compelling ideas for boosting authentic, realistic positive-thinking and enhancing resilience.

First, we need to be an example for our children. When difficult experiences beset us, it is natural to wallow in self-pity and feel defeated. But only for a short time. Then it's time to critically examine our thinking, question it, argue with it and find alternative ways of looking at the situation. We need to remind ourselves that our beliefs about a situation can make the situation better or worse. And then we need to identify the temporary, impersonal, specific reasons it happened this time, and why that is unusual.

Second, surround yourself and your child with optimistic people. That optimism will rub off on you – and your child. I recently made a new friend. He is an optimist. His perspective on why things happen and what will happen is enlivening and enlarging. I love being around him. When we spend time together I leave feeling invincible. Being around him makes me better, and when I interact with my family, they catch that same optimism and resilience. It's actually contagious. It's terribly hard to become an optimist if you're surrounded by doom and gloom people. An important sidenote to this principle is that this does not mean we should tell our children to abandon friends with challenges in their lives. Such an approach will hardly teach our children to give people a hand up when they need it. Rather, we can encourage our children to be understanding, compassionate and positive influences in the lives of those who struggle.

Third, teach your children to challenge themselves. If something bad happens to them and they begin talking themselves down or saying they want to give up, leave or stay in bed, steer them to alternative perspectives. But ask – don't tell. If you *tell* them they are wrong, they'll become even more entrenched in their negative appraisals. Instead, ask, 'Is there another way to look at it?' Teach them to interrupt themselves while they're on one of those pessimistic spirals, saying, 'There you go again,' and then stop it.

And work through these models with your children regularly. Once you have both been through it a few times, it will start to click, make sense and change the way you perceive situations. What was once a resilience-busting, painful adverse experience can become a growth opportunity that allows for psychological flexibility, optimism and resilience.

Hollow optimism

Some people think the idea of positive thinking is nothing more than hollow words. They will argue that teaching kids to have a positive mental attitude in the face of evidence that clearly points in a negative or challenging direction is inauthentic, and sets them up with a shaky foundation. In some instances, they may be entirely right. Trying to convince our children that they should 'always look on the bright side of life' when there does not appear to be a bright side is likely to be unhelpful. The idea that affirmations and positive 'booster' statements aimed at increasing self-esteem can make children more resilient has little empirical support – there may be slight increases in mood or motivation, but small setbacks stifle self-belief and those affirming statements leave a person's sense of self falling like a house of cards.[157] Their identity is questioned, they become psychologically rigid in their thinking, and their resilience takes a dive. They question everything they had believed about themselves. This is particularly the case for those already battling low levels of resilience and low self-worth.

The ideas in this chapter are not about building false foundations. Instead, the ideas are about teaching children to think clearly, flexibly and accurately. We want them to see a challenging situation and consider what *other* explanations there might be to account for what initially appears to be a negative.

We want them to see challenge as an opportunity for learning and growth. In both cases, this approach promotes a realistic and well-founded sense of optimism that lifts resilience, promotes effort, and attributes positive outcomes to personal, permanent, pervasive characteristics. This is a powerful formula for resilience.

School, friends, family, sport, music or other pursuits can be painful from time to time. Things don't always work out. When our children respond to these events with a negative attribution style, or when they allow their negative beliefs to determine the consequences of the events, those setbacks and failures can define them and also define their resilience level.

Take-home message

Regardless of the outcomes, being optimistic and having a positive attribution style actually makes us happier and more resilient. We're more likely to have a go. And we are more likely to anticipate great things in our future. Optimism predicts success. A life without optimism is a life without hope, without vision, and without resilience. A life with optimism is a life with hope, possibility and a greater likelihood of joy. Optimism can change our attitudes, which changes our actions ... which changes our reality. In short, optimism – realistic, accurate optimism built on a positive explanatory style – can change resilience.

CHAPTER 5

There's no such thing as smart

You are not born with a fixed amount of resilience.
[It's] like a muscle; you can build it up.

Sheryl Sandberg

Bertha was married to a man who was either a fool or a genius. She believed he was a genius. Unfortunately, he was a failing genius, which meant that nobody else believed in him like she did. It was the 19th century and Karl's bad business decisions had left the family in challenging circumstances. He was depressed and full of self-doubt. And so his wife, Bertha, decided to take matters into her own hands.

Without telling Karl her plans, she rose before dawn one morning and woke her two eldest boys, Eugen (aged 15) and Richard (aged 13), and left, leaving a note for Karl explaining that they were heading to her mother's home and that they would be back soon enough. They hit the road on a warm August morning in 1888. Of course, being 1888, there were actually no 'roads' to hit. Rather, they headed out along a track used by horses and carts, knowing that their 106-kilometre journey was going to test all of their resolve and capacity.

Their vehicle did not respond well to the trip. It was insufficiently geared to get up hills, so Eugen and Richard would get out and push it while Bertha steered. It didn't take too long before they ran out of fuel. Because it was 1888 there were no petrol stations. In fact, there was no 'petrol'. Leaving the boys with the car, Bertha walked into the nearest village and purchased ligroin, a solvent she hoped would act as fuel. It worked. A few hours later another problem arose: the car's wooden brakes began to fail. Bertha sought help from a local village cobbler. They worked out how to place leather over the wooden brake blocks, providing padding and durability to allow the trip to continue. Next challenge: the ignition cable broke. Bertha couldn't call roadside assistance — there was no such thing. Besides, phones hadn't been invented yet. Instead, she saw another opportunity to learn what worked and what didn't, removed her garter and used that to fix the problem.

Almost 15 hours after leaving home, Bertha and the two boys arrived at her mother's house. It was almost dark. Bertha explained all of her family's challenges to her mother, who was supportive. Bertha was from a wealthy family and had access to significant resources. Once she had arranged affairs, she sent a telegram home, letting Karl know to expect her soon and that everything would work out. A few days later the return journey took place — not without incident. Similar challenges kept Bertha and her boys on their toes.

Karl was waiting for Bertha when she returned. So were the journalists and everyone else who was interested in the journey. The real reason Bertha had taken the trip was for the publicity. She had a sense that this invention — what would eventually become the car — would change the world. Her husband had given all he had trying to convince people of its merit but they hadn't believed him. He didn't know if he would ever succeed, or convince anyone else of its potential. Bertha knew that with new ideas, new strategies and new thinking, it could work. They just had to learn from what didn't work and try again. Now Bertha had done something previously never done. And the media were absorbed.

The longest ever drive in a 'car' before Bertha's adventure was approximately 15 metres! Now, because of this woman's remarkable resilience and mindset, people caught a glimpse of how Karl Benz might change the world. Her husband's business grew until it became one of the world's most prestigious car brands – Mercedes Benz. And it all happened because of the remarkable growth mindset of one remarkable person. Not Karl, but Bertha Benz, his wife.[158]

Where her husband's concerns had led to a narrowed perspective and an inability to see options and possibility, Bertha had remained flexible and confident that she and Karl could build their knowledge and technology to literally change the world. Bertha Benz had a growth mindset: a hallmark of a resilient way of being, and something to foster in our children.

Mindset

To what extent do you agree with these statements in relation to your children?

- You can't change your intelligence much.
- You're born with a certain amount of intelligence and it's up to you to make the most of it.
- Even when you learn new things, that's not changing your intelligence.

Do you agree with the statements? Or is there something inside you that protests? What about these statements?

- Anyone can change their intelligence.
- You can improve your intelligence by learning new things.
- You're born with incredible potential, and it is ultimately up to you to decide how intelligent you'll become.[159]

If you answered yes to the first three statements, you believe that intelligence is set, firmly established and limited. You have a 'fixed' mindset. If you responded positively to the second trio of items, then you have an 'incremental' or 'growth' mindset. You see intelligence as something that can be developed, grown and improved through experience and even failure.

So who is correct?

Research seems to indicate that another motor industry heavyweight, Henry Ford, had it correct way back in the early 20th century when he said, 'Whether you think you can, or you think you can't, you're right.' Whatever we believe in relation to intelligence (or any other ability that we may possess, such as athletic ability, social skills, artistic capacity or even music) becomes a self-fulfilling prophecy. We're right either way. Therefore, if we believe that our morality, our intelligence or our musical or sports ability is something that can grow, we'll achieve far more because of that belief than we will if we believe it is fixed. If we believe we only have so much intelligence and that's all there is, the obvious extension of this thinking is that we shouldn't try to do things we are no good at, because trying isn't worth the effort. We're either good at something or lousy at it, and all the trying in the world won't make much difference. If you've ever caught yourself saying, 'Yeah, I wasn't much of an athlete either. It must be in the genes,' when your child is struggling, you may be teaching them that ability is fixed rather than malleable. Perhaps you've groaned, 'Oh, I hated maths too. I just don't have a maths head.' Or 'I think the apple hasn't fallen far from the tree in regards to our singing ability.' Such statements convey the idea that abilities are set in concrete and either present or not. And the same goes if we're great at something and we believe our children have the same capacity. These statements, flipped to the positive, still convey the belief that ability is fixed.

We're either good at something or we're not. There's nothing that can be done about it.

When we examine these mindsets through the lens of resilience, there is an obvious bias towards resilience with one mindset, and away from resilience with the other mindset. I am yet to uncover research specifically investigating the relationship between resilience and mindsets, but theoretically, a person with a growth mindset *is* resilient, because they have a mastery and learning (growth) mindset. So while setbacks hurt, they also motivate and inspire. They push a person towards trying again with a belief that through effort and persistence, excellence and success can be achieved. This leads to dramatic, positive adaptation specifically in the face of adversity. But if a person lacks resilience, that person will often possess a fixed mindset. Their focus is rigid. Failure will be seen as terminal. There will be no hope for the future. And there will be no point to trying harder.

To go back to a theme that has been repeated over and over again throughout this book, resilience is the default. For most people, resilience is the very typical and completely ordinary thing we show when times are tough. We all showed it, as did our children, when we couldn't walk, talk, ride a bike, scribble our name or do whatever other hard thing we struggled with. And curiously, we didn't see our failings as failure. Instead, it was all simply learning, improving, practising – part of the process.

As we, and our children, got older, however, we started experiencing evaluations and expectations. Some were from others. Some were internal, within us. And we started seeing failure as something serious, something painful, and something to be avoided.

Modelling growth mindset

How do you feel when you fail at something. Do you get excited? Do you say, 'Wow, I really stink at that. This is so exciting. I'm about to learn something new.' Or do you pretend that you know the answer, or that the answer or the skill or ability isn't actually that important anyway? Do you embrace getting it wrong with humility, curiosity and anticipation? Or are you defensive or dismissive? One approach represents the incredible resilience of a growth mindset, while the other is indicative of a fixed mindset that disallows vulnerability, mistakes and the learning and resilience that come from the alternative approach.

When was the last time you set yourself a challenge to do something you could not do? Perhaps you decided to increase your intelligence and capacity by returning to education? Maybe you thought you were never really very fit and healthy so you decided you could grow (rather than remaining fixed where you were), and you began a program to be able to run 5 kilometres in a month? Or perhaps you commenced guitar or piano lessons so you could learn that skill? If not, why not? We need to demonstrate that growth is possible so our children can learn from our example.

Here's another question about your own approach to mindsets. When do you feel smart? Is it when you're getting everything right, making a perfectly flawless performance? Or is it when you're learning, struggling through a challenge, and building on your experiences and mistakes to finally get 'there'?

There is a critical reason that I have asked these questions about you, rather than your children. Our children will follow our example in the mindset that they adopt. They follow our lead, modelling our beliefs and behaviours. So how do you respond to challenges? Do you embrace them, or worry about how you'll look if things don't go so well? Do you only approach challenges you know you can get over, or do you look forward to opportunities to learn and develop?

If you really want to teach a resilient, growth mindset to your children, take on new challenges yourself. Perhaps you can't run around the block because you've let your health and fitness drop.

Talk to your children about what you're doing and how it relates to a growth mindset – then take on the challenge. Show them it's okay to FAIL because it signifies your First Attempt In Learning.

The IQ test

One of the central reasons that we adopt less helpful mindsets, such as the fixed mindset, is because of the way that we measure intelligence. If we want to know a person's cognitive capacity, we ask them to sit a test – called an IQ test – to assess their intelligence. At the conclusion of the test, they are given a number which represents their intelligence. High numbers mean a person has a lot of intelligence. Low numbers mean they have less intelligence. But either way, intelligence is portrayed as a fixed quantity. There's only so much of it, and this number represents the amount.

The first IQ test was developed by Alfred Binet, a Frenchman, because schools were concerned that some children were not being taught well in their classroom environment and were falling through the cracks. The test was developed to try and identify which students might need extra help. Binet's argument was that intelligence could be developed through effort and practice, and the IQ test was to work out which children needed that little bit of extra help. Before too long, however, the test was being used the way we use it today – to provide a fixed number that signifies a person's absolute, fixed level of intelligence. Many people, if not most, read that number as a label that identifies the extent to which they or their child has this magical, indefinable thing called intelligence. And if a child (or adult) gets a low number on an intelligence test, they're likely to shrug their shoulders and say, 'Hmph. I'm not that smart, really.' Then they stop trying. Their resilience takes a pummelling. But the purpose of these intelligence tests, originally, was to develop intelligence, not quantify it. Binet, himself, reacted to those misusing his tests, saying:

A few modern philosophers assert that an individual's
intelligence is a fixed quantity which cannot be increased.
We must protest and react against this brutal pessimism.
With practice, training, and above all method, we manage to
increase our attention, memory, our judgement, and literally
to become more intelligent than we were before.[160]

I *love* that. We *must* protest and react against this *brutal*
pessimism. This is the kind of pessimism that undermines
resilience and reduces a child's willingness to keep on trying.
(High-stakes standardised tests have taken the brutality to new
levels and at younger and younger ages, and should be protested
against even more vigorously![161])

Binet suggested that, 'It's not the ones who start the smartest
who end smartest.' This is the ultimate in growth mindsets and
resilient thinking. Resilience and ultimately success are much more
dependent on the approach we bring to challenges rather than on
our inbuilt capacity. Yes, we all have strengths – and we will talk
about that more in Chapter 8 when we discuss strengths-based
parenting. And yes, we should absolutely utilise and capitalise on
those strengths. But no matter what we tackle, we will do better
with a growth mindset. As a child and teenager I was constantly
told I could do better. In fact, one high school teacher, perhaps
quite rightly, told my parents I was 'a classic underachiever'. But I
also had a fixed mindset. I did not enjoy school. I was forced to sit
in a classroom learning material every adult I knew had forgotten.
This told me it was not important. And frankly, I found a lot of
it hard. I did not believe I could do much of it. And socially, I felt
like a loser at school. A well-meaning relative heard my complaints
about how much I hated school and reassured me that I should
enjoy it because 'Your school years are the best years of your life!'
If this was true, I now felt I had *nothing* to look forward to, and
my resilience took a dive. I stopped trying. And when I finally

graduated at the end of my final year, my tertiary entrance score was so low I never even had a chance of attending university. I was given a number that confirmed I was dumb and my fixed mindset told me that score was an indicator of my future. I suspect my experience was similar to that of tens of thousands of disengaged students throughout our communities.

Then I discovered the radio industry. I loved it. I was good at it. And to get better I had to have daily feedback, which could have potentially *crushed* me. My boss would sit down with me most days and tell me everything I had done wrong on air. But it was also focused on how I could be better tomorrow. And this was thrilling. I developed a growth mindset. I recognised that feedback about failure made me better. It boosted my resilience. And it led to a relatively successful radio career. At the peak of my radio career, still in my 20s, I quit so I could return to school with an all-new mindset. I'd learned my lesson from radio, and this time I knew anything was possible if I worked like crazy and focused on growth and mastery rather than whether or not I was smart. I worked, developed strategies, and graduated with first class honours after a four-year psychology degree, went on to complete a PhD and write a book and build my own business. With three exceptions, in my entire degree all of my marks were distinctions and high distinctions, but I just loved the study. I loved the learning. And when I got those three credits (two of which were in my first year) I didn't feel like a failure. I just committed to change my study habits. But what I didn't know was that other people did it differently. Many other students would read over their notes, skim the textbook, try and memorise the bits they thought would be examined, and if it was not embedded in memory they might try and repeat it. But I got a group of people around me who were enthusiastic. We did group quizzes. We linked our quizzes across lectures and subjects. We rehearsed our mistakes. We talked psychology endlessly. When our results were handed out, other people would enviously tell me that they would do anything for my marks – except work hard and be committed. Their motivation wasn't to learn and master the content. It was to ace the test. And when some of them failed (especially stats) they would say, 'That subject isn't for me.' Conversely, my newfound growth mindset led to a different perspective. I'd see my mistakes as an opportunity to figure this stuff out.

This example is not to brag. Rather, it highlights that children have experiences that lead them to feel that they 'can't' do something. It's all too hard. They feel bored, frustrated or disengaged. As a result, they struggle with their schooling or their sports or whatever other activity they might choose. They get poor marks and evaluations. This reinforces the negative feelings they have towards the activity or learning. It undermines their resilience. It leaves them feeling that they only have so much ability – not much in this case – and reduces their motivation to try. The next mark or report is similarly dismal and a self-fulfilling prophecy eventuates. But if we can help our children understand that they can grow and develop and master, and if we can point them to engaging, exciting activities, their success experiences will see them resiliently push towards ever-higher attainment. And the same process occurs when our children excel with a fixed mindset. One failure can be punishing to resilience. After all, if ability is fixed and I just failed, it doesn't matter how many previous successes I've had. I'm only as good as my last performance, and that was bad. Or perhaps, rather than considering how to do better next time, a talented person with a fixed mindset might blame the teacher, the weather or any other thing. After all, it couldn't be 'me'. 'I'm talented.'

Teaching growth mindset

Here are a few tips to teach your children to have a growth mindset.

1. Encourage your children to let go of ego and performance and, instead, focus on learning and improving.
2. Teach your children that when they confront a challenge, they shouldn't ask, 'Can I _____?' Instead, they should ask, '*How* can I _____?' And when you ask your children about a challenge, it will be helpful to adopt the same approach. Rather than, 'Can you do this?' ask, 'How can you do this?'
3. Teach them the power of the word 'YET'. If they say they can't do it, remind them they can't do it YET. This is a resilient approach to challenges.
4. Ask yourself what message are you sending your kids when you say:
   - You learned that so quickly. You're so smart.
   - Wow, that picture is amazing. You're going to be a superstar artist.
   - You're a natural. You did that effortlessly.

   Stop praising talents and attributes like intelligence and talent. Get rid of words such as 'genius' and 'natural'. Instead, focus on drawing attention to specifics such as effort, persistence and strategy.

Alfred Binet said that through effort and study you can change the quality of a person's mind. You can literally become more intelligent. This is a remarkable, positive approach to challenges that promotes resilience. When our child complains that another kid outdoes them – or that their entire year outdoes them – ask them, 'Were they really smarter or sportier or more talented? Or just better prepared or more experienced?' Help them to recognise that it is hard work and commitment that leads to the best outcomes – if they want them.

And if your child frequently or always comes in last and does not seem to improve with practice, there may be some questions to consider. Is your child motivated to compete? After all, competition is not good for resilience, and it pushes kids into a fixed mindset anyway. Are there alternative activities that are both non-competitive and will utilise your child's strengths better?

If your child insists on competing – even with a strong risk of repeatedly losing – then allowing them to autonomously pursue a task for whatever motive they hold may be fine. Some children want to get better and are willing to suffer tremendously for it. Some are motivated because of the relationships that they enjoy. But when their resilience starts to suffer, some gentle guidance towards more fulfilling activities aligned with their strengths will typically be more satisfying for everyone.

Take-home message

Is there such a thing as natural ability? Of course there is, but there are so many 'naturals' who go nowhere, or who fail to achieve their potential because of a fixed mindset. Does this mean it's possible that you might be able to do *anything*? I don't know ... but neither do you unless you try.

I teach my children there is no such thing as smart or dumb. Instead there are people who keep on trying to learn new things, and people who do not. Of course, this is not entirely true. There probably are limits to what we are each capable of achieving, but I'm not going to be the one who puts limits on my child by telling her, 'I don't think you're really smart enough to be a vet, or a doctor, or that you're talented enough to be a sports star, or coordinated enough to play drums or be a hairdresser.' My preference is that my children find something they love to do and work at it with passion and excitement. They'll go further with a growth mindset than they will with a fixed mindset.

CHAPTER 6

It's all about relationships

The most important work we will ever do is
within the walls of our own home.

Harold B Lee

In this chapter I want to introduce you to two girls, Tayah and Hollie. The girls are cousins, and are only nine months apart in age. Tayah is the younger of the two, and has just turned 16. Hollie is close to 17. For the first 12 years of their lives, Tayah and Hollie were best friends. They looked forward to every opportunity that the family would get together so they could play. As they entered early adolescence, however, their relationship changed; according to Hollie, her friendship with her cousin changed because Tayah changed. The lessons from their adolescent years teach us a lot about resilience.

Hollie is the kind of girl who enters a room and lights it up with her energy and smile. She is trendy, loves to imitate her favourite internet video stars, and cannot get enough of time with her friends. Hollie is not particularly popular. She only has a few friends, but those friends are a tight-knit group. Hollie has decided against a boyfriend, preferring to hang out with a bunch of friends than get too serious about anyone in particular. She complains boys get in the way of friendships and cites examples of jealousy, breakups and other relationship difficulties she has observed over the past few years as she and her friends have had boys in their lives. Hollie also comes from a family that is, while far from perfect, pretty much together. Her mum and dad are busy but available. Hollie loves talking late into the night with her mum, and goes on runs with her dad regularly. She recently told me she had achieved her goal to run 10 kilometres in less than an hour. She also complained – with a big smile on her face – that her dad doesn't have to run very hard to keep up with her, so he uses that time to talk about all the 'parent stuff' with her while they run. They talk about boys, technology limits, educational goals and progress, and life. Hollie holds down a part-time job, gets above-average marks at school, and wants to be a paediatrician.

Tayah's story began similarly, but diverged early in her life. Her parents split when she was just three years old. In spite of her father's absence from her life, Tayah was a talented, excited and vivacious child. Naturally gifted in both sport and music, and with a remarkable academic capacity, she seemed to be thriving. Tayah could be verbally sharp – even aggressive – but her radiant smile and easy laughter would always return quickly. An attractive girl, she was very popular at school among both boys and girls. But things began to change for Tayah around the age of nine or ten. Her mother remarried and had another child with her new husband. Tayah began puberty before all of her friends. This made her more popular, particularly with older boys, but also changed the nature of her relationships. Her father had re-entered her life, but was inconsistently involved with her and her siblings. And her mother was distant and angry, and from time to time, she was also physically and verbally abusive to Tayah.

By the time Tayah was 14 and almost finished Year 8, things were changing dramatically. She had begun to experiment with alcohol and other drugs, and was sexually active. Her mother wanted to keep her relationship with her daughter positive, so she laughed about, and even encouraged, her daughter's partying ways. As Year 9 concluded, Tayah had been in trouble with the police for breaking and entering. Her sexual history was significant, and her academic history was almost non-existent. She had all but stopped attending school. Her mum had split from her second husband, and her dad had told her that if she couldn't make better decisions then he wanted nothing to do with her. Over the previous six months, Tayah had been living between homes, spending some nights at her grandmother's house and a few nights at home. She had also been couch-surfing – sleeping wherever she landed on any given night. When Tayah and I spoke, shortly after her 16th birthday, she had just re-enrolled in school. She had also just left the police station after being questioned over a physical assault on another young woman, and she was feeling low about life.

As we spoke, Tayah told me about her relationship with Hollie. They had recently spent a few days together while she had been with her grandmother. She and Hollie had not seen each other much in the past year. Hollie knew how Tayah lived and Tayah felt judged by her cousin. The two girls had spent time together, awkwardly, with no foundation to support their troubled relationship. 'I hate her. I hate everything about her. She's such a goody-goody.' Tayah told me that Hollie had everything she had never had. And she felt entirely inferior. She also felt alone.

She told me that her mother had asked her to come home again in recent days. Following the separation from her second husband, Tayah's mum had spent a couple of months getting back on her feet and had just purchased a brand-new townhouse – absolutely perfect – in a beachside suburb of Sydney. Tayah had called in to see the place, but told me, 'It doesn't feel nice to be there. All mum does is yell and get angry. It doesn't matter how nice the house is. It's the people in the house that make it good to live in.'

As Tayah and I spoke, she confided that she felt as though her life was challenging because she did not have parents in her life. She felt uncared for and unloved. At the time I talked with Tayah, she told me her mum had not asked her where she was staying since she left home. Tayah understandably took that as a sign that 'Mum doesn't care.'

In speaking to Tayah's mum, I saw a great deal of defensiveness. More than once, she stated, 'I am a good mother!' and she assured me that she loves her children. I believe her. She does love her children. But Tayah did not feel that love. And her mother appeared to lack the skills and capacity to show that love. Tayah showed me her mum's social media profile (Instagram and Facebook). It was filled with pictures of Mum doing things with her kids. 'If my family was like it is on Facebook in real life, it would be awesome,' she told me. 'But it's not. Mum makes out that she's devoted. But she makes us feel like she hates us when there's no one watching.'

I asked Tayah what three things she wished her mum would do so she felt loved. Her answers almost made me weep for their simplicity.

'I just want her to actually listen to me. She won't listen. Ever. She just tells me to get over it when I have a problem and she's never interested.

'If she would talk to me nicely. She doesn't have to yell all the time.

'I wish she would hug me.'

Tayah then mentioned a fourth item. 'My dad hasn't called to say hi or ask me how I'm going for more than a month. It's not that hard to pick up the phone and say hi.'

Tayah and Hollie started life in similar fashion. Over time, however, their paths diverged enormously. The key contributor to the change was the love that was felt in their families. While there is tremendous evidence supporting the importance of fathers in the lives of children,[162] I suspect that the biggest impact on the different levels of resilience that the two girls now experience is ultimately related, perhaps in part to family structure, but predominantly due to whether they feel like they matter and are loved. Over time, Hollie continued to have the foundations of her resilience supported by engaged, involved, loving parents who took time to be in her life and have her in theirs. Conversely, her cousin, Tayah, was routinely verbally and physically abused, ignored, pushed away, scolded, called names, and left to fend for herself. The nature of her relationships, according to her recollection, began to change from around the age of six or seven, when her mother invited new men into her life, before ultimately finding her second husband. Tayah felt she needed to compete for attention and affection. Her neediness seemed to become a barrier that interfered with positive relationships, making her increasingly desperate for that attention, and ultimately leading her to make unhealthy, unwise decisions.

Our children are wired to connect to us. Even as adults we *want* to be close to our parents. And in spite of their challenging behaviours, our children have an innate desire to be close to us. It is the quality of this connection, perhaps more than anything else, that matters most for resilience.

Being responsive

Earlier in this book, I described the research conducted by Harry Harlow on monkeys who were given the choice between a 'wire mother' and a 'cloth mother'. He went further too – conducting even less ethical experiments in which the artificial 'mothers' hurt the babies, or the infants were left in solitary confinement, and later showed signs of immense damage. This research, which rightly damaged his reputation, nevertheless confirmed the idea that for true, strong resilience, it is *all* about the quality of relationships that children share with their caregivers.

From Harlow through to today, increasing evidence is showing us that our children's developing brains and identities rely on a consistent process of engaged interactions between parent and child. This means that when they seek us in some way, we respond warmly and kindly – with love. And when we seek them in some way, they feel safe in responding however they need to in that moment, knowing we will provide the support and scaffolding that helps build crucial capabilities that are the foundation of resilience: the ability to plan, monitor and regulate behaviour, and adapt to changing circumstances.

But in the absence of these responsive relationships, the brain's architecture doesn't develop optimally and nor do these capacities and capabilities. The body perceives the absence of a warm and responsive caregiver as a threat. It then activates a stress response that — when prolonged — leads to physiological changes that affect the brain and overall systems of physical and mental health. That is what happened to Tayah. Her experience was much like Harlow's mistreated monkeys. A lack of access to warmth and responsiveness – a listening ear, a gentle touch – created a long-term stress response that changed the way her brain responded to potentially stressful events. She became highly stressed, lacked resilience and responded to challenging circumstances in unhelpful and unhealthy ways. These responses further alienated the people in her life, setting up a negative cycle that continually pushed people away and reduced resilience.

Are you speaking my language?

How do we make sure we are responsive? How can we be sure we are available, warm and sufficiently providing the support and scaffolding that builds resilience?

The answers are on every page of this book. But there's one idea, specifically, that may be particularly helpful in the context of our relationships with our children. The idea builds on the work of Gary Chapman and my mentor, Professor H Wallace Goddard. In 1995, Gary Chapman wrote a book called *The 5 Love Languages*. In his book, he argued there are five different ways we can show someone we love them, and that each person has their own unique preference for how they are shown love. That is, each person has his or her own love language.

Chapman's five love languages are:

- using words of encouragement
- providing acts of service
- giving gifts
- offering quality time
- reaching out with physical touch.

He suggests that to discover a person's language of love we should watch the way they express love towards others, and consider what they most ask of their significant other. If they're a gift-giver, that's the sign that their language is gifts. If you give them gifts, you're showing love in their language. If they make themselves available and spend time, that's what they'll respond to best.

Often we have problems in our relationships (including with our children) because we show love in *our* preferred love language, but our loved ones seem unresponsive. They speak a different language and so they're not aware we are trying to show them love. We reach out to touch our teenager and he says, 'Hey, don't touch!' Or we give and give and give to our school-aged children and they never say thanks or show any love to us, because they want our time instead.

Current research gives us clues as to how Chapman's love languages can be modified to strengthen relationships and improve the way we show love. Using Goddard's insights, here's how we could arrange them. Rather than having five languages to choose from, evidence implies that all people (including partners/spouses and children) have two universal 'love languages'. These are:

- time (which Chapman identifies)
- understanding.

In addition, there are three additional languages that may or may not be applicable to others. Some may respond well to one, while others may respond well to all three. They are:

- show me (which consolidates Chapman's acts of service and receiving gifts)
- tell me (which includes words of encouragement but goes further)
- touch me (again shown in Chapman's initial five).

How they work

Every single person on the planet – and especially our children – respond to the two languages of time and understanding. An old saying reminds us that 'To a child, love is spelled T-I-M-E.' I know of no intervention more powerful than simply spending time with another person to create a strong and positive relationship. I have written dozens of articles about understanding. While the topic is only loosely and briefly mentioned in this book, my previous book, titled *21 Days to a Happier Family*, discusses how to really understand children in great detail.

In addition to time and understanding, the three additional languages work like this:

Show me

Some people, children included, feel most loved when we show them our love. Sometimes this might be by giving gifts. Other times it may be by making some kind of sacrifice or special effort to help them or please them. (We should remember that children have a tendency to expect us to do things for them, so we may not see this as their language of love until they've left home and become adults themselves!)

Tell me

Being told 'I love you' is all some children (and adults) need to feel loved. They don't need gifts or special or expensive experiences. A love note, an acknowledgment, a statement of appreciation or affirmation; these are the expressions of love that create a sense of love in a 'tell me' person.

Touch me

The 'touch me' language is simple. These are the huggers, the snugglers, the strokers, the caressers. These are the ones who, if you walk past them without squeezing their elbow or running your finger across their shoulder or neck, will wonder if they've done something wrong. The touch me language craves physical contact to express love.

What are your family members' love languages?

Sometimes it can be tricky to work out what language of love your family members respond to best and understand the most. Focus on the first two, and experiment with the next three. Watch how they respond. And look for the ways they express their love. It may help to make your family happier. It will almost certainly set up a lovely feedback loop that helps your child feel supported, loved and ultimately more resilient.

Outside the family matters too

If resilience is built on a foundation of solid relationships, we should also consider the impact of relationships outside the walls of our home. Our children's experiences with school friends, teachers, aunts and uncles, and other significant people in their lives can build a successful relationship foundation that supports resilience. But bullying, being ignored or being left to feel unworthy or lacking in value can reduce resilience. Helping children establish and maintain healthy relationships outside the family structure is so important.

One of my daughters was celebrating a successful swimming carnival. She had competed well and enjoyed the opportunity to go to a representative swimming event. We asked her, 'What was the best part about your day?' She responded instantly. 'Winning all my races!' Then she paused. 'No, hang on. It was really nice to win, but the best part of my day was hearing all my friends cheering me on.'

Take-home message

One-on-one, parent-to-child, is where the real work of the family is done. We build resilience in the minute-by-minute micro-interactions we have with our children where we tap into their lives and shore up their confidence and feelings of worth. While we are doing chores, tucking them in to bed, bathing them, sharing a meal, driving to preschool (or big school), listening to them practise the piano or helping them with their homework, our investment in making our relationship with our children right forms their feelings of worth, experiences of success, and opportunities to grow in capacity, competence, confidence and resilience.

CHAPTER 7

Boosting resilience by supporting autonomy

I teach them correct principles and they govern themselves.

Joseph Smith Jr

My 16-year-old daughter was upset. Through her tears she explained to me that, 'My friends had a party last week and they didn't invite me.'

I empathised. 'You must have felt awful. No wonder you're feeling horrible.'

'Dad, they didn't invite me because they said it was the kind of party Dr Justin Coulson wouldn't approve of.'

It took a few seconds for my daughter's statement to register. Then it occurred to me. Over the years we have discouraged our children from attending parties where alcohol and other drugs would be consumed. We have talked to our children about the risks of being at parties where kids consume alcohol or take drugs, or disappear into bedrooms for intimate encounters. Like all parents, we want our children to be safe, and to make good decisions.

'So it sounds as though there was stuff happening at that party that they know you've been taught to avoid.'

My daughter's response surprised me. 'Dad, some of the kids were drinking, but not all of them. I'm not upset I wasn't there. I'm upset they never gave me the option to decide for myself.'

One of the central tasks of adolescence is identity development. Tweens and teens ask themselves, 'Who am I? What am I about? What do I stand for and what do I value?' Part of this identity development requires that they separate from their parents. And part of this identity development often entails them making their own decisions.

Sometimes, children make decisions rebelliously in order to show that they really are their own person – and that they have separated from their parents. But research tells us our kids do not *have* to rebel. Parents can reduce the risk by maintaining a healthy and open relationship with their children. In fact parents who know what's going on with their children and their friends can minimise the likelihood that their children will make poor choices – just by talking with their children.

In one study, a research team observed children in Year 5 and again in Year 7. For too many, this age range is a starting point or baseline for alcohol, tobacco and other drug use. It's also a time when parents may be caught off guard by changes in their child's behaviour. Nearly 675 children were included in the study. Researchers observed mothers and fathers separately as they interacted with their children. They found that parents could make a difference in influencing their children's behaviour by having conversations with them, knowing who their children were with and what they were doing, and setting basic limits around what behaviour was acceptable and what behaviour was not. It can be that simple to reduce risk.[163]

Another study, this time from Brigham Young University, investigated teens' behaviour based on parenting styles. The researchers found that teenagers with parents who used a strategy called *reasoned deference* made better decisions around friends, school participation, alcohol and other drug use, and pro-social behaviour.[164]

Reasoned deference means that parents spent time talking with their teens about expected behaviour. They provided them with a rationale, or clear reasons why they had certain rules. And then they deferred to their child. 'What do you think you should do? We'll leave it up to you.'

As I sat with my crestfallen daughter I heard myself saying something difficult. I began to defer to her.

'Do you think we need to review the rules and talk about why they matter?'

'No, Dad. I know why they matter.'

'I think they're good rules,' I responded. 'They keep you safe. It only takes one drunken or drug-affected person to put you in hospital, or to hurt you in other ways.' I found myself taking it up a notch. 'I think they're good rules. But let me defer to you on this one. Do you think we need to change the rules? You're nearly 17.'

My daughter was quiet for a moment. Tentatively and thoughtfully, she replied, 'Dad. I don't like the rules. They make life horrible sometimes.'

I held my breath.

She added, 'But they're good rules. I don't like them, but they're good rules.'

Autonomy support

Autonomy support is not about letting children do what they want. That is called permissiveness. Research has abundantly demonstrated that permissiveness leads to poor child outcomes and undermines resilience. Nor is autonomy support about neglect or lack of involvement. There is perhaps even more research pointing to the undermining effects of neglect and parental inattention on wellbeing and resilience in children than anything else.

Autonomy support is built on encouraging our children to act for themselves in volitional, harmonious and integrated ways. That means they choose for themselves in ways that reduce pressure and that are consistent with their values (and ideally, ours!). This is in contrast to more pressured, conflicted behaviour, where they are behaving a certain way because they feel they *have* to, or because they will feel alienated or isolated from us if they choose otherwise. This type of control seeks to *change the child* through force, coercion, manipulation, guilt induction, love withdrawal and invalidating feelings. It is a form of psychological control, aligned with those unhealthy outcomes described in my earlier material in Myth 3 about helicopter parenting and over-involved parenting.

As I highlighted in my daughter's story, she had the opportunity to be self-initiating based on my several years of working with her, teaching her and encouraging her to make safe and healthy decisions for herself with the input of both her parents. And when the pressure and control were removed from the situation, she had no one to fight against. There couldn't be a power struggle against the 'power/authority' because it was absent. I was absolutely present and involved, but not over-involved. And I was clear on what limits I believed were appropriate and why, but was not forceful in my demands.

So what does autonomy support actually 'look like'? How do we break it down so that we as parents can use this process with our children? And does it work the same for children at any age?

The structure of autonomy-supportive parenting

Unlike permissive or neglectful parenting, autonomy-supportive parenting is hard work. The key word is 'pro-active'. To be autonomy-supportive for our children, regardless of whether they are 2 or 22, we need to work on the following four key elements.

1. Provide a clear explanation (or rationale) for what we are asking our children to do.

2. Recognise the feelings and perspective of our child; see the world through their eyes.
3. Offer choice and encourage initiative.
4. Minimise the use of controlling techniques.

These are *not* steps to be followed sequentially. This is not a technique or a process. Autonomy support is a way of working with our children to help them understand values and principles, and to *internalise* them. And when we support our children's autonomy, something interesting happens to them: we support the development of competence and foster healthy development – or resilience.

Most parents usually cope with the first idea – explaining. We know that when someone helps us to understand *why* something should be done, we feel better about doing it. For example, at an organisation I do some work for, their receptionist put a sign on the door saying, *Please close the door as it helps to regulate the air-conditioning.* I asked her why she had changed the sign from the old one, which had read *Please shut the door.* Her response: 'No one was closing the door.' When I asked how compliance was now, she replied, 'It's amazing! Everyone closes the door.'

As nice as it would be, we struggle to provide a clear rationale to our children at times. This is especially the case when we are under pressure, or when we feel as though our children 'should know' what we are asking and why. We snap and say, 'Because I said so!' or 'You know why. Don't be so silly. Just do it.' But for our children to internalise values, act volitionally without outside control, and feel good about their behaviour, they need to know why we want them to behave in a particular way. This is why teaching them, clearly, matters so much. As a brief aside, trying to teach them 'in the moment' or at the moment of decision is a fraught pastime. Our child is distracted or emotional. We are concerned or frustrated.

The second principle is about perspective. Unfortunately we usually struggle to *really* see the world through our children's eyes. They do something challenging, say something wrong, or fail to follow a simple instruction. In those instances when we are tired, distracted, stressed, dealing with another child or another issue, we sometimes snap and say something like, 'Do you think the world revolves around you?' While we don't mean it, in that moment we may actually be thinking, 'Well it doesn't! It revolves around me! And you're throwing my world off balance!' No parent would intentionally become their child's enemy and abandon them as they struggle, but sometimes we all do things we do not mean to, and we turn against our child. In those circumstances where we aren't capable of being present and engaged with our child, they feel our disapproval. Alternatively, sometimes we turn away from them, telling them to figure it out for themselves, or 'Come to me when you can speak without blubbering and I can understand you.' The soft version of this is, 'You'll be right.' This lack of empathy is often unintentional and unthinking, or if it is done purposefully it may be done under the guise of 'steeling' our children. After all, we reason, they need to be resilient. We have discussed, at length, what happens with this approach earlier, in Myth 2.

To see the world through our children's eyes and investigate their perspective means we slow down, listen and understand – not just in our heads, but in our hearts. We hear our child crying that she can't clean up her room and we respond with compassion, recognising that while she may be developmentally capable of cleaning it up, perhaps tonight she is overtired or overwhelmed with the size of the mess. Perhaps we might walk to her room and offer gentle guidance. Maybe we can clean it up together. Or we could sit on the bed and say, 'Can you just do five things and we'll see how it looks? Good. Now perhaps another three? Okay. We're really getting somewhere. Let's just do another few things while I chat with you about why things have been so hard today.'

When we take our children's perspective and see the world through their eyes, we show them we value them and their feelings. We demonstrate that we see our children as real people with real feelings, challenges, hopes and dreams. And we are better able to work together on solving challenges.

Next, we encourage initiatives, offer choice and problem-solve. This is where the real work (and magic) of building resilience happens.

When our children understand what we want and why we want it, and they feel as though we really do understand them, we get to start problem-solving together. This is the most pivotal moment of the autonomy support process, and it is also the exciting resilience formation moment. In an environment where a child feels safe and secure, and is then given choice and responsibility for their own life, they begin to be the governors of their own life. They are the ones who are accountable and responsible. They get to own their decisions. We could say, 'Well … now you know how I feel about this, and I can see how you feel. So, what do you suggest we do?' Alternatively, we might gently ask, 'Where to from here?' Or simply, 'How can I help?' Then we sit and wait as our child makes a decision. The crucial aspect of autonomy support is that if a child chooses poorly we don't criticise or laugh or belittle. We just respond, 'Hmmm. That's one option. I wonder what might happen if you choose to do that?' We then walk through consequences, and ask again, 'So what other options are there that could work out better?'

Young children may not know what to say. Older children may run out of options before they get to a suitable one. In either case, we respond by saying, 'I have an idea or two that could work. Would you mind if I shared them with you? Are you interested in hearing them?' When children have felt understood and have been given an opportunity to use their own voice, they are no longer disempowered by us.

In essence, autonomy support is like saying to a child, 'Here's a situation. I know how you feel and you know how I feel. I trust you. Let's pretend we're on a soccer field. I'm putting the ball right in front of you and you get a free kick. You know where the sidelines are. Where do you want to kick it to?' Then we wait while they take their kick. If the kick goes in the wrong direction, we simply put the ball back in front of them and make the same offer. 'Try again. That one went out of bounds. We can do better.'

Autonomy support builds resilience because children feel empowered. We demonstrate our faith in their ability to develop solutions and strategies for the complex and challenging circumstances in which they find themselves – sometimes by foolishness and other times by accident. Autonomy support builds hope as we point them to a future orientation and ask them how they can make things better. It offers an opportunity for us to guide them to psychologically flexible responses rather than rigid, formulaic thinking as we problem-solve together.

Timing is everything

Effective teaching is more likely to happen in emotionally cool climates, where time is plenty and decisions are not pending. When emotions are high and hot, it is better to stay calm and kind and, where possible, hold off on discipline or other in-depth discussions. Here's a simple example. In teaching our children about values related to alcohol and other drugs, and intimacy, my wife, Kylie, and I have not spoken to them with urgency as we drop them off at their first high school party. Instead, we have talked with them each year as they started in a new class at school, discussing what they have observed in older children, what they might expect now they're in a new year, and how they could approach some of the moral dilemmas they may face. We have worked hard to provide clear counsel, explanation and rationale for what we expect and why, and then we have problem-solved. We have asked questions like, 'So if this happened to you, how would you feel? What would a wise response be? Why do you think we would be concerned about this? How could we help you? Where else could you get help?' This discussion takes place in the days preceding school commencement while everyone is relaxed and far-removed from the challenging situations that may confront them later. (I will share an example of how to deal with things 'in the moment' in Chapter 9, about screen time.)

The studies support autonomy

Experimental studies show that when parents behave in autonomy-supportive ways towards their children, the outcomes are better all around. Whether children are toddlers, teens or even adults, studies have shown that autonomy support leads to greater persistence, competence, intrinsic motivation, internalisation of values and principles, compliance and more.[165] In a study of toddlers, mothers and their children were videotaped while they performed various tasks. In one task, the mother was asked to stop the child from touching attractive objects. After the interaction with Mum, the child was left alone with the prohibited attractive objects for a few minutes to measure the degree to which they had internalised the prohibition and were able to comply with Mum's requests or demands. Then the experimenters reviewed the video to examine how different mothers controlled their children and how compliant their children were without an authority figure to stop them touching things. The mothers who used *gentle guidance*, a concept similar to autonomy support, were not power assertive (for example, they used reasoning, polite requests, positive comments, suggestions, distractions). Many mothers used negative control – defined as using threats, harsh physical interventions and negative statements. Children's compliance was associated with gentle guidance. The children whose mothers used gentle guidance showed a high level of *committed compliance* across a range of tasks. Committed compliance shows the child is trying to follow the mother's agenda; it is a preliminary form of genuine internalisation. The alternative is *situational compliance*, which refers to superficial obedience to a request, and usually occurs when a child is worried about being in trouble.[166]

Other studies point to autonomy support as predicting better school adjustment,[167] as well as school performance, friendship choices, avoidance of alcohol or other drugs, and pro-social behaviour.[168] In short, all of the hallmarks of resilience in children are facilitated through an autonomy-supportive approach in our relationship with them.

While 'do as I say' autocracy gets things done, it undermines resilience – for the individual and the family. Resilient families and individuals rely on gentle guidance and a collaborative approach for their strength.

What gets in the way?

A number of factors affect our capacity to be autonomy-supportive. This way of being requires time. It is effortful. We need to be psychologically balanced and available to our children. When we are stressed, anxious or worried, we step away from being autonomy-supportive and towards being controlling. And this may be particularly true when we are stressed, anxious or worried *about our child*!

Sometimes we don't know how to do it. Other times, we may want to do it but can't get past the fact our child is driving us around the bend. We may be ego-involved too. If we see that our children's performance, ability, social skills or some other outcome could be a reflection on how we see ourselves as parents, we are more likely to try to control that outcome rather than support its development and evolution.

What helps us be autonomy-supportive?

Skills and knowledge help us to be autonomy-supportive. But there may be something more foundational, and thus infinitely more important. What do we believe about our children's ability to develop in healthy, functional ways?

Our children are *designed* to develop and grow, to explore their environments, pursue their interests and build on strengths, take on challenges that inspire and excite them, and participate in activities that will allow them to develop their mastery and competence. They are intrinsically, autonomously driven to develop themselves in ways that feel natural and authentic to them. But we parents have a wide range of opinions regarding whether our children will naturally experience this process. When we possess rigid, inflexible goals for our children's growth and development, we become more ego-involved. Our children's outcomes matter to us, not because we want the best for our children (though we all do), but because their outcomes will reflect on what kind of parents we are. This increases the likelihood that we will be controlling – not trusting the natural yearning for growth inside each child. In so doing, our control may actually short-circuit their intrinsic development, disempowering them, and lowering their motivation, internalisation and resilience in the process. We may do this unconsciously but that does not mean it is not happening.

The more likely reason for our controlling parenting is that we don't want our children to make mistakes. And when we see them getting it wrong, we dive in. But if we trust in these inbuilt growth and mastery processes within our children, we are less likely to thwart and frustrate their development through interfering with their autonomous decisions. We are less likely to rupture our relationships with them by being overly controlling. And we are more likely to facilitate their growth and competence.

So perhaps the key word here is trust. Do we really trust our children? Do we trust them to make good decisions? Do we trust in the innate growth tendencies they possess?

Maybe a child has given us reasons not to trust. Perhaps their ongoing displays of untrustworthy behaviour leave us feeling we have to force them to behave in particular ways. If this is the case, we should consider two things: first, what resistance am I creating in my child by forcing them? And second, how have I interfered with my child's inbuilt strivings towards development? Have I been too untrusting in the past, leading to frustration on the part of my child? Can this now explain my child's behaviour? And if so, how can I change this?

Studies assessing the extent to which parents believe children's positive development will naturally take place show that those parents who *trust* are more relaxed, make fewer social comparisons about their children, and are better adapted adults whose children are, unsurprisingly, also better adapted. They are more likely to be autonomy-supportive of their children, and those children are more likely to be thriving – and resilient.[169]

Take-home message

When parents support their children's autonomy by trusting in their natural tendency towards growth and mastery, they are not being detached and uninvolved. Nor are they being permissive. Instead, they work with their children in understanding and compassionate ways to guide them and offer support in their children's own decision-making processes. This approach is associated with tremendous positive outcomes in both the short and long term.

CHAPTER 8

Strengths-based parenting

Strengths are potentials for excellence that can be cultivated through ... awareness, accessibility and effort.

Robert Biswas-Diener, Todd Kashdan and Gurpal Minhas[170]

Mandy was organising a 'night of excellence' for the girls aged 12–17 in her local church group. This was to be a celebration to wind up the year. But as Mandy considered her plans for the event, she realised that the night of excellence might be a night of humiliation for some of the girls.

'We're supposed to be recognising the achievements and milestones that each of the girls has reached this year. But some of them are struggling. Some of them haven't really *achieved* anything to speak of. And if we were to acknowledge some of their "achievements" it would seem tokenistic, particularly when they're being compared to the other girls' achievements.

'We have girls who are from families where they have lots of resources, and so they receive lots of opportunities. And we have girls from families where they are really struggling, and so they don't really receive any opportunities. And if we want to acknowledge every girl so no one is left out, some of the awards and recognition will look really slack. Are we better to acknowledge minor accomplishments and stuff that's not really that excellent? Or should we leave out the girls who don't really have much to show for the year?'

My suggestion was a simple one, and I had no idea if it might work. 'Why don't you invite each of the girls' mums to prepare a two- or three-minute talk, detailing their daughter's character strengths? Instead of focusing on their external achievements, shift the focus to internal growth and character.'

The idea was novel, but Mandy liked it. Several weeks later I heard back from her.

'It was amazing!' Her excitement and enthusiasm were bursting through the phone line. I listened intently as she described the beautiful, kind things that the mothers had said about their daughters the previous night. She described the tremendous outpouring of emotions that everyone had experienced as mothers spoke of the remarkable strengths, attributes and character their daughters possessed. Several boxes of tissues had been required, and a feeling of psychological and emotional safety had encompassed all who attended.

Mandy continued. 'Something even more incredible happened today though.' Her voice caught. Then came the tears, flowing freely as she told me of a phone call she had received from an overwhelmed and profoundly grateful mother who had attended the evening.

'Nikki is a mum who has it all together. She has a master's degree, the big house, the wealthy husband who loves her like mad. She has the perfect, happy family. She's got the whole package. This morning she called me to say thanks for last night. Nikki's 14-year-old daughter, Penelope, was really emotional when her mum shared her thoughts. Like, almost out of control emotional.' Mandy explained that the tears had turned into uncontrollable heaving sobs and Penelope had to leave the room to compose herself. By the end of the evening Penelope had calmed down, but she was still weeping openly, and clinging to her mother's side.

'When they got home,' Mandy continued, 'Nikki sat with Penelope on the couch while she cried. After a while she finally said, "What is going on with you? I've never seen you cry like this. Is everything okay? Did I say something wrong?"

'Penelope let go of her mum and asked, "Mum, do you really believe those things that you said about me tonight?"

"'Of course I do, sweetheart. I would never say it if I didn't mean it. Why do you ask?"

"'I've never heard you say anything like that to me before. I just thought you always saw me as a nuisance.'"

Mandy described how overwhelmed Nikki and her daughter were, and how the experience had drawn them closer together. Through the experience, Penelope had an opportunity to see herself differently, recognise her strengths, and use them as resources to build her resilience.

What are strengths?

How would you define a strength? We use the term all the time. But what does it mean? Like most things, scholars argue over what a strength is and how it works. But what they don't argue about so much is that strengths predict wellbeing, and strengths predict resilience. My favourite definition of a strength is that it is a 'potential for excellence' that is inside each of us. Strengths are cultivated through developing an awareness they exist, finding ways to access them, and making the effort to both expand them and utilise them *every day*. Deep inside each of our children is a remarkable capacity to be excellent in something. Some people call it their 'spark'. This suggests a few important things that we should consider. First, strengths are intrinsic, or authentic, or pre-existing. They're a part of who we are and we just need to tap into them. Strengths allow us to perform at a high and consistent level of competence. But there's more to it than that. We *feel* strong when we use our strengths. They help us to feel energised, positive and passionate. This means it's more than just doing something well. It's doing something that enlivens us, lifts us up, engages us, and makes us feel we are being who we were born to be!

Researchers have shown that using our strengths guards against negative psychological symptoms like lowered resilience, depression, anxiety and stress.[171] This is a good thing! Studies in educational settings have shown that using strengths increases intrinsic motivation in students, and students who can use their strengths best are most likely to succeed academically and socially.[172] For us, as adults, using strengths is associated with work satisfaction, work engagement and work performance. And people quit their jobs less when they use their strengths at work.[173] When people use their strengths they just do better. They have higher emotional and psychological wellbeing and less stress, and they are more likely to accomplish goals. They have higher levels of happiness and less depression, even up to six months after they have been shown how to identify and use their strengths.[174] The capacity to identify, use and develop our strengths builds self-esteem and resilience.

Think of what this means in regards to our children. Are they aware of their strengths? Or are we like Nikki, failing to identify and encourage our children to use their strengths? Crucially for their resilience, each day at school, what opportunities do they have to use their strengths? For some children it is easy to feel strong at school. These children have remarkable academic aptitude, or resonate with a particular subject. Some children thrive in social situations and school feeds that strength, buoying them through the day. But for others, school can be a place that suffocates strengths. They may have strengths in domains outside of the typical structures that schools create and demand conformity to. They may be creatives, or energisers. Perhaps they prefer manual manipulation of matter, or have exceptional mechanical aptitude or athletic strength, but the school day offers (in some cases) little to enhance those strengths. Of course, school requires our children to demonstrate competencies that are important for getting along in life. But when strengths aren't an integral part of our children's day, is it any wonder that they feel weakened, disengaged, and that their resilience drops? Days become drudgery when we do not use our strengths.

When school does not offer the opportunities our children require to develop and utilise their strengths, we can look elsewhere to help bolster and develop our children's strengths. The most obvious option is after-school activities including sport, art, writing, music, languages, drama or community-based opportunities like scouts, guides, cadets or other groups. Participation in these activities will be most helpful when it aligns with children's natural strengths, and when they experience high levels of engagement. Our children will develop competence, which builds confidence. They'll learn to think more flexibly, develop relationships, create a sense of identity, and persist in order to develop. And we will be able to learn to be patient and encouraging, and find that balance between pushing our children to continue in an activity when they struggle, and letting them stop because it does not align with their strengths, their values or their passions.

How do I know what my child's strengths are?

Sometimes strengths are immediately conspicuous. When a child demonstrates obvious flair for art, music, dance or sport, we recognise that, relative to other children, our child is remarkably capable. Even when this is the case, however if we do not develop our children's strengths, others who do not have the innate capacity naturally may still improve and excel because of their willingness to practise and strive. They can turn something that is not quite so innate into a developed and practised strength. But other times, strengths may not be discovered until we are well into adulthood.

The list of possible strengths a person could possess is long. We might divide them into two groups: character strengths and performance-based strengths. The performance-based strengths focus on the ability to *do* things like play sport or music, or to demonstrate capacity by *performing*. The list of character strengths is long, and includes head strengths such as wisdom, creativity, curiosity, love of learning, discernment and judgement, and perspective. Strengths might be capacities of the heart, including courage or bravery, love, humanity, kindness, gratitude, forgiveness, compassion or appreciation of beauty. Some have strengths aligned with being authentic, responsible, self-controlled/disciplined, or even having transcendence. Others have strengths in working with people, such as teamwork, fairness, helping, being a change agent, and more.[175]

Take an inventory right now. Go through the list and see if you can identify which of these character strengths your children possess. Create your own list of strengths for each member of your family. Consider ways that you can encourage and facilitate opportunities for your children to develop and use these strengths each day, at home and at school. Perhaps you might do the same for yourself and your spouse or partner. It may also be helpful to pause and write down which performance-based strengths you have seen demonstrated in your children. How can you provide opportunities for your children (or yourself) to use those strengths more often, and to increase in both competence and confidence as a result?

Overplaying strengths

Failing to use our strengths each day can and will reduce our vitality and our resilience. But overplaying our strengths can also work against us. More is not always better. For example, let's take a look at the character strength of curiosity. If we choose not to use or develop this strength at all, we end up bored. But if we use it too much, that curiosity might be interpreted by others as being nosy. It might lead to distraction. It could stop us from being effective in one area because we are constantly becoming curious about other areas. Character strengths can almost all be overplayed and lead to less-than-optimal outcomes, and perhaps even a weakening effect rather than the strengthening that we hope for. Thus we should be mindful of what they are, encourage their use in prudent and positive ways each day, but moderate them to ensure they do not cause our children to become unbalanced.

The strengths most related to wellbeing

Not all strengths boost wellbeing (and potentially resilience) in the same way. Some strengths may have a more powerful impact on the quality of wellbeing and the capacity to bounce back from trials that we experience than other strengths. Gratitude, forgiveness, compassion, optimism, grit and persistence – each may be powerful and positive in one way or another. But these potentials for excellence are within all of us to varying degrees. It would be helpful to identify which is the most predictive of positive outcomes and develop that strength. Ken Sheldon and a team of psychology researchers examined ten prime candidate strengths to do precisely this.

So which strengths did they find boosted wellbeing once goals were achieved? In this study, the *only* strength to do this consistently across the duration of the study was curiosity. Again, this makes sense because when we are curious, we are engaged in doing something, we are developing our strengths and competencies, and we are learning and growing. In the face of adversity, curiosity fuels development and insight. Indifference and disinterest (the opposite of curiosity) lead to apathy and stagnation. Which do you think is more likely to build resilience?[176]

These results are, well … curious. There are, of course, many other strengths that can enhance wellbeing that were not studied, so we should not imagine it is all about curiosity. And the emphasis was on goal attainment. It may be that other strengths matter more for strengthening relationships, or for doing well at school or work. The context matters.

Do strengths really predict resilience?

With so many studies showing that some things are related to things *like* resilience, it is nice to be able to point to a specific study on strengths and resilience! Maria Martínez-Martí and Willibald Ruch, two psychology researchers in Switzerland, carried out a study with just over 360 participants. The study showed significant positive correlations between character strengths and resilience. Strengths mattered for the development of resilience over and above variables like income and education. Strengths contributed to wellbeing beyond the contribution of people feeling positive, having self-belief, being optimistic, having good relationships, enjoying high self-esteem, and being satisfied with life. That means that this stuff really does matter. Using strengths actually *does* build resilience.[177]

Using strengths to help

I believe that we find the greatest happiness in life when we (or our children) use our strengths to serve other people. One of the best things we can do to build resilience is to help our children help others. This is the time when we particularly use our strengths. When we forget ourselves and focus on using our strengths to give to, help and do for others what they may not be able to do for themselves, we forget about our dramas and problems. We are somehow lifted out of our own ruts of selfishness, or sadness, or difficulty and adversity as we lift others out of theirs. And we become more resilient.

When we let go of ourselves and tap into things that are bigger than us, we usually find more happiness and resilience. As such, it makes sense that character strengths that foster these self-transcendent connections are also the ones most closely linked to happiness.

How to create a strengths-focused family

So long as your kids are over about ten years of age, try the free viame.org website and discover their top five signature character strengths. In 20 minutes you'll get an idea of what their strengths are. (Remember that these character strengths are not the same as performance-based strengths, such as artistic, sport or academic strengths.)

If your child is under ten, talk with your spouse or partner – or even your child – about the various strengths listed in this chapter and identify those strengths your child possesses as best you can while they're young.

Ask yourself which of these strengths your child uses and when – and importantly, how does it make your child feel?

Work out how you can help your child to use those strengths more, particularly to help others.

Remember, though, that it is important not to decide what your child's strengths are while they are too young. Strengths emerge as we develop. Some of us are discovering new strengths and capacities well into our adulthood. A growth mindset teaches us that we can become stronger in anything we want to – but of course there are some things we and our children will be naturally drawn towards because they feel authentic and make us feel strong.

If you can do this for your child, try it for yourself too. Chances are that you'll feel stronger – and more vital and resilient.

Here are some other simple ideas:

- Show your child pictures of various pop-culture icons, cartoon characters or other famous-ish people and have them identify their strengths. Do the same with characters in books you read to (or with) them.
- Get your child to identify the strengths of parents or friends (but be warned that this can backfire with witty adolescents).
- Find private and sincere ways to emphasise your child's strengths (positive psychologists call this strength-spotting) and invite them to find opportunities to use them more each day.
- Give your child assignments about various strengths in order to develop their understanding and language around what these strengths are and how they work.

Take-home message

Using strengths daily – particularly in the service of others – builds wellbeing, increases engagement, improves productivity, and makes people more resilient. But we need a clear language around strengths. Our young people need to know what they are, be able to identify them, and work out how to use them in order to get the benefits. Practise spotting strengths in your family members and give them opportunities to use these strengths, and their resilience will increase.

CHAPTER 9

Screen time vs green time

Resilience may, at least in part, be child's play. Literally.

There may be no more contentious parenting challenge in today's always turned on world than how much screen time is okay, and how we can limit our children's access to screens without our interactions turning into full-scale conflict. Children (and some adults) of all ages get angry, tantrum and act out when we ask them to get off their screens. Screens may be the issue that I am asked about more than any other. I am forever hearing parents tell me things like:

- He never leaves his room.
- She won't go to sleep.
- He is glued to his screen.
- She is not contributing to the house.
- He is starting to miss school and fail his subjects.
- She is becoming more secretive and I'm sure she's hiding things from me.
- He is getting angry and aggressive.

While most of these complaints come from parents of children in early adolescence, it is not uncommon for parents of children as young as four or five to be struggling with at least some of these issues. Conflicts in the kitchen and down the hallway are growing as parents feel powerless to stop the screen tsunami engulfing their children. Hand-wringing is followed up with threats, removal of privileges, and all kinds of punitive parenting to get children off their devices. Doing as some experts suggest and laying down the law may be effective with younger children, but adolescents tend to respond particularly poorly to overly controlling parenting.

Yet we are right to be concerned, and to want to act. In fact we need to. Excessive screen and device usage is depriving our children of the opportunity to genuinely play, and to have a healthy, balanced childhood. As parents, we are the first generation to ever have to face such challenging circumstances regarding screens. Toddlers and preschoolers are armed with tablets while still in their prams, our young school-aged children are being given smart devices at ever-younger ages, and our teens appear glued to their screens. We were born in the olden days, BC: Before Computers. Our children have been born in a new era, AD: After Digital.

What's the attraction?

Children seem captivated by their screens. Why are they so compelled to play their games, use social media, or while away the hours in front of their screens – and from such a young age? Here are a few reasons:

1. **Screens are fun.** Pure and simple. Watching and interacting with screens can produce huge amounts of dopamine. This is a chemical in the brain that is usually produced to make us feel great. It is associated with a variety of addictions. Some researchers suggest that dopamine production as a result of game playing and screen activity is beyond anything the real world can produce. But just because our children have a lot of dopamine whizzing around their brains making them feel good, it doesn't mean they're happy, or that they're resilient.

2. **It's rewarding.** Not only is playing on a screen a lot more fun than writing an essay or reading a book (or even kicking a footy with a mate), but the reward schedule of games, and the constant social reinforcement from social media – or just the pure entertainment and escapism of screens generally – are designed to provide the ultimate positive reinforcement. Just when you think you'll run out of fuel the checkpoint appears in the distance. That little red notification gives you the signal that someone wants to talk to you. The commercial break comes on just in time to leave you in full suspense, itching to know what happens next.

3. **Screen time is an escape.** Switching on a screen allows our children to forget all about what's troubling them. Unfortunately this is a poor coping strategy (similar to turning to alcohol and drugs), but it does provide temporary relief. Some kids acknowledge that they don't even enjoy the game, but flicking it on has become a habit.

4. **It creates a feeling of social inclusion.** Social media and games promote peer support. Even if our children aren't old enough for the social aspects of being online, they talk about what they play at school. Screen time is still a form of social currency. Being the only one who doesn't play a certain game or watch a particular program can lead to ostracism.

5. **I need something to do.** Like adults checking their email or social media, or playing a quick game while waiting in the doctor's surgery (or sitting at traffic lights!), kids see screens as an easy way to fill in time, be amused and not have to think or make an effort.

There are other reasons, of course, but these are central to why screens now occupy such a significant part of our children's lives.

Are screens damaging to resilience?

There are dozens and dozens – if not hundreds – of research articles that tell us that screens bring benefits. And they do ... when we use them in positive ways. Context matters. From education and creativity to building social relationships in a global way, or just for some basic rest and relaxation, screens bring benefits. But they also bring a level of risk for ill health and reduced resilience.

Our devices bring a faraway world into the palms of our hands. Our lives are potentially enriched as we scan and scroll through more information in a moment than previous generations could have imagined. But as world events, natural wonders, social media, comedians and other information and entertainment sources crowd into our lives via our screens, the people and opportunities directly in front of us give way to our distracted way of being. Further, entertainment often fails to provide the consumer with anything enriching or memorable. Not every parent, however well-meaning, has the capacity to monitor and limit screen usage either. When single parents are away from the home for long periods throughout the day, or when both parents work long hours and commute, or when a parent is a shift-worker and screens assure the tired breadwinner that sleep will be uninterrupted, it can be tremendously difficult to get the screen time balance 'right'. Under such circumstances it can be very difficult to find the time, the energy and the resources to get outside and play with the kids. And in today's world, some children are living in units without backyards. In these locations, it is typically no longer appropriate to simply send the children off to the park or out into the street to play. In some communities, this decision would be met with frowns of disapproval and potentially even calls to child protection agencies!

There are some significant ways screens can impact on resilience – and they tend to be in a negative direction. When young children (under the age of around five years) get hooked on screens, they can permanently damage their still-developing brains. We want our children to be focused, attentive and cognitively attuned. When they are on screens they appear to be precisely that. But it does not auger well for their life away from the screen. In fact, too much screen time too early in life literally impedes the development of those attributes. Screens have been shown to impact negatively on the capacity for concentration and focus, and the ability to develop an enlarged vocabulary.

Why is this? The devices do the thinking for our children, and so our children's cognitive muscles don't have as many opportunities to strengthen. The neurological connections are not made. The necessary stimulation is missing.

The most critical period to keep our children away from screens is up until age three, because the significant brain developments at this stage of life are literally the foundation of all later neurological development. And for optimal development, our children need stimulation from a much broader environment than screens can provide. The technical, scientific word for this broader environment is called *outside*. The more time a child can spend 'outside', the more benefit their brain receives.

It is not just cognitive resilience that is undermined through excessive device and screen time. Social resilience is impacted too. The brain's frontal lobe is crucial in understanding and framing social interaction, and the bulk of its development is throughout childhood. A simple experiment demonstrates how easily phones and screens impact on social success and resilience. A researcher sent 51 kids on a five-day nature camp where television, computers and mobile phones were not allowed. They were compared with 54 children who stayed home and used devices as normal.

Prior to the children's separation, they had taken part in a test of emotional intelligence, looking at photos and watching videos (with no sound) to identify non-verbal emotion cues. After five days interacting face-to-face without the use of any screen-based media or using devices as usual, all children were tested again. Recognition of non-verbal emotion cues for both facial expressions and videotaped scenes was significantly higher for the children who had been on the camp than that of the control group. Time with friends combined with time away from screen-based media and digital communication tools had a positive impact on their social and emotional intelligence.[178] With lower quality, less cohesive relationships that lack empathy and sociality, children are at risk of being less resilient because social relationships are the bedrock of resilience.

Screens are also impacting on physical activity levels, with health professionals increasingly concerned about the growing problem of weight gain and obesity. There are clear links between these issues and children's resilience levels. Lack of physical health is associated with lack of both physical resilience (poor sleep, lowered immunity) and psychological and emotional resilience – the kind of resilience this book is all about. Evidence even suggests that screens are affecting eyesight, with medical professionals indicating that more children have myopia than ever before due to screen time.[179] And screens *are* affecting wellbeing.

The more we provide access to screen time, and the earlier we allow children to use screens, the greater the risk is that they may become compulsive screen users. A colleague of mine, Professor Joseph Ciarrochi, conducted a study on just over 2000 Aussie school kids through most of their high school years. He and his team found that compulsive internet use (CIU) increased through high school, but especially in the Year 8 to Year 9 period. The most important finding from his research showed that compulsive internet and screen usage led to worsening mental health. The more time on screens, the lower the resilience. But the reverse was not true. Children did not seem to spend too much time on screens because of poor mental health.[180]

So should we get rid of screens?

Research from the Longitundal Study of Australian Children has shown we aren't doing so well with the amount of screen time our children get. Around two-thirds of our early adolescents were exceeding two hours per day on all screens, and in some cases children were spending as much as one-third of their day glued to the screen.[181] Potentially, we might argue that with the decreases in wellbeing associated with screen time, the digital revolution is reducing resilience in our children – and parents know it but don't know what to do about it.

But does screen time include Skype with grandparents? What about homework? Aren't these good things? Before the internet, screen time was usually staring dumbly at a television screen. But our screens are far more interactive now. The jury is still out regarding how much is too much, but experts err on the side of caution, and with good reason. Guidelines still firmly state that little ones under two should not see screens at all. This is good counsel. But limits for kids aged 5–17 need to be developed for each family's unique circumstances.

To be clear, research shows that a *moderate* amount of screen time, whether gaming, exploring or on social media, is positively correlated with wellbeing, but the evidence does not support the possibility that screens make our children 'happy', help them achieve anything particularly productive, or live well-balanced lives. And the current data indicates that our children are not utilising screens at a moderate level. They're over and above the reasonable recommendations. So it's up to parents to actively monitor their children's screen usage and, where necessary, set limits on the extent to which they have access to it. Failure to do so will increase the likelihood of any number of issues including those outlined above and more, ultimately reducing resilience in our children. But we cannot walk into the room, cut the cords and ban screens forever! Such an approach will only create conflict. Instead, the following tips may be helpful.

First, talk it through. Choose a time that works to have a conversation about what you want and why. It is best that emotions are cool rather than hot. If your child is on a screen, it's probably not the right time to have a careful, logical, sensitive conversation. Nor is late at night, or when you or your child are tired. It can help to ask your child if they know why you are worried about the amount of screen time they are getting. If they do not, you might discuss issues like sleep, schoolwork, physical activity, being outside, learning skills, spending time with friends and family, and other aspects of life that lead to a whole, balanced life.

Second, work out why it means so much to them. This may be a bigger issue for older children than younger children. But it's important to acknowledge that you understand *why* they're so into their screens. (That's the purpose of the previous section that highlighted their central motivations.) When our children feel understood, they are far more likely to engage in a productive conversation with us.

Third, problem-solve together. This may mean that you make suggestions and they negotiate with you. Or you may invite their initiative, and then you trial their ideas to see how they work. This phase of the discussion will not usually work effectively unless the first two elements have been effectively and patiently worked through.

Fourth, minimise control. It is tempting to write up an 'internet contract' with children, promising rewards or goodies if they keep to the agreed limits and removing privileges if they do not. Such an approach seldom works, though. Instead, children become motivated to not get caught. They become despondent and feel that we are their enemies once they've failed to reach a certain target and their devices are removed from them. They see themselves as helpless victims when we indicate that they'll be missing out on a reward because they didn't stick to the contract, or they lose all motivation once they realise that the reward is no longer on offer. And there are the endless negotiations about whether time on the device is school-related or entertainment-related. In short, rather than being controlling, we want to work through those first three principles to be as supportive of our children's autonomy as possible – within reasonable limits.

Putting it into practice

One of my daughters, at around age 14, was using screens in an excessive and unhealthy way. For several months I had attempted to discuss the issue with her, but we were getting nowhere. Requests were ignored. Conversations were shut down. Tempers flared on a few occasions. Nothing seemed to be working. I had even resorted to controlling techniques a couple of times and removed her devices, but that had simply resulted in power plays, obstinance and occasional sneaky behaviour. She spent extra time at friends' homes where device usage was unlimited rather than being in our home. And when she did receive her device back, the problem behaviour continued.

But we had not worked through those first two steps effectively. We couldn't problem-solve when neither of us really understood what the issue was or what a suitable solution looked like for the other person. I had just returned from a week of travelling and giving talks, and knew we needed some time together. Exhausted, but committed to working things out with my daughter, I suggested a Saturday evening run – something I knew she would be responsive to. She agreed. We drove to a nearby running track and set off. After a short while I told her I was unhappy about our arguments regarding technology and whether she felt the same. The answer was brief: 'Yes.' I asked whether we could talk it over and, with her agreement, began the discussion. We talked about my rationale for wanting clearer, more sustainable limits. We discussed the pressures she was feeling with schoolwork and other commitments, along with her enjoyment of Netflix and social media. And I asked her what she saw as a solution. A confusing and convoluted answer left us stuck, so I asked if I could tell her what would work for me and perhaps we could start from that position instead. Agreement. Phew. After I had shared my preferences, my daughter's response was, 'Is that all you want? I thought you were going to tell me I wasn't allowed to do anything. I thought you were going to take my screens from me completely.'

Whether your child is a toddler or a teenager, you will find this is harder than it seems. The truth is that there are *no* easy answers. It's hard work. Screens are here to stay, and they do tend to create conflict when not used in healthy, positive ways – which is all too often. But getting the conversation right will aid you enormously. Even so, your child will still struggle to regulate their usage, even after discussions and agreements are reached. Our children have far more energy for this battle than we do. They are more persistent, more motivated and far more invested in the outcome than most parents. In such cases, the following ideas may be helpful.

- Agree ahead of time how long is suitable on games and other media.
- Agree ahead of time what time devices will go off at night.
- Agree ahead of time on a strategy for getting them to switch off when asked. I find that the oven timer works very well with all ages.
- Agree ahead of time to keep devices out of bedrooms and in public areas to the extent that it is reasonable and possible.

- Agree ahead of time that text messages, a tap on the door or the oven timer will be used for a 15-minute (or a 5-minute) warning.
- Agree ahead of time that your child must acknowledge and respond to those warnings.
- Agree ahead of time what the consequences of refusal to get off the screens will be – but remember not to be too punitive, and remember to be flexible. Rigidity to rules can be the enemy of family functionality. Be aware that the more you emphasise consequences (read: punishments), the bigger the impact on the relationship and your child's transparency. If punishment/consequences are required, talk through things with your child and focus on helping them get it right next time.
- Agree ahead of time that schoolwork and other priorities will be completed ahead of screen time for fun.

In serious cases, there may not be many options aside from getting professional help. Reasoning and logic are unhelpful, as are consequences when things get this serious. Indeed, becoming controlling usually only deepens the crisis. Remember resilient families have buy-in – not autocracy.

There are three other variables to help us in making wise decisions about our children's access to screens: content, context and your child.

Consider content

When your child is on the screen what are they doing/watching? Is it active or passive? Is it content that is time-wasting? If so, keep time limits short. Is it something constructive, open-ended or educational? If so, you may be open to allowing additional time for learning and exploration. It is safe and appropriate? The content they consume must be discussed, monitored and limited.

Consider context

There are times when screen time is inappropriate. It may be a particular place (for example, a schoolroom or church building), a specific time (like dinnertime), or when a particular person is visiting. Or perhaps there are some contexts that justify specific decisions around technology and that may require specific rules. A long car trip may mean relaxed rules. A busy day where you are completely overwhelmed and just need an extra 30 minutes to get your head around things may also mean relaxed rules. Or a special family day may mean tightened rules. So too might an overdue assignment or a stressful schedule.

Consider your child

The rules you develop to help your child use technology appropriately may differ based on their specific needs. If your child is experiencing learning difficulties a computer or screen may be helpful (or detrimental). If your child is tired and putting them to bed is not an option, maybe a screen can get you through a tough spot. If your child is advanced or gifted and requires extra stimulation, or if your child finds digital creativity more inspiring than other kinds you may want to take that into account.

All of these rules, ideas and strategies are useful and important, but only to the extent that they serve the effective functioning of your family and your child. Ultimately, this is about strengthening your child's resilience. And there's something far more effective at boasting resilience than screen time.

Green time

Play, particularly outside play, brings with it elements that powerfully promote resilience: risk, ambiguity and uncertainty. For young children, climbing a fortress or sliding down a slippery dip are exhilarating confidence builders. Older children might follow a parent along a scary precipice, or abseil down an escarpment on a school camp. And because most play is social, the role-playing, identity-building processes that emerge through interactions with others provide additional scaffolding that builds and develops a child's resilience. There are many excellent books, research articles and TED talks about why play matters for children and adults. So if we are going to replace screens, this is what to replace them with.

Cutting-edge research from Professor Richard Ryan at the University of Rochester highlights the incredible value of green time (over screen time) for our children's vitality, wellbeing and resilience. According to Ryan, nature is fuel for our souls. Being outside makes our children feel more alive, more vital and perhaps even more resilient. And the research shows that sense of increased vitality exists above and beyond the boost we get from physical activity and social interaction.[182]

For example, an analysis of 19 studies from around the world found that the availability of parks, playgrounds and recreation areas plays an important role in wellbeing.[183] And a study in the United Kingdom looked at changes in mental health over several years as people moved home. When people moved to areas with more green space, including tree-lined streets, private gardens and public parks, they were happier for at least three years after their move, and this feeling of contentment grew over time. The move to a less green environment showed a decline in wellbeing for a time, before mood returned to what it had been prior to the move.[184] Getting good-quality green time has been shown to reduce cortisol and lower blood pressure. And time in nature is a legitimate intervention to help those suffering mental illness.[185] Green time is associated with improved mood, enhanced wellbeing and better concentration and attention. A teacher recently told me her Year 3 boys were rowdy, disrespectful and impossible to teach. A shift of emphasis towards green time and outdoor activity in the morning changed things within three days. The class took a 20-minute walk outside to exercise and experience a little bit of nature to start each day, and the difficult and challenging behaviour stopped.

We have all had that experience where it has rained for days and 'the kids are climbing the walls'. A bright sunny day and the opportunity to get outside and expend energy is all it takes to restore peace and balance.

Take-home message

If your child wants screens, make sure that:

- they're using screens in public areas (where reasonable and appropriate)
- they've had some outside activity
- they've played with friends
- they've done what they are expected to do around the house (if they're old enough)
- they're up to date with schoolwork
- the context is appropriate – it's not meal time or family time
- the content of what they're viewing is in line with family values.

Screen time can be fun and it has its place. But to raise resilient children, green time should be the focus. Play – open-ended and active (and social where possible) – is the real work of childhood, and doing what we can to keep our children outside will be better for their resilience than all the time in the world on screens.

Conclusion

John's eyes opened slowly. Everything looked blurry. Everything looked unfamiliar. And the pain was excruciating.[186]

John was confused. It looked like he was in a hospital room. Why was he here?

Realising he had a buzzer tucked under his left hand, John pushed the button and a nurse entered his room. She explained to him he had been involved in a serious accident while riding his bike and that it would take him a long time to recover. John passed out.

It had been three days since the accident. It was 1988 and John, aged 22, had been training for a triathlon when he was hit by a truck.

He was knocked unconscious instantly. Emergency services were called and John's comatose body was rushed to hospital. Fifteen bones were broken. His back had three breaks, his pelvis sustained four, one of his arms was broken in two places, and the other was broken as well; he had a punctured lung, a fractured sternum, broken ribs and more.

As John returned to consciousness, he was slowly able to begin to comprehend the repercussions of his accident. Like most serious cyclists, John's first question for his dad was, 'How's my bike?' But as the days passed, the reality of his situation became increasingly evident. He was now a paraplegic. The condition of his bike was irrelevant. He would probably never ride again. Or walk. John was told that he was paralysed from around his belly button down. The paralysis was called 'incomplete', however, because some nerve pathways remained intact. John was able to move his left side minimally. His doctors were hopeful that he might recover some capability. They never told him, 'John, you won't walk again.' But over time he realised for himself that it was not going to happen. Medical professionals told him that after 12–24 months, whatever movement he had was all he would likely ever have. He would have to come to terms with it.

John had wanted to be the guy that proved the doctors wrong. In his mind, he was going to get back on the field, 'playing and running and doing all that I did pre-injury'. John had shown promise as an athlete, and was heavily into football and triathlon. And so he pushed as hard as he could, training his upper body and attempting to improve his mobility by taking weight through his arms on Canadian crutches and hobbling up and down his street. A little after the 12-month mark, John said, 'I realised I was not going to improve. So I sat with Dad, cried, and we talked about what I could do now – in a wheelchair. I had to make the most of the cards I'd been dealt.'

His dad said, 'Son, look at how far you've come. Now ... how far can you go?' This inspired John, and he began to set and achieve unprecedented goals. John's first goal – complete the Nepean Triathlon as a paraplegic athlete. That was the triathlon he had been training for when he was hit by the truck. He said, 'What you hold onto in life holds onto you.' He completed the triathlon in 1994, six years after the accident. In so doing, he became Australia's first paraplegic triathlete. And then he let go of the pain and baggage related to that triathlon ... but not quite.

John went on to become the first paraplegic to complete the Hawaii Ironman Triathlon: a 3.8-kilometre swim, 180-kilometre ride, and 42-kilometre run, in 1995. He raced again the two following years, and in 1997, he finished before the cut-off time for able-bodied athletes. In 1998, ten years after the crash, John became the first paraplegic to swim the English Channel. It took 12 hours and 55 minutes. This also made him the first man to complete an Ironman triathlon *and* swim the Channel. And John represented Australia in rowing at both world championships and the Paralympic Games in Beijing, winning silver in both events with his rowing partner, Kathryn Ross.

John achieved what was thought to be impossible. He demonstrated a resilience that seems unusual. But there was more to come.

He wanted to walk again. And so John began working with therapists, specialists and people who believed he could do the impossible. He tried new technologies. He did new exercises. And he got it into his head that he could and would walk again. He began to move a little. He progressed from movement to being able to spin his legs on a stationary spin bike. Some carbon fibre braces were made for his legs. This allowed him to apply some load to his legs and build muscle. His next step: a conventional bike. In 2014, John returned to the Nepean Triathlon and competed as an able-bodied athlete.

Following the swim and the ride, his 'run' leg was a slow walk, using the carbon fibre braces and walking poles for support. John Maclean completed the run leg of the race, one careful and intentional step at a time, holding hands with his wife and son as they crossed the finish line together.

Is this possible?

I asked John about his experiences. He told me, 'I had to learn to let go of the internal dialogue. Those conversations I have with myself. They are only our thoughts. Just because you think something is true doesn't mean it *is* true. I had to teach myself not to believe everything I think. I just focused on what I have control over.' He emphasised that when we let the past interfere with, and override, the present, it limits our potential. 'You cannot let the past hold you back. That's not resilient. That's being a victim. Just worry about what is right now and create a future that is hopeful.'

I asked him if he was different from other people. Did he have some special resilience gene? John laughed. 'No, not at all. I had a rough start to life. Mum suffered from schizophrenia and I spent my first five years in a foster home. When Mum committed suicide I got to live with Dad. He worked three jobs to give me a chance and opportunities. But I'm no different to anyone. We've all got the same capacity – but I won't be defined by my path. I just want to explore.' John's life (so far) is chronicled in his book, *How Far Can You Go?*[187]

A resilient world?

This book has described a small handful of people who have demonstrated what appears to be remarkable resilience. Perhaps it is. But perhaps it is actually entirely normal, and we have somehow lost the capacity to allow our children (and ourselves) to naturally and authentically tap into it so powerfully. After all, we have created a world that actively undermines resilience. We are surrounded by a culture – a system – that sets our children up in competitions, comparisons and the fear of never being enough. There is so much pressure. There is so much expectation. There are so many 'shoulds' and 'have-tos'. As parents, we watch our children lying in bed asleep, staring in wonder at their perfection, knowing life is going to present them with challenges, difficulties, adversities and problems that we – and they – may have no idea how to overcome.

It's frightening.

But it is also beautiful, if we can trust in our children's inbuilt capacity for growth, mastery and resilience. We don't need to know how to overcome every problem or difficulty. Nor do our children. Instead, we need to focus on providing the right environment – the kind of environment we have focused on in this book – and help our children to authentically and innately develop the self-confidence to face adversity with a secure self-belief that they will work it out, and succeed.

Sometimes we mistakenly believe that happiness is the absence of a load. We feel our children would be so much more resilient without the need to carry the heavy burdens life places on their shoulders. My research suggests the opposite. An absence of a 'load' can in fact weaken or incapacitate us, or our children, and leave us stuck. As hard as it is to see at the time, adversity can fuel growth, learning and development.

As you think back over all of the remarkable stories of resilience in this book, and as you think about the resilience you have experienced in your own life, or witnessed in the lives of those closest to you, perhaps you might think of resilience just slightly differently.

Resilience is partly related to an individual's psychological traits and the environment in which they are raised. But it is also an ordinary adaptation to challenge, built in to every one of us and designed to activate when given the right resources and support to make those adaptations. Despite this, so many people are suffering under burdens that may be too big for them to be able to easily and quickly bounce back from. What can each of us do to curb that experience in ourselves and others?

The secrets and strategies detailed in this book can help. But ultimately it's all about relationships. Relationships lie at the heart of resilience. Relationships with self, family, friends and the broader community (via school, work, sport, church and so on) – ultimately it is this love that builds resilience as well as the skills and capacity to be resilient. Having those crucially important people who act as support and scaffolding when times are both good and bad is the central, critical factor in raising a resilient child. Our children are relying on us to be that support, to give them that relationship.

We know how resilience works. We can do better. We *must* do better.

We have work to do.

Endnotes

1   All statistics in this section found here: Australian Bureau of Statistics. (2015). *National Health Survey first results – Australia 2014–15.* Canberra: ABS

2   More information on these statistics and associated reports and research can be found at the following references:
Kessler, R.D. et al. (2005). *Lifetime prevalence and age-of-onset distributions of DSM-IV disorders in the National Comorbidity Survey Replication.* Archives of General Psychiatry, 62: p. 593–602
Lawrence, D., Johnson, S., Hafekost, J., Boterhoven De Haan, K., Sawyer, M., Ainley, J., Zubrick, S.R. (2015). *The mental health of children and adolescents. Report on the second Australian Child and Adolescent Survey of Mental Health and Wellbeing.* Canberra: Department of Health
Accessed from http://www.abs.gov.au/ausstats/abs@.nsf/Lookup/by%20 Subject/4364.0.55.001~2014-15~Main%20Features~Psychological%20 distress~16 on 22 November 2016

3   I am grateful to Andrew for his generosity in sharing some of his data with me for this. More information about Resilient Youth Australia can be found at www.resilientyouthaustralia.org.au

4   More examples here: These statistics are consistent with other data that indicates children's wellbeing is highest around age eight and drops consistently through to around the age of 16–17 years. Other Australian research combines with global studies pointing to a pattern showing that adolescence is not just a time of potential turmoil for a large percentage of our children. It is a time where resilience and wellbeing drop significantly.
For example, see http://www.unicef.org/polls/cee/happiness/; https:// www.unicef-irc.org/Report-Card-11/; https://www.childrenssociety.org. uk/sites/default/files/TheGoodChildhoodReport2015.pdf
Commissioner for Children and Young People WA. (2015). *Our children can't wait – review of the implementation of recommendations of the*

2011 Report of the inquiry into the mental health and wellbeing of children and young people in WA, Perth: Commissioner for Children and Young People

Australian Bureau of Statistics. (2015). *Causes of death, Australia, 2014. Catalogue No. 3303.0.* Canberra: ABS. Accessed from http://www.abs. gov.au/ausstats/abs@.nsf/mf/3303.0?OpenDocument on 2 March 2015

5   Taleb, N. (2012). *Antifragile: Things That Gain from Disorder.* New York: Random House

6   Accessed 24 May 2016 from https://en.wikipedia.org/wiki/Rosie_Batty

7   View the Harvard report here: http://developingchild.harvard.edu/ resources/reports_and_working_papers/working_papers/wp13/

8   The work of Jane Gillham and Karen Reivich describes longitudinal studies of children and adolescents where resilience 'skills' have been taught, with ensuing improvements in wellbeing and resilience outcomes. For two examples see

Gillham, J. E., et al. (2007). School-based prevention of depressive symptoms: a randomized controlled study of the effectiveness and specificity of the Penn Resiliency Program. *The Journal of Consulting and Clinical Psychology, 75,* 9–19

Gillham, J., & Reivich, K. (2004). Cultivating optimism in childhood and adolescence. *The Annals of the American Academy of Political and Social Science, 591,* 146–163. The work of Martin Seligman, Carol Dweck, Ann Masten and many others is also illustrative.

9   For those seeking a deeply thoughtful scholarly review of resilience definitions, theories, interventions and issues, you may find it helpful to read the academic literature. I have relied on resilience research from all of the leading names in the area, including Garmezy, Masten, Werner, Rutter, Lurhar, Cicchetti and Ungar. There's information here based on Bronfenbrenner and other classic theorists too. But I've stayed largely out of the quagmire of resilience research. Furthermore, for those seeking a perfectly cohesive 'bringing together' of disparate theories and definitions, again, that is beyond the scope of this book. Finally, I acknowledge that in much academic research, 'risk factors' are often described as significantly more serious than many of the issues I'll write about in this book. The colloquial way that we refer to resilience (and risk factors) means that for most ordinary families, they simply want their children to respond well to challenge and setback, develop positively and adaptively and increase wellbeing. While this will be dissatisfying to some readers, the purpose of this book is to review the basics of helping children thrive, regardless of their situation. (It may be

worth noting that the same principles that help a child with significant risk factors to be resilient will have positive impacts on a child with minor risk factors.)

10   Wyman, P. A., Cowen, E. L., Work, W. C., Hoyt-Meyers, L., Magnus, K. B., & Fagen, D. B. (1999). Caregiving and developmental factors differentiating young at-risk urban children showing resilient versus stress-affected outcomes: a replication and extension. *Child Development*, 70, 645–659

11   Masten, A. S. (2014). Global perspectives on resilience in children and youth. *Child Development*, 85, 6–20. DOI: 10.1007/s10567-013-0150-2

12   Evans., G. W., Li, D., & Whipple, S. S. (2013). Cumulative risk and child development. *Psychological Bulletin*, 139, 1342–1396. DOI: 10.1037/a0031808

13   Ibid. See also Patterson, J. M. (2002). Integrating family resilience and family stress theory. *Journal of Marriage and Family*, 64, 349–360. DOI: 10.1111/j.1741-3737.2002.00349.x

14   Guy, S., Furber, G., Leach, M., & Segal, L. (2016). How many children in Australia are at risk of adult mental illness? *Australian and New Zealand Journal of Psychiatry*. Published online before print on 23 March 2016. Accessed from http://anp.sagepub.com/content/early/2016/03/22/0004867416640098.abstract on 24 May 2016

15   Weissman, M. M., et al. (2016). Offspring of depressed parents: 30 years later. *American Journal of Psychiatry,* online first. Accessed from DOI: 10.1176/appi.ajp.2016.15101327 on 16 May 2016

16   Qu, Y., Fuligni, A. J., Galvan, A., Lieberman, M. D., & Telzer, E. H. (2016). Links between parental expression and longitudinal changes in youths' neural sensitivity to rewards. *Social Cognitive and Affective Neuroscience,* online first. Accessed from DOI: 10.1093/scan/nsw035 on 16 May 2016

17   For a detailed review of this devastating research see the recent report by Cicchetti, D. (2013). Annual research review: resilient functioning in maltreated children – past, present, and future perspectives. *Journal of Child Psychology and Psychiatry*, 54, 402–422. DOI: 10.1111/j.1469-7610.2012.02608.x

18   Huizink, A. C., Bartels, M., Rose, R. J., Pulkkinen, L., Eriksson, C. J. P., & Kapiro, J. (2008). Chernobyl exposure as a stressor during pregnancy and hormone levels in adolescent offspring. *Journal of Epidemiology and Community Health*, 62(4), 1–6. DOI: 10.1136/jech.2007.060350

19   Newbury, J., Arseneault, L., Caspi, A., Moffitt, T. E., Odgers, C. L., & Fisher, H. L. (2016). Why are children in urban neighbourhoods at

increased risk for psychotic symptoms? Findings from a UK longitudinal cohort study. *Schizophrenia Bulletin*. Accessed from DOI: 10.1093/schbul/sbw052 on 17 May 2016

20   McEwen, B. S., & Gianaros, P. J. (2011). Stress and allostasis-induced brain plasticity. *Annual Review of Medicine*, 62, 431–445. DOI: 10.1146/annurev-med-052209-100430

21   Masten, A. S., & Monn, A. R. (2015). Child and family resilience: a call for integrated science, practice, and professional training. *Family Relations*, 64, 5–21. DOI: 10.1111/fare.12103

22   American Academy of Pediatrics (2016). Factors that help children thrive in the face of adversity. *Science Daily*, 30 April

23   Masten, A. S. (2001). Ordinary magic. Resilience processes in development. *American Psychologist*, 56, 227–238. DOI: 10.1037//0003-066X.56.3.227

24   Knost, L. R. (2013). *Two Thousand Kisses a Day: Gentle Parenting through the Ages and Stages*. USA: Little Hearts Books

25   Most of Narvaez's work quoted here comes from her 2015 Kohlberg Memorial Lecture on moral development, which she sent to me in personal correspondence. It is available in the 2016 *Journal of Moral Education*, 45 (3)

26   Narvaez, D. (2014). *Neurobiology and the Development of Human Morality: Evolution, Culture and Wisdom*. New York, NY: W.W. Norton

27   Swain, J. E., Tasgin, E., Mayes, L. C., Feldman, R., & Leckman, J. F. (2008). Cesarean delivery affects maternal brain response to own baby cry. *Journal of Child Psychology and Psychiatry*, 9, 1042–1052

28   See Jan Blustein's article at *The Conversation*: http://theconversation.com/do-kids-born-by-c-section-have-a-higher-risk-of-chronic-disease-a-new-study-looks-at-the-evidence-43033, accessed 28 April 2016

29   Accessed from http://www.who.int/healthsystems/topics/financing/healthreport/30C-sectioncosts.pdf on 22 November 2016

30   Data accessed from http://www.sbs.com.au/news/thefeed/story/women-are-feeling-bullied-and-coerced-australias-rising-c-section-rate on 5 May 2016

31   Shu, X. O., et al. (1999). Breast-feeding and risk of childhood acute leukaemia. *Journal of the National Cancer Institute*, 91, 1765–1772. doi: 10.1093/jnci/91.20.1765

32   For more information about the protective factors of breastfeeding, see the World Health Organization at http://www.who.int/elena/titles/bbc/breastfeeding_childhood_obesity/en/

33   There are dozens of studies to support this. Here are just a few that will guide the reader to primary sources:

American Academy of Pediatrics Section on Breastfeeding. (2005). Breastfeeding and the use of human milk. *Pediatrics*, 115, 496–506

American Academy of Pediatrics Work Group on Breastfeeding. (1997). Breastfeeding and the use of human milk policy statement. *Pediatrics*, 100, 1035–1039

Delgado, P. L. (2006). Monoamine depletion studies: implications for antidepressant discontinuation syndrome. *Journal of Clinical Psychiatry*, 67 (Suppl. 4), 22–26

Goldman, A. S. (1993). The immune system of human milk: antimicrobial, anti-inflammatory and immunomodulating properties. *Pediatric Infectious Disease Journal, 12*, 664–671.

Goldman, A. S., Goldblum, R. M., Garza, C., Nichols, B. L., & O'Brien Smith, E. (1983). Immunologic components in human milk during weaning. *Acta Paediatrica Scandinavica*, 72, 133–134

Martin, L. J., Woo, J. G., Geraghty, S. R., Altaye, M., Davidson, B. S., Banach, W., & Morrow, A. L. (2006). Adiponectin is present in human milk and is associated with maternal factors. *American Journal of Clinical Nutrition*, 83, 1106–1111

Slusser, W., & Powers, N. G. (1997). Breastfeeding update 1: immunology, nutrition, and advocacy. *Pediatrics in Review*, 18, 111–119

Yehuda, S., Rabinovitz, S., & Mostofsky, D. I. (1999). Essential fatty acids are mediators of brain biochemistry and cognitive functions. *Journal of Neuroscience Research*, 56, 565–570

34   Oddy, et al. (2010). The long-term effects of breastfeeding on child and adolescent mental health: a pregnancy cohort study followed for 14 years. *Journal of Pediatrics*, 156, 568–574

35   Carter, C. S. (2003). Developmental consequences of oxytocin. *Physiology and Behavior*, 79, 383–397

Feldman, R., Weller, A., Sirota, L., & Eidelman, A. I. (2002). Skin-to-skin contact (kangaroo care) promotes self-regulation in premature infants: sleep-wake cyclicity, arousal modulation, and sustained exploration. *Developmental Psychology*, 38, 194–207.

36   For a fascinating, broad-ranging and expansive overview of this and much more of Harlow's research and thinking, this original source that is available free online will be useful: Harlow, H. F. (1958). The nature of love. *American Psychologist*, 13, 673–685. Accessed from http://psychclassics.yorku.ca/Harlow/love.htm Accessed on 5 May 2016

37 Ardiel, E. L., & Rankin, C. H. (2010). The importance of touch in development. *Paediatrics and Child Health*, 15, 153–56

38 Ferber, S. G., Feldman, R., & Makhoul, I. R. (2008). The development of maternal touch across the first year of life. *Early Human Development*, 84, 363–370
    Hertenstein, M. J. (2002). Touch: its communicative functions in infancy. *Human Development*, 45, 70–94
    Hertenstein, M. J., & Campos, J. J. (2001). Emotion regulation via maternal touch. *Infancy*, 2, 549–566

39 Dettling, A. C., Gunnar, M. R., & Donzella, B. (1999). Cortisol levels of young children in full day childcare centers: relations with age and temperament. *Psychoneuroendocrinology*, 24, 519–536
    Moszkowski, R. J., Stack, D. M., Girouard, N., Field, T. M., Hernandez-Reif, M., & Diego, M. (2009). Touching behaviors of infants of depressed mothers during normal and perturbed interactions. *Infant Behavior and Development*, 32, 183–194

40 Takeuchi, M. S., Miyaoka, H., Tomoda, A., Suzuki, M., Liu, Q., & Kitamura, T. (2010). The effect of interpersonal touch during childhood on adult attachment and depression: a neglected area of family and developmental psychology? *Journal of Child and Family Studies*, 19, 109–117

41 Donzella, B., Gunnar, M. R., Krueger, W. K., & Alwin, J. (2000). Cortisol and vagal tone responses to competitive challenge in preschoolers: associations with temperament. *Development Psychobiology, 37*, 209–220

42 The easiest-to-read example of Halfon's ideas, as well as a summary of the research, can be found at his blog article: http://blog.nj.com/njv_guest_blog/2012/06/could_texting_while_parenting.html, accessed in September 2016

43 Sheldon, K. M., Kashdan, T. B., & Steger, M. F. (Eds). (2011). *Designing Positive Psychology: Taking Stock and Moving Forward*. New York, NY: Oxford University Press

44 Knost, L. R. (2013). *Two Thousand Kisses a Day: Gentle Parenting through the Ages and Stages*. USA: Little Hearts Books

45 Rutter, M. (2012). Resilience as a dynamic concept. *Development and Psychopathology*, 24, 335–344. DOI: 10.1017/S0954579412000028

46 Lyons, D. M., et al. (2010). Stress coping stimulates hippocampal neurogenesis in adult monkeys. *Proceedings of the National Academy of Sciences of the United States of America*, 107, 14823–14827

Lyons, D. M., & Parker, K. J. (2007). Stress inoculation-induced indications of resilience in monkeys. *Journal of Trauma Stress*, 20, 423–433.

Lyons, D. M., Parker, K. J., Katz, M., & Schatzberg, A. F. (2009). Developmental cascades linking stress inoculation, arousal regulation, and resilience. *Frontiers in Behavioral Neuroscience*, 3, 32

Parker, K. J., Buckmaster, C. L., Schatzberg, A. F., & Lyons, D. M. (2004). Prospective investigation of stress inoculation in young monkeys. *Archives of General Psychiatry, 61,* 933–941

Parker, K. J., & Maestripieri, D. (2011). Identifying the key features of early stressful experiences that produce stress vulnerability and resilience in primates. *Neuroscience & Biobehavioral Reviews,* 35, 1466–1483

47 While there are dozens of examples of studies that support such a decision, my favourite examples are those found in work by Bart Soenens and Maarten van Steenkiste, as well as (from an entirely different theoretical perspective) Dr John Gottman (see note 48).

48 Another view of these ways of relating to our children is described in Dr John Gottman's 1998 book, *Raising an Emotionally Intelligent Child.* New York: Simon & Schuster, Gottman describes these ideas as turning against or turning away from our children.

49 Lythcott-Haims, J. (2015). *How to Raise an Adult: Break Free of the Overparenting Trap and Prepare Your Kid for Success.* New York: Macmillan

50 Keppler, K., Mullendore, R.H., & Casey, A. (2005). *Partnering with Parents of Today's College Students.* Washington, DC: National Association of Student Personnel Administrators

51 Tyler, K. (2007). The tethered generation. *HR Magazine, 52,* 5

52 Wendy Mogel's book *The Blessing of a Skinned Knee* contains more examples of this overparenting.

53 Locke, J., Campbell, M. A., & Kavanagh, D. J. (2012). Can a parent do too much for their child? An examination by parenting professionals of the concept of overparenting. *Australian Journal of Guidance and Counselling,* 22, 249–265

54 Ginott, H. (1969). *Between Parent and Teenager.* New York, NY: Scribner. The quote is found on page 18 where a teen states, 'Mother hovers over me like a helicopter.'

55 Cline, F.W., & Fay, J. (1990). *Parenting with Love and Logic: Teaching Children Responsibility.* Colorado Springs, CO: Pinon Press

56 Segrin, C., Woszidlo, A., Givertz, M., Bauer, A., & Murphy, M. (2012). The association between overparenting, parent-child communication,

and entitlement and adaptive traits in adult children. *Family Relations*, 61, 237–252

57 In my previous book, *21 Days to a Happier Family*, I point out that authoritative parenting is NOT actually the gold standard due to more research around autonomy-supportive parenting indicating that *this* approach is optimal. However, for simplicity, and because most research refers to authoritative parenting as ideal, I have stuck with this theme for this chapter. (Additionally, given the limited research on autonomy-supportive parenting, we are probably on more conservative – read: safer – scholarly ground here.)

58 Padilla-Walker, L. M., & Nelson, L. J. (2012). Black hawk down?: establishing helicopter parenting as a distinct construct from other forms of parental control during emerging adulthood. *Journal of Adolescence*, 35, 1177–1190

59 Ibid.

60 Hastings, P. D., Nuselovici, J. N., Rubin, K. H., & Cheah, C. S. L. (2010). Shyness, parenting and parent–child relationships. In K. H. Rubin & R. J. Coplan (Eds), *The development of shyness and social withdrawal*. NY: Guilford, pp. 107–130

61 Ibid.

62 Rubin, K. H., Burgess, K. B., & Hastings, P. D. (2002). Stability and social-behavioural consequences of toddlers' inhibited temperament and parenting behaviours. *Child Development*, 73, 483–495

63 Ibid. Hastings 2010

64 Bayer, J., Sanson, A., & Hemphill, S. (2006). Parent influences on early childhood internalising difficulties. *Journal of Applied Developmental Psychology*, 27, 6, 542–559

65 Bayer, J., Hastings, P., Sanson, A., Ukoumunne, O., & Rubin, K. (2010). Predicting mid-childhood internalising symptoms: a longitudinal community study. *The International Journal of Mental Health Promotion*, 12, 5–17

66 Emerson, L., Fear. J., Fox, S., and Sanders, E. (2012). *Parental engagement in learning and schooling: lessons from research*. Canberra: A report by the Australian Research Alliance for Children and Youth (ARACY) for the Family-School and Community Partnerships Bureau

67 Segrin, C., Woszidlo, A., Givertz, M., Bauer, A., & Murphy, M. T. (2012). The association between overparenting, parent-child communication, and entitlement and adaptive traits in adult children. *Family Relations*, 61, 237–252. DOI: 10.1111/j.1741-3729.2011.00689.x

68　Brummelman, E., Thomaes, S., Overbeek, G., Orobio de Castro, B., van den Hout, M. A., & Bushman, B. (2014). On feeding those hungry for praise: person praise backfires in children with low self-esteem. *Journal of Experimental Psychology*, 143, 9–14

69　Bradley-Geist, J. C., & Olson-Buchanan, J. B. (2014). Helicopter parents: An examination of the correlates of over-parenting of college students. *Education and Training*, 56, 314 - 328. DOI 10.1108/ET-10-2012-0096

70　Padilla-Walker, L. M., Nelson, L. J., & Knapp, D. J. (2014). 'Because I'm the parent, that's why!' Parental legitimate authority during emerging adulthood. *Journal of Social and Personal Relationships*, 31, 293–313

71　Padilla-Walker, L. M. (2008). 'My mom makes me so angry.' Adolescent perceptions of mother-child interactions as correlates of adolescent emotions. *Social Development*, 17, 306–325

72　Darling, N., & Steinberg, L. (1993). Parenting style as context: An integrative model. *Psychological Bulletin*, 113, 487–496

73　Bugental, D. B., & Grusec, J. E. (2007). Socialization process. *Handbook of Child Psychology* III: 7
Joussemet, M., Landry, R., & Koestner, R. (2008). A self-determination theory perspective on parenting. *Canadian Psychology*, 49, 194–200
Pomerantz, E. M., & Moorman, E. A. (2007). The how, whom, and why of parental involvement in children's academic lives: More is not always better. *Review of Educational Research*, 77, 373–410

74　Padilla-Walker, L. M. (2008). 'My mom makes me so angry.' Adolescent perceptions of mother-child interactions as correlates of adolescent emotions. *Social Development*, 17, 306–325

75　Bradley-Geist, J. B., & Olson-Buchanan, J. (2014). Helicopter parents: an examination of the correlates of over-parenting of college students. *Education and Training*, 56, 314–328. DOI: 10.1108/ET-10-2012-0096

76　The best two examples are Duckworth, A. L. (2016). *Grit*. New York: Simon & Schuster. And Tough, P. (2014). *How Children Succeed*. New York: Houghton Mifflin Harcourt

77　Duckworth, A. L., Peterson, C., Matthews, M. D., & Kelly, D. R. (2007). Grit: perseverance and passion for long-term goals. *Journal of Personality and Social Psychology*, 92, 1087–1101

78　Duckworth, A. L., & Seligman, M. E. P. (2005). Self-discipline outdoes IQ in predicting academic performance of adolescents. *Psychological Science*, 16, 939–944. DOI: 10.1111/j.1467-9280.2005.01641.x

79　Eskreis-Winkler, L., Duckworth, A. L., Shulman, E., & Beal, S. (2014). The grit effect: predicting retention in the military, the workplace, school and marriage. *Frontiers in Personality Science and Individual Differences*, 5, 1–12

80 Duckworth, A. L., Peterson, C., Matthews, M. D., & Kelly, D. R. (2007). Grit: Perseverance and passion for long-term goals. *Personality Processes and Individual Differences*, 92, 1087–1101. DOI: 10.1037/0022-3514.92.6.1087

81 Accessed from http://lsi.gse.harvard.edu/individual-mastery on 11 June 2016

82 Deci, E. L., & Ryan, R. M. (1985). *Intrinsic Motivation and Self-determination in Human Behavior*. New York, NY: Plenum
Deci, E. L., & Ryan, R. M. (2000). The 'what' and 'why' of goal pursuits: human needs and the self-determination of behavior. *Psychological Inquiry*, 11, 227–268
Ryan, R. M., & Deci, E. L. (2000). Self-determination theory and the facilitation of intrinsic motivation, social development, and well-being. *American Psychologist*, 55, 68–78

83 Vansteenkiste, M., Simons, J., Lens, W., Sheldon, K. M., & Deci, E. L. (2004). Motivating learning, performance, and persistence: the synergistic effects of intrinsic goal contents, and autonomy-supportive contexts. *Personality Processes and Individual Differences*, 87, 246–260

84 Covey, S. R. (1989). *The 7 Habits of Highly Effective People*. Melbourne, Australia: The Business Library

85 Talbot, J. C. (2009). *The Road to Positive Discipline: A Parent's Guide*. Los Angeles, CA: TNT. See also Youngs, B. B. (1991). *How to Develop Self-esteem in Your Child: Six Vital Ingredients*. New York, NY: Fawcett Columbine

86 Bandura, A. (1977). Self-efficacy: toward a unifying theory of behavioral change. *Psychological Review*, 84, 191–215. See also Bandura, A. (1997). *Self-efficacy: The Exercise of Control*. New York: Freeman

87 Deci, E. L., & Ryan, R. M. (1985). *Intrinsic Motivation and Self-determination in Human Behavior*. New York: Plenum Press

88 O'Leary, K. D., & O'Leary, S. G. (1977). *Classroom Management: The Successful Use of Behavior Modification* (2nd ed.). New York: Pergamon Press

89 Madsen, C. H., Becker, W. C., & Thomas, D. R. (1977). Rules, praise, and ignoring: elements of elementary classroom control. In K. D. O'Leary & S. G. O'Leary (Eds), *Classroom Management: The Successful Use of Behavior Modification* (2nd ed.). New York: Pergamon Press, pp. 63–84
Schunk, D. H. (1983). Ability versus effort attributional feedback: differential effects on self-efficacy and achievement. *Journal of Educational Psychology*, 75, 848–856

Schunk, D. H. (1984). Sequential attributional feedback and children's achievement behaviors. *Journal of Educational Psychology*, 76, 1159–1169

90   Koestner, R., Zuckerman, M., & Olsson, J. (1990). Attributional style, comparison focus of praise, and intrinsic motivation. *Journal of Research in Personality*, 24, 87–100

Dweck, C. S. (1986). Motivational processes affecting learning. *American Psychologist*, 41, 1040–1048

91   Meyer, W. (1992). Paradoxical effects of praise and criticism on perceived ability. *European Review of Social Psychology*, 3, 259–283. DOI: 10.1080/14792779243000087

92   Brummelman, E., Thomaes, S., Orobio de Castro, B., Overbeek, G., & Bushman, B. (2014). 'That's not just beautiful. It's incredibly beautiful!' The adverse impact of inflated praise on children with low self-esteem. *Psychological Science*, 25, 728–735. DOI: 10.1177/0956797613514251

93   Baumeister, R. F., Hutton, D. G., & Cairns, K. J. (1990). Negative effects of praise on skilled performance. *Basic and Applied Social Psychology*, 11, 131–148

94   Kamins, M. L., & Dweck, C. S. (1999). Person vs process praise and criticism: implications for contingent self-worth and coping. *Developmental Psychology*, 35, 835–847

Mueller, C. M., & Dweck, C. S. (1998). Praise for intelligence can undermine children's motivation and performance. *Journal of Personality and Social Psychology*, 75, 33–52

You can read the article that describes the studies and analysis here: http://www.uky.edu/~eushe2/mrg/MuellerDweck1998.pdf accessed June 16, 2016

95   Kohn, A. (1993). *Punished by Rewards: The Trouble with Gold Stars, Incentive Plans, A's, Praise, and Other Bribes*. New York: Houghton Mifflin

Lepper, M. R., Greene, D., & Nisbett, R. E. (1973). Undermining children's intrinsic motivation with extrinsic reward: a test of the 'overjustification' hypothesis. *Journal of Personality and Social Psychology*, 28, 129–137

Lepper, M. R., & Henderlong, J. (2000). Turning 'play' into 'work' and 'work' into 'play': 25 years of research on intrinsic versus extrinsic motivation. In C. Sansone & J. M. Harackiewicz (Eds), *Intrinsic and Extrinsic Motivation: The Search for Optimal Motivation and Performance*. San Diego, CA: Academic Press, pp. 257–307

Lepper, M. R., Henderlong, J., & Gingras, I. (1999). Understanding the effects of extrinsic rewards on intrinsic motivation – uses and abuses of meta-analysis: comment on Deci, Koestner, and Ryan (1999). *Psychological Bulletin*, 125, 669–676.

96 Kohn, A. (1993). *Punished by Rewards: The Trouble with Gold Stars, Incentive Plans, A's, Praise, and Other Bribes.* New York: Houghton Mifflin

97 Deci, E. L., & Ryan, R. M. (1985). *Intrinsic Motivation and Self-determination in Human Behavior.* New York: Plenum Press

98 Kohn, A. (1986). *No Contest: The Case against Competition.* Boston: Houghton Mifflin. And see also Kohn, A. (2005). *Unconditional Parenting.* New York: Atria Books.

99 Meyer, W. (1992). Paradoxical effects of praise and criticism on perceived ability. *European Review of Social Psychology*, 3, 259–283. DOI: 10.1080/14792779243000087

100 Kamins, M. L., & Dweck, C. S. (1999). Person vs process praise and criticism: implications for contingent self-worth and coping. *Developmental Psychology*, 35, 835–847
Mueller, C. M., & Dweck, C. S. (1998). Praise for intelligence can undermine children's motivation and performance. *Journal of Personality and Social Psychology*, 75, 33–52
You can read the article that describes the studies and analysis here: http://www.uky.edu/~eushe2/mrg/MuellerDweck1998.pdf accessed June 16, 2016

101 See Grusec, J., & Redler, E. (1980). Attribution, reinforcement, and altruism: a developmental analysis. *Developmental Psychology*, 16, 525–534.
Bryan, C. J., Adams, G. S., & Monin, B. (2013). When cheating would make you a cheater: implicating the self prevents unethical behaviour. *Journal of Experimental Psychology*, 142, 1001–1005. doi.org/10.1037/a0030655
There are many other studies that continue to shed patchy and at times confusing light on the issue. For more resources, contact the author

102 These four variables are described in depth, and adapted from Henderlong, J., & Lepper, M. R. (2002). The effects of praise on children's intrinsic motivation: A review and synthesis. *Psychological Bulletin*, 128, 774–795

103 I retrieved specific details on the Steven Bradbury story from http://profilemag.com.au/up-to-speed-with-steven-bradbury/, http://www.dailytelegraph.com.au/sport/q-a-with-steve-bradbury/story-fn9dirj0-1226419900202, and https://en.wikipedia.org/wiki/Steven_Bradbury_(speed_skater), all accessed on 18 June 2016

104 I had my own experience of this at a netball game for one of my children. The referee was clearly biased (no... honestly, she was!), and called penalty after penalty against my daughter's team. After the umpteenth occurrence I found myself becoming increasingly vocal, attempting to point out with my one eye what the referee clearly could not see with her two perfectly good eyes. After a particularly noisy complaint, I recognised that I was getting upset at a 16-year-old girl who was learning, and that the game was an unimportant fixture between two 11-year-old girls' teams. I pulled my head in, apologised and just let the girls enjoy the game

105 Schurr, A., & Ritov, I. (2016). Winning a competition predicts dishonest behaviour. *Proceedings of the National Academy of Science*, 113, 1754–1759

106 This effect has been shown by a number of studies, such as:
Poon, K. T., Chen, Z., & Dewall, C. N. (2013) Feeling entitled to more: ostracism increases dishonest behaviour. *Personality and Social Psychology Bulletin*, 39, 1227–1239
Zitek, E. M., Jordan, A. H., Monin, B., & Leach, F. R. (2010) Victim entitlement to behave selfishly. *Journal of Personality and Social Psychology*, 98, 245–255

107 Madigan, D. J., and Stoeber, J. and Passfield, L. (2016) Perfectionism and attitudes towards doping in junior athletes. *Journal of Sports Sciences*, 34(8), 700–706. doi:10.1080/02640414.2015.1068441

108 http://cyclingtips.com/2016/03/opinion-why-van-den-driessches-decision-to-walk-away-from-cycling-is-a-regrettable-one/

109 See more about Turing's then CEO, Martin Shkreli, and his unique story here: http://www.vanityfair.com/news/2015/12/martin-shkreli-pharmaceuticals-ceo-interview

110 See http://mashable.com/2015/09/27/vw-dieselgate/ or http://www.businessinsider.com.au/this-is-the-real-cause-of-the-vw-cheating-scandal-2015-10?r=US&IR=T

111 See http://www.economist.com/news/schoolsbrief/21584534-effects-financial-crisis-are-still-being-felt-five-years-article

112 In recent years, most of this research has been conducted by Paul Piff and his colleagues. You can see a few examples here:
Piff, P. K., Krausm, M. W., Côté, S., Cheng, B. H., & Keltner, D. (2010). Having less, giving more: the influence of social class on prosocial behaviour. *Journal of Personality and Social Psychology*, 99, 771–784
Piff, P. K. (2014). Wealth and the inflated self: class, entitlement, and narcissism. *Personality and Social Psychology Bulletin*, 40, 34–43

Piff, P. K., Stancato, D. M., Côté, S., Mendoza-Denton, R., & Keltner, D. (2012). Higher social class predicts increased unethical behaviour. *Proceedings of the National Academy of Science*, 109, 4086–4091

113 For more evidence on each of these points, see:
John., L. K., Loewenstein, G., & Rick, S. I. (2014) Cheating more for less: upward social comparisons motivate the poorly compensated to cheat. *Organisational Behaviour and Human Decision Processes*, 123, 101–109
Zitek, E. M., Jordan, A. H., Monin, B., & Leach, F. R. (2010) Victim entitlement to behave selfishly. *Journal of Personality and Social Psychology*, 98, 245–255
Pittarello, A., Rubaltelli, E., & Rumiati, R. (2013) You can't be better than me: the role of the reference point in modulating people's pursuit of wealth. *Journal of Economic Psychology*, 37, 65–76
Major, B. (1994) From social inequality to personal entitlement: the role of social comparisons, legitimacy appraisals, and group membership, pp. 293–355. In Zanna, M. P. (Ed.) *Advances in experimental social psychology*. San Diego, Academic
Major, B., & Testa, M. (1989) Social comparison processes and judgements of entitlement and satisfaction. *Journal of Experimental Social Psychology*, 25, 101–120

114 Gino, F., & Pierce, L. (2009). The abundance effect: unethical behaviour in the presence of wealth. *Organisational Behaviour and Human Decision Processes*, 109, 142–155
Gino, F., & Pierce, L. (2009). Dishonesty in the name of equity. *Psychological Science*, 20, 1153–1160
Wakeman, W., Moore, C., & Gino, F. (2014) *Competence by Any Means: Cheating as a Response to Ego Threat*. Philadelphia, PA: Academy of Management

115 Elliot, A. J., & Dweck, C. S. (2005). *Handbook of Competence and Motivation*. New York: Guilford Press

116 Vallerand, R. J., et al. (2003). Les passions de l'ame: on obsessive and harmonious passion. *Journal of Personality and Social Psychology*, 85, 756–767

117 You can find terrific resources and information about this research in two of Carol Dweck's books. The first is *Mindset*, and is for a popular audience. The second is *Self-theories*, and is written for an academic audience.
Dweck, C. S. (2008). *Mindset: The New Psychology of Success. How We Can Learn to Fulfil our Potential*. New York: Ballantyne Books

Dweck, C. S. (2000). *Self-theories: Their Role in Motivation, Personality, and Development*. Philadelphia, PA: Psychology Press

118 http://www.theaustralian.com.au/sport/the-times-sport/ nick-kyrgios-god-help-me-if-im-playing-at-30/news-story/ bcf10b7a56a5e18b888778076d13e1a5

119 Kohn, A. (1986). *No Contest: The Case against Competition. Why We Lose in Our Race to Win*. New York: Houghton Mifflin
Amabile's study is:
Amabile, T. M. (1982). Children's artistic creativity: detrimental effects of competition in a field setting. *Personality and Social Psychology Bulletin*, 8, 573–578

120 Fox, M. (2002). *Lucky Man*. New York: Hyperion

121 Tauer, J. M., & Harackiewicz. (2004). The effects of cooperation and competition on intrinsic motivation and performance. *Interpersonal Relations and Group Processes*, 86, 849–861

122 Sherif, M., Harvey, O. J., White, B. J., Hood, W., & Sherif, C. W. (1961). *Intergroup Conflict and Cooperation: The Robbers Cave Experiment*. pp. 155–184
Note that some have argued that the 'vandals' that were introduced as being responsible for many of the challenges that the new combined group of boys had to overcome simply changed the competition by introducing a common enemy. That is, the boys were now in competition with the vandals. However, this is not necessarily the case. While they had to work against a new 'enemy', there was no competition. They weren't trying to outmanoeuvre, outscore, outlast or outwit the enemy. They simply had to work together when things went wrong, collaborate with one another and develop the capacity to solve challenges. Life consistently pits us against challenging situations that don't demand we 'beat' someone else. This was no different.

123 Deci, E. L., Koestner, R., & Ryan, R. M. (1999). A meta-analytic review of experiments examining the effects of extrinsic rewards on intrinsic motivation. *Psychological Bulletin*, 125, 627–668
Note that the study does not focus on wellbeing or resilience. I take the logical step of suggesting that increased intrinsic motivation would boost both wellbeing and resilience because when a person is intrinsically motivated, particularly when that motivation is autonomous, they are going to be far more likely to have their basic psychological needs of autonomy, competence and relatedness met. In so doing, their wellbeing and resilience should be higher. Conversely, if a person is amotivated, or externally motivated (or even experiencing introjected motivation – a

controlled sense of intrinsic motivation) then their psychological needs are likely to be frustrated or thwarted in some way. Relationships may feel askew, competence may be low, or the person may feel controlled. As such, Self-Determination Theory predicts – through a mountain of studies – that the person will experience suboptimal motivation, wellbeing and resilience.

124 Ellison, R. (1952). *Invisible Man.* New York: Signet Books

125 While I used a number of resources for this story, they all came from the references list from this Wikipedia article about Bruno Mars: https://en.wikipedia.org/wiki/Bruno_Mars#2012.E2.80.9314:_Unorthodox_Jukebox_and_Super_Bowl_XLVIII_Halftime_Show, accessed on 16 June 2016

126 Steinberg, L. (2015). *Age of Opportunity: Lessons from the New Science of Adolescence.* Boston: Houghton Miflin Harcourt Publishers

127 The background to this story is well described in Bruce Feilor's 2013 book, *The Secrets of Happy Families: How to Improve Your Morning, Rethink Family Dinner, Fight Smart, Go Out and Play, and Much More.* New York: Harper Collins

   Duke, M.P., Lazarus, A., & Fivush, R. (2008). Knowledge of family history as a clinically useful index of psychological well-being and prognosis: a brief report. *Psychotherapy Theory, Research, Practice, Training,* 45, 268–272

   See also Fivush, R., Bohanek. J. G., & Duke, M. P. (2008). The self in time: subjective perspective and intergenerational history. In F. Sani (Ed.), *Continuity and Self.* New York, NY: Psychology Press, pp. 131–143

128 Fivush, R., Duke, M. P., & Bohanek. J. G. (2010). 'Do you know?' The power of family history in adolescent identity and family wellbeing. Accessed from http://publichistorycommons.org/wp-content/uploads/2013/12/The-power-of-family-history-in-adolescent-identity.pdf on 24/6/16

129 Thank you to Professor Marshall Duke for his generous input into aspects of this chapter related to his research.

130 Permission to reprint the 'Do You Know' scale was provided by Professor Marshall Duke in personal correspondence, dated 24 June 2016

131 Harris, R. (2007). *The Happiness Trap.* Boston: Trumpeter

132 Fredrickson, B. L., & Branigan, C. (2005). Positive emotions broaden the scope of attention and thought-action repertoires. *Cognition & Emotion,* 19, 313–332. http://doi.org/10.1080/02699930441000238

   More of this work is cited and expanded upon in the following articles: Fredrickson, B. L. (1998). What good are positive emotions? *Review of General Psychology: Journal of Division 1, of the American Psychological Association, 2,* 300–319. http://doi.org/10.1037/1089-2680.2.3.300

Fredrickson, B. L. (2001). The role of positive emotions in positive psychology: the broaden-and-build theory of positive emotions. *The American Psychologist, 56,* 218–226

Fredrickson, B. L. (2004). The broaden-and-build theory of positive emotions.*Philosophical Transactions of the Royal Society B: Biological Sciences, 359,* 1367–1378. http://doi.org/10.1098/rstb.2004.1512

Tugade, M. M., & Fredrickson, B. L. (2004). Resilient individuals use positive emotions to bounce back from negative emotional experiences. *Journal of Personality and Social Psychology, 86,* 320–333. http://doi.org/10.1037/0022-3514.86.2.320

133 Much of the work described in this chapter is taken from Kashdan, T. B., & Rottenburg, J. (2010). Psychological flexibility as a fundamental aspect of health. *Clinical Psychology Review, 30,* 865–878. DOI: 10.1016/j.cpr.2010.03.001

134 Gjerde, P. F., Block, J., & Block, J. H. (1986). Egocentrism and ego resiliency: personality characteristics associated with perspective-taking from early childhood to adolescence. *Journal of Personality and Social Psychology, 51,* 423–434

Klohnen, E. C. (1996). Conceptual analysis and measurement of the construct of ego-resiliency. *Journal of Personality and Social Psychology, 70,* 1067–1079

135 Accessed from https://workingwithact.com/what-is-act/what-is-psychological-flexibility/ on 30 June 2016

136 The content related to mindfulness in this section comes from the work by Harvard psychology professor Ellen Langer. Langer, E. J. (1989). *Mindfulness.* Addison-Wesley/Addison Wesley Longman

137 Todd Kashdan and his colleagues have written that no emotion is negative or positive. Rather, all emotions are just that – emotion. It is the context that determines the negativity or positivity of the emotion. For example, grief following death is a positive and helpful emotion that facilitates mourning and allows us to process the pain that we experience at the loss of a loved one. They also argue that emotions such an anger are positive – but they add that the emotion can only be positive if we can remove ourselves some distance from the emotion and then think about how to use that emotion in aid of our highest values. If justice is something that matters more to us than relationships, we will use that anger to right a wrong or demand

recompense in an unjust situation. Thus, anger can be seen as positive. While I understand and appreciate their argument, my feeling is that for most people – and especially children – those emotions we would typically term 'negative' are often far too strong and internalised for us to be productive with them. The psychological flexibility process helps us to do something with them in a positive way, but it requires following the steps and ultimately reducing the strength of the emotion to a point where flexible thinking is possible. Hence, Fredrickson's broaden-and-build theory of positive emotions comes into play because as emotions subside we begin to think more clearly and broadly, and thus respond more flexibly.

138 Creswell, J. D., Way, B. M., Eisenberger, N. I., & Lieberman, M. D. (2007). Neural correlates of dispositional mindfulness during affect labeling. *Psychosomatic Medicine, 69*, 560–565

139 In their article, Kashdan and Rottenberg cite several other studies that corroborate this process. See:
DeYoung, C. G., Peterson, J. B., & Higgins, D. M. (2005). Sources of openness/intellect: cognitive and neuropsychological correlates of the fifth factor of personality. *Journal of Personality, 73*, 825–858
Kalisch, R. et al. (2005). Anxiety reduction through detachment: subjective, physiological, and neural effects. *Journal of Cognitive Neuroscience, 17*, 874–883
Ochsner, K. N., & Gross, J. J. (2008). Cognitive emotion regulation: insights from social cognitive and affective neuroscience. *Current Directions in Psychological Science, 17*, 153–158

140 Garland, E. L., & Fredrickson, B. L. (2013). Mindfulness broadens awareness and builds meaning at the attention-emotion interface, pp 30–67. In T. B. Kashdan and J. Ciarrochi (Eds), *Mindfulness, Acceptance, and Positive Psychology. The Seven Foundations of Well-being.* Oakland, CA: Context

141 You can watch some very funny examples of re-enactments of the marshmallow test online. It could be a great activity for the family to watch the video and talk about what your child would do and why.

142 Mischel, W. (2014). *The Marshmallow Test. Why Self-control is the Engine of Success.* New York: Little, Brown and Company

143 Hoffman, W., Luhmann, M., Fisher, R. R., Vohs, K. D., & Baumeister, R. F. (2013). Yes, but are they happy? Effects of trait self-control on affective wellbeing and life satisfaction. *Journal of Personality, 82*, 265–277

144 Ibid.

145 Accessed from http://www.alfiekohn.org/blogs/lots-of-love/ on 4 July 2016

146 Deci, E. L., and Ryan, R. M. (n.d.). Intrinsic motivation inventory. Available at http://www.selfdeterminationtheory.org/questionnaires/10-questionnaires/50

Deci, E. L., & Ryan, R. M. (2000). The 'what' and 'why' of goal pursuits: human needs and the self-determination of behavior. *Psychological Inquiry*, 11, 227–268

Deci, E. L., Ryan, R. M., & Williams, G. C. (1996). Need satisfaction and the self-regulation of learning. *Learning and Individual Differences*, 8, 165–183

Sanli, E. A., Patterson, J. T., Bray, S. R., & Lee, T. D. (2013). Understanding self-controlled motor-learning protocols through the self-determination theory. *Frontiers in Psychology*, 3, 611. DOI: 10.3389/fpsyg.2012.00611

Vansteenkiste, M., Simons, J., Lens, W., Sheldon, K. M., and Deci, E. L. (2004). Motivating learning, performance, and persistence: the synergistic effects of intrinsic goal contents and autonomy-supportive contexts. *Journal of Personality and Social Psychology*, 87, 246–260

147 Miller, G. E., Yu, T., Chen, E., & Brody, G. H. (2015). Self-control forecasts better psychosocial outcomes but faster epigenetic aging in low SES youth. *Proceedings of the National Academy of Sciences*, 112, 10325-10330. doi: 10.1073/pnas.1505063112

148 Shoda, Y., Mischel, W., & Peake, P. K. (1990). Predicting adolescent cognitive and self-regulatory competencies from preschool delay of gratification: identifying diagnostic conditions. *Developmental Psychology*, 26, 978–986

149 There are countless books that promote the idea that attitude is everything and we only need to think positively or have big, hairy, audacious goals, or WHOOP it up and our problems will go away. Some even lean on some questionable evidence to support their claims. These include: Norman Vincent Peale's classic, *The Power of Positive Thinking*; Napoleon Hill's classic, *Think and Grow Rich*; Gabriele Oettingen's bestselling *Rethinking Positive Thinking*; Darren Hardy, *The Compound Effect*.
And other books with titles like 'attitude is everything', and so on. While they may offer inspiring principles, these books, ideas, theories and approaches are being ignored here for approaches with a more sound evidence base.

150 Taylor, S. E., & Brown, J. D. (1988). Illusion and well-being: a social
    psychological perspective on mental health. *Psychological Bulletin*, 103,
    193–210
    Taylor, S. E., & Brown, J. D. (1994). Positive illusions and wellbeing
    revisited: Separating fact from fiction. *Psychological Bulletin*, 116, 21–27

151 Chapin, J., & Coleman, G. (2009). Optimistic bias: what you think, what
    you know, or whom you know? *North American Journal of Psychology*,
    11, 121–132

152 Sharot, T. (2011). The optimism bias. *Current Biology*, 21, R941–R945.
    DOI: 10.1016/j.cub.2011.10.030. See also Taylor, S. E., Collins, R. L.,
    Skokan, L. A., & Aspinwall, L. G. (1989). Maintaining positive illusions
    in the face of negative information: Getting the facts without letting them
    get to you. *Journal of Social and Clinical Psychology*, 8, 114–129

153 Ciarrochi, J., Parker, P., Kashdan, T. B., Heaven, P. C. L., & Barkus, E.
    (2015). Hope and emotional well-being: a six-year study to distinguish
    antecedents, correlates, and consequences. *The Journal of Positive
    Psychology*, 10(6), 520–532, DOI: 10.1080/17439760.2015.1015154

154 Ellis, A. (1957). Rational psychotherapy and individual psychology.
    Journal of Individual Psychology, 13: 38–44. See also Ellis, A. (1962).
    Reason and Emotion in Psychotherapy. New York: Stuart

155 Hollon, S. D., & Beck, A. T. (1994). Cognitive and cognitive-behavioral
    therapies. In A. E. Bergin & S.L. Garfield (Eds), *Handbook of
    psychotherapy and behavior change*. New York: Wiley. pp. 428–466
    Kendall, P. C., & Kriss, M. R. (1983). Cognitive-behavioral
    interventions. In C. E. Walker (Ed.) *The handbook of clinical
    psychology: theory, research and practice*, Homewood, IL: Dow Jones-
    Irwin, pp. 770–819

156 The evidence base for attribution style is extensive. For a popular outline
    of the idea in regards to children, see Seligman, M. E. P. (1995). *The
    Optimistic Child*. Sydney: Random House.
    For a scholarly description of the validation of the attribution style
    questionnaire, see Peterson, C., Semmel, A., von Baeyer, C., Abramson,
    L. Y., Metalsky, G. I., & Seligman, M. E. P. (1982). The attributional
    style questionnaire. *Cognitive Therapy and Research*, 6, 287–300

157 In spite of the many advocates of this kind of thinking, a search of
    the psychological database PSYCinfo yielded few, if any, studies that
    could demonstrate anything empirically substantive when it comes
    to 'affirmations' and the blind form of positive thinking that is often
    prescribed in concert with such techniques. There aren't many studies to
    cite, but this one appears to offer a wise and balanced view: Wood, J.,

Elaine Perunovic, W., & Lee, J. (2009). Positive self-statements: power for some, peril for others. *Psychological Science*, 20, 860–866 DOI: 10.1111/j.1467-9280.2009.02370.x. In short, the researchers divided participants into high and low self-esteem categories (without them knowing) and had them practice an affirmation: 'I am a lovable person.' They then measured the participants' mood and their self-worth. In the same way that praise from others led to inferences of low ability in research cited in this book, the low-esteem group felt worse afterwards compared with those with higher self-esteem. And people with high self-esteem felt better after repeating the positive affirmation. But this increase in this group was minor. Perhaps the most interesting finding from this study was when the researchers invited participants to list negative and positive thoughts about themselves. Those with low self-esteem actually felt better when they were allowed to have negative thoughts about themselves than when they were asked to focus exclusively on the affirmations. There is a sense that forcing a statement that is hollow and unbelievable creates resistance in the participants in the study. If they see themselves as unlovable, being forced to say how lovable they are only serves to strengthen their perception rather than reversing it.

158 More details on the remarkable story of Karl and Bertha Benz can be found at *Bertha Benz hits the road, 125 years ago – history in the headlines*. Accessed from http://www.history.com/news/bertha-benz-hits-the-road-125-years-ago on 25 May 2016

159 Dweck, C. S. (2000). *Self-theories: Their Role in Motivation, Personality, and Development*. Philadelphia, PA: Psychology Press

160 Binet, A. (Suzanne Heisler, translation). (1975). *Modern Ideas About Children*. Menlo Park, CA: Suzanne Heisler. (original work, 1909)

161 In typical standardised tests, the stakes could barely be higher. A child sits that test and is given a mark, or a 'band', which they are told represents their academic ability. And while many educators emphasise that this number represents a simple moment in time, and that children develop at different times and in different ways, the eight-year-old third-grader who reads that she is in the lowest band is most likely going to feel 'you're dumb' reinforced with incredible power on an official document, and this is not going to inspire a belief that her intelligence can be enhanced through effort.

162 There has been a large increase in literature showing the importance of fathers in the past one or two decades. Curiously, prior to that, fathers were largely overlooked in academic studies. A nice starting point for those interested in more information would be a concise summary by

journalist Paul Raeburn, or a slightly more academic overview in an edited book by Sean Brotherson and Joseph White:

Raeburn, P. (2014). *Do Fathers Matter? What Science is Telling Us About the Parents We've Overlooked.* New York: Scientific American/ Farrar, Straus and Giroux

Brotherson, S. E., & White, J. M. (2007). *Why Fathers Count: The Importance of Fathers and Their Involvement with Children.* Tennessee: Mens Studies Press

163 Schofield, T. J., Robins, R. W., & Conger, R. D. (2015). Early adolescent substance use in Mexican Origin families: Peer selection, peer influence, and parental monitoring. *Drug and Alcohol Dependence, 157,* 129–135.

164 Padilla-Walker, L. M., Christensen, K. J., & Day, R. D. (2011). Proactive parenting practices during early adolescence: A cluster approach. *Journal of Adolescence, 34,* 203-214. DOI: 10.1016/j.adolescence.2010.05.008

165 Wendy Grolnick is the researcher I cite most in regards to these ideas, though there are many, many other examples that support these ideas:

Grolnick, W. S. (2003). *The Psychology of Parental Control: How Well-meant Parenting Vackfires.* Mahwah, NJ: Erlbaum Publishers

Grolnick, W. S., Frodi, A., & Bridges, L. (1984). Maternal control style and the mastery motivation of one-year-olds. *Infant Mental Health Journal, 5,* 72–82

Grolnick, W. S., Gurland, S. T., DeCourcey, W., & Jacob, K. (2002). Antecedents and consequences of mothers' autonomy support: an experimental investigation. *Developmental Psychology, 38,* 143–155

Grolnick, W. S., Price, C. E., Beiswenger, K. L., & Sauck, C. C. (2007). Evaluative pressure in mothers: effects of situation, maternal, and child characteristics on autonomy supportive versus controlling behaviour. *Developmental Psychology, 43,* 991–1002

Frodi, A., Bridges, L., & Grolnick, W. S. (1985). Correlates of mastery-related behaviour: a short-term longitudinal study of infants in their second year. *Child Development, 56,* 1291–1298

Deci, E. L., Driver, R. E., Hotchkiss, L., Robbins, R. J., & Wilson, I. M. (1993). The relation of mothers controlling vocalizations to childrens intrinsic motivation. *Journal of Experimental Child Psychology, 55,* 151–162

166 Kochanska, G., & Aksan, N. (1995). Mother-child mutually positive affect, the quality of child compliance to requests and prohibitions, and maternal control as correlates of early internalization. *Child Development, 66,* 236–254

Kochanska, G., Coy, K. C., & Murray, K. T. (2001). The development of self-regulation in the first four years of life. *Child Development*, 72, 1091–1111

167 Joussemet, M., Koestner, R., Lekes, N., & Landry, R. (2005). A longitudinal study of the relationship of maternal autonomy support to children's adjustment and achievement in school. *Journal of Personality*, 73, 1215–1236

168 Padilla-Walker, L. M., Fraser, A. M., & Harper, J. M. (2012). Walking the walk: the moderating role of proactive parenting on adolescents' value-congruent behaviour. *Journal of Adolescence*, 35, 1141–1152 See also Padilla-Walker, L. M. (2014) Parental socialization of prosocial behaviour: A multidimensional approach. L. M. Padilla-Walker & C Gustavo (Eds); *In Prosocial Development: A Multidimensional Approach*. New York: Oxford University Press

169 Landry, R. et al. (2008). Trust in organismic development, autonomy support, and adaptation among mothers and their children. *Motivation and Emotion*, 32, 173–188

170 Biswas-Diener, R., Kashdan, T. B., & Minhas, G. (2011). A dynamic approach to psychological strength development and intervention. *Journal of Positive Psychology*, 6, 106–118. DOI: 10.1080/17439760.2010.545429

171 Seligman, M., Rashid, T., & Parks, A. C. (2006). Positive psychotherapy. *American Psychologist*, 61, 774–788. See also Fluckiger, C., & Grosse Holforth, M. (2008). Focusing the therapist's attention on the patient's strengths: a preliminary study to foster a mechanism of change in outpatient psychotherapy. *Journal of Clinical Psychology*, 64, 876–890

172 Louis, M. C. (2009). A summary and critique of existing strengths-based educational research Utilizing the Clifton Strengths Finder. Internal paper, The Gallup Organization. And see also Bowers, K. M., & Lopez, S. (2010). Capitalizing on personal strengths in college. *Journal of College and Character*, 11, 1–11

173 Peterson, C., Stephens, J. P., Park, N., Lee, F., & Seligman, M. E. P. (2009). Strengths of character and work. In P. A. Linley, S. Harrington, & N. Garcea (Eds), *Oxford Handbook of Positive Psychology and Work*. Oxford, UK: Oxford University Press, pp. 221–234 Harter, J. K., Schmidt, F. L., & Hayes, T. L. (2002). Business-unit-level relationship between employee satisfaction, employee engagement, and business outcomes: A meta-analysis. *Journal of Applied Psychology*, 87, 268–279

Corporate Leadership Council. (2002). *Performance Management Survey.* Washington, DC: Corporate Leadership Council

Stefanyszyn, K. (2007). Norwich Union changes focus from competencies to strengths. *Strategic Human Resources Review,* 7, 10–11

174 Govindji, R., & Linley, A. (2007). Strengths use, selfconcordance and well-being: implications for strengths coaching and coaching psychologists. *International Coaching Psychology Review,* 2, 143–153

Proctor, C., Maltby, J., & Linley, P. A. (2009). Strengths use as a predictor of well-being and health-related quality of life. *Journal of Happiness Studies,* 10, 583–630

Wood, A. M., Linley, P. A., Maltby, J., Kashdan, T. B., & Hurling, R. (2011). Using psychological strengths leads to less stress and greater self-esteem, vitality, and positive affect: longitudinal examination of the strengths use questionnaire. *Personality and Individual Differences,* 50, 15–19

Linley, P. A., Nielsen, K. M., Wood, A. M., Gillett, R., & Biswas-Diener, R. (2010). Using signature strengths in pursuit of goals: effects on goal progress, need satisfaction, and well-being, and implications for coaching psychologists. *International Coaching Psychology Review,* 5, 6–15

Seligman, M., Steen, T., Park, N., & Peterson, C. (2005). Positive psychology progress: empirical validation of interventions. *American Psychologist,* 60, 410–421

Minhas, G. (2010). Developing realised and unrealised strengths: implications for engagement, self-esteem, life satisfaction and well-being. *Assessment and Development Matters,* 2, 12–16

175 This list of character strengths is drawn from two central sources:

The VIA character strengths survey, which is an empirically based, theoretically derived survey that can be taken for free via the website: http://www.viacharacter.org/www/Character-Strengths/VIA-Classification. Accessed August 2016

Clifton Strengthsfinder, used by Gallup, which has been taken by some 14 million people worldwide. You can also take a free version of this survey at this website: https://www.gallupstrengthscenter.com/ Accessed August 2016

176 Sheldon, K. M., Jose, P. E., Kashdan, T. B., & Jarden, A. (2015). Personality, effective goal-striving, and enhanced well-being: comparing 10 candidate personality strengths. *Personality and Social Psychology Bulletin,* 41, 575–585

177 Martínez-Martí, M. L., & Ruch, W. (2016). Character strengths predict resilience over and above positive affect, self-efficacy,

optimism, social support, self-esteem, and life satisfaction. *Journal of Positive Psychology*. Published online April 2016, 1–10. DOI: 10.1080/17439760.2016.1163403

178 Uhls, Y. T., Michikyan, M., Morris, J., Garcia, D., Small, G. W., Zgourou, E., & Greenfield, P. M. (2014). Five days at outdoor education camp without screens improves preteen skills with nonverbal emotion cues. *Computers in Human Behaviour*, 39, 387–392. DOI: 10.1016/j.chb.2014.05.036

179 http://www.abc.net.au/news/2015-12-19/childrens-eyesight-damaged-from-lack-of-outdoor-time/7040942

180 Ciarrochi, J., Parker, P., Sahrdra, B., Marshall, S., Jackson, C., Gloster, A, & Heaven, P. (2016). The development of compulsive internet use and mental health: a four year study of adolescence. *Developmental Psychology*, 52, 272–293. DOI: 10.1037/dev0000070

181 Accessed from http://growingupinaustralia.gov.au/pubs/asr/2015/asr2015e.html on 7 October 2016

182 Accessed from http://selfdeterminationtheory.org/living-green-magazine-being-in-nature-makes-us-healthier-happier/ on 6 December 2016

183 van den Berg, M., Wendel-Vos, W., van Poppel, M., Kemper, H., van Mechelen, W. & Maas, J. (2015). Health benefits of green spaces in the living environment: a systematic review of epidemiological studies. *Urban Forestry and Urban Greening*, 14, 806–816. DOI: 10.1016/j.ufug.2015.07.008

184 Alcock, I., White, M. P., Wheeler, B. W., Fleming, L. E., & Depledge, M. H. (2014). Longitudinal effects on mental health of moving to greener and less green urban areas. *Environmental Science & Technology*, 48, 1247–1255. DOI: 10.1021/es403688w

185 See this review for more: http://publications.naturalengland.org.uk/publication/4513819616346112

186 A very big thank you to John Maclean for his willingness to share his story with me personally, and allowing me to share it here.

187 Maclean, J. (2016). *How Far Can You Go? My 25-year Quest to Walk Again*. New York: Hachette.

Acknowledgements

Thanks so much to so many people who have been shoulders for me to stand on during the writing of this book.

Firstly, to the team at kidspot.com.au, thank you for the trust you place in me. I joined the Kidspot team near their beginning and our relationship has continued in a strong and positive way ever since, even as Kidspot has changed and shifted to NewsCorp. Thanks to Alex Brooks (former editor), Ella Walsh, Marg Rafferty, Melissa Wilson, Jeni O'Dowd, Rhett Watson and everyone else behind the scenes for such stellar support. And a special thanks to Nicole Sheffield at NewsLifeMedia – you made it happen!

At ABC Books, I have had a tremendously patient publisher in Katie Stackhouse. Katie has endured questions, quarrels and crazy ideas via email and phone at all hours as crises of confidence or questions around content have pummelled my brain. Katie, thank you. Additional thanks to Kate O'Donnell, whose fairness and perspective contributed to an enormously improved and compassionate manuscript. Barbara McClenahan and Bronwyn Sweeney took this book and reviewed, edited and improved so much that I think they must know the contents and concepts as well as I do. They make me look like a much better writer than I actually am, and I thank them for their awesome work and attention to detail. I hope it's helped to make your families more resilient, too. If so, mission accomplished.

I had valuable input for which I'm grateful from a range of people with incredible insight into what makes resilience happen. Thank you to Andrew Fuller, Professor Darcia Narvaez, Professor

Marshall Duke and Professor H Wallace Goddard. Your generous gift of time to answer questions for a book that doesn't bear your names has been appreciated.

I'm particularly appreciative to John Maclean, who spent an hour talking to me about his incredible story of resilience and courage. I hope that this book honours your legacy, John.

There have been many parents who have shared stories, experiences and heartfelt challenges with me over the years. I am grateful to them for allowing me to share aspects of their stories in this book, and for their trust in me to help them.

Writing this book has been a test of resilience for my family. Researching and writing requires significant sacrifice, and it is not just the author who gives things up. To my children, who went to bed with far too little attention on too many nights during the months I was working on this book, I owe you a tremendous debt of gratitude. Your resilience is a beacon to me of how to be hopeful and happy in spite of an over-tired, grumpy dad who should know better. I love you all: Chanel, Abbie, Ella, Annie, Lilli and Emilie. And we'll make up for this ten times over.

Mum and Dad, and also Les and Natasha, my in-laws. I'm grateful for the influence you've had in my life and the belief you've shown over the many years. Your support and belief in me and your unconditional love have contributed to my resilience.

Finally, to my wife, my eternal sweetheart. I owe the resiliency of our relationship to you and your support. The world is all gates, all opportunities. Let's open them and see where they take us – together.

Index

Kidspot parenting expert Dr Justin Coulson knows how to make families happier! *21 Days to a Happier Family* combines cutting-edge insights from positive psychology with classic psychological research to help parents identify and develop habits that will strengthen their family. In his trademark warm and empathic style, Dr Coulson covers topics such as finding the most effective parenting style for your child, getting relationships right and how that leads to effective discipline, using mindfulness in parenting, being emotionally available to your children – and so much more.

'Parenthood can be a jungle, but Justin's advice and simple strategies will help you find that path back to sanity, stability and smiling kids.'
Lisa Wilkinson

'Justin Coulson's compassionate and helpful advice helps me unravel my many parenting dilemmas.'
Jessica Rowe